The GOLDEN WALLABIES

Spiro Zavos has been the rubgy columnist for the *Sydney Morning Herald* for the past twenty years. Having written five books on the subject, he is regarded as one of Australia's leading rugby writers. In 1995 he was awarded the Ford Rugby Writer of the Year. He is also the author of a bestselling, controversial biography of the former New Zealand Prime Minister Sir Robert Muldoon, *The Real Muldoon*, and a collection of short stories, *Faith of Our Fathers*, which won the NSW Premier's Award in 1983. He is one of a handful of players of full Greek parentage who have played first-class cricket.

The GOLDEN WALLABIES

The Story of Australia's Rugby World Champions

Spiro Zavos

Penguin Books

Penguin Books Australia Ltd
487 Maroondah Highway, PO Box 257
Ringwood, Victoria 3134, Australia
Penguin Books Ltd
Harmondsworth, Middlesex, England
Penguin Putnam Inc.
375 Hudson Street, New York, New York 10014, USA
Penguin Books Canada Limited
10 Alcorn Avenue, Toronto, Ontario, Canada M4V 3B2
Penguin Books (NZ) Ltd
Cnr Rosedale and Airborne Roads, Albany, Auckland, New Zealand
Penguin Books (South Africa) (Pty) Ltd
5 Watkins Street, Denver Ext 4, 2094, South Africa
Penguin Books India (P) Ltd
11, Community Centre, Panchsheel Park, New Delhi 110 017, India

First published by Penguin Books Australia Ltd 2000

1 3 5 7 9 10 8 6 4 2

Design by David Altheim, Penguin Design Studio
Cover photograph courtesy of Allsport Australia
Typeset in Bembo by Midland Typesetters, Maryborough, Victoria
Made and printed in Australia by Australian Print Group, Maryborough, Victoria

National Library of Australia
Cataloguing-in-Publication data

Zavos, Spiro, 1937– .
Golden wallabies.

Includes index.
ISBN 0 14 029601 8.

1. Wallabies (Rugby team). 2. Rugby football – Australia –
History. I. Title.

796.3330994

From decades of watching rugby and after a long study of the history of Australian rugby, this is the Dream Time Team that in my opinion best represents the vibrancy of the Australian rugby community:

Matthew Burke, Dally Messenger, Trevor Allan, Tim Horan, David Campese, Mark Ella, Ken Catchpole, John Ford, Colin Windon, Simon Poidevin, Stephen Williams, John Eales, Jonathon White, Phil Kearns, Enrique Rodriguez.

This book is dedicated to the Wallaby Dream Time Team and all the tens of thousands of rugby players who have played the great game of rugby in Australia since some students at Sydney University in the 1860s decided to give it a go.

ACKNOWLEDGEMENTS

The lyrics on page 4 are reproduced from 'A Number on My Back' (The Wallaby Anthem), written and recorded by John Williamson © 1999 Emusic Pty Ltd. Available through EMI Music Australia on CD/cassette *The Way It Is* by John Williamson. Reproduced by permission.

Peter Fenton's poem on the 1927–28 Waratahs on page 125 was published in *For the Sake of the Game* (Little Hills Press, Sydney, 1996). Reproduced by permission.

CONTENTS

PART I
Bill Is Back!
How the Wallabies Captured the 1999 Rugby World Cup   1

PART II
1991 World Cup Triumph
'Kick It to the Shithouse!'   55

PART III
Golden Wallabies
1908 Olympic Gold Medal   83

PART IV
A Half-century of Wallaby Triumphs
Eye Witness to the State of Rugby   139

PART V
Australian Rugby into the Twenty-first Century
'Making a Little Winter Love'   251

Appendix
Australian Rugby Milestones   279

Index   293

PART I: Bill Is Back!

How the Wallabies Captured the 1999 Rugby World Cup

Advance Australia Fair

On 6 November 1999, at Cardiff, on a piercingly cold afternoon towards five o'clock, with the crowd in the steepling stands of the new Millennium Stadium roaring, Andre Watson raised his arm dramatically to the heavens and gave a resounding blast of his whistle. The final of the 1999 Rugby World Cup tournament was over. The world champions of rugby were the Australian Wallabies.

Like the previous two World Cup finals, it had not been pretty rugby. The Wallabies defeated France 35–12 by use of boa constrictor tactics – metaphorically swallowing their opponents with a defence that allowed them nowhere to run. Then, when the vital juices had been squeezed out of the French, the Wallabies ran in two tries towards the end of the match to put an end to any French hopes of a victory. The tries, though, were the first scored in a World Cup final since the inaugural encounter in 1987.

The Wallabies hugged one another. A sense of their Australianness flooded through them. Back in 1991, after the Wallabies went back to their changing room as world champions with the William Webb Ellis trophy and their medals, they had sung chorus after rousing chorus of 'Advance Australia Fair'. That expression of national pride had taken place in the sanctuary of the changing room, a gesture for themselves. Now they sang 'Advance Australia Fair' as the officials busily set up the presentation ceremony on the field of the Millennium Stadium. This was a proclamation to the world of their pride in their country.

The French wandered around the field, duplicating the bewilderment they experienced during the final, not knowing where to go and what to do. A red carpet was rolled out in front of the main stand. The trophies were placed on the table. Minutes later the Queen, tiny, frumpy, in what looked like a French-blue outfit, walked slowly on to the field. The Duke of Edinburgh and Princess Anne deferentially followed her.

The Wallaby captain, John Eales, accepted the golden William Webb Ellis trophy from the Queen. Towering over her, he held the trophy aloft like a priest raising the chalice at benediction. Earlier in the week George Gregan, the vice-captain of the Wallabies, had told reporters he would prefer to win the vote for a republic that was being held hours before in Australia, also on 6 November, than win the World Cup final, if it came to a trade-off. Now he accepted his winner's medal from the Queen. He moved towards Eales, took the William Webb Ellis trophy and held it aloft. As each Wallaby received his medal, he in turn took the cup from his team-mate and raised it, too, in a benediction to all parts of the ground. The crowd greeted each blessing with a cheer.

Eye Witness, 18 September 1999

At the Darling Harbour Convention Centre, 2500 laughing and singing rugby supporters, paying $250 each, gave the Wallabies a rousing farewell before they travel to Britain to win the 1999 Rugby World Cup . . . Like the 1991 side, the 1999 Wallabies are a team on the up. The victory against the All Blacks at the Olympic Stadium was more convincing than any of the three victories in 1998 . . . John Williamson has written a song for the Wallabies to give them the lift they need to combat the rampant Welsh nationalism in the quarter-final at Cardiff on 23 October. The melody is catchy and the words rousing:

> *I will seize the day,*
> *Because it belongs to me.*
> *I have a number on my back.*
> *I am a Wallaby.*

Generally the Welsh win the singing (if nothing else) at rugby tests. The Wallabies this time, though, are primed to win the singing and the rugby at Cardiff . . .

Nothing Is Inevitable

There is always the temptation to read history backwards. After an event has happened it is seen as inevitable. But this is a false way of reading life and history. Nothing is inevitable, until it happens. Up to the occurrence of the event there are an infinite number of variables that might be able to come into play, affecting the final outcome.

The capture of the 1999 Rugby World Cup by the Wallabies became inevitable after Andre Watson blew the final whistle. There was nothing inevitable about the triumph, though, until about three minutes or so before the end of the final, when Wallaby coach Rod Macqueen accepted the fact that he and his team had made history and that all the planning, training, the agonies of coping with disasters and the joy of the adventure were to be crowned with success. He quietly withdrew from his seat and in a corridor of the Millennium Stand embraced his wife and son, while the voice of the vast crowd surged in waves of sound.

Going into the World Cup tournament the Wallabies were ranked with the All Blacks, the Springboks and England as the strongest candidates for victory. Some British journalists believed that France, the unpredictable geniuses of rugby, might like their soccer team have a magical run once they reached the finals. Others fancied the chances of Wales, reinvigorated by their New Zealand coach, Graham Henry, 'The Great Redeemer'. The logic behind this prediction was that, of the three previous World Cup tournaments, two had been won by the host nation. Wales was the host nation and was going to play the tournament, except for a semi-final (if the Red Dragons got this far in the tournament), at the new Millennium Stadium, a temple built for the glory of Welsh rugby in the heart of Cardiff.

The logic behind the nomination of the three southern-hemisphere favourites was driven by the strength and intensity of Super 12 and Tri Nations rugby. The Wallabies, however, were going into the World Cup carrying a double burden: an Australian side never having won the Super 12 competition and the Wallabies never having won the Tri Nations tournament. The Springboks had not been defeated by the Wallabies in South Africa since 1993, either. If the seeding system used in the RWC draw worked, the Wallabies were due to confront the Springboks at Twickenham in the first semi-final.

The King Is Dead, Long Live Macqueen

If one moment has to be selected as pivotal for the capture of the 1999 William Webb Ellis trophy it is when Paddy O'Brien, the New Zealand referee, blew the full-time whistle at Loftus Versfeld Stadium in Pretoria on 23 August 1997. The scoreline was South Africa 61, Australia 22. This result represented the worst defeat suffered by the Wallabies in 352 Tests. The half-time score was 18–15 to the Springboks. In the second half the Wallabies literally gave up playing.

During the 1997 rugby season a dispirited Wallaby told Bob Dwyer, the coach of the 1991 world champion team, that his play had been poor because the team was so depressed. Teams are like people. When they get depressed they find it hard to function effectively or produce their best form. The depressed Wallabies of 1997 lost it at Loftus Versfeld Stadium.

How were they to get their attitude and commitment back?

The chief executive of the ARU, John O'Neill, believed he knew the answer. The Wallaby coach, Greg Smith, had to be sacked. O'Neill came to this decision while observing the shattered Wallabies as they moped around a tourist resort, Sun City, for two days while they waited for their flight home. This decision was hardened in his mind by an incident on the bus as the team was on its way to the airport. O'Neill saw Smith reading through a file of newspaper clippings faxed from Australia. Smith was drafting something on a piece of paper, which he passed to one of the members of the team.

'Could you get me that piece of paper, please?' O'Neill asked the team manager, John McKay.

When he read it, O'Neill saw that it was a petition to be signed by the players, supporting their coach. O'Neill ripped it up. 'That's a good way to get the sack,' he told Smith. After some bitter negotiations, in private and in public, where O'Neill kept to himself the fact that Smith was suffering from a potentially fatal illness, Greg Smith's contract was ripped up.

The new coach was Rod Macqueen. Macqueen had had a successful two years creating the ACT Brumbies team in the Super 12 tournament. Earlier, in 1991, he had coached the NSW Waratahs to a nine-match unbeaten season. This Waratahs side had formed the heart of the triumphant 1991 World Cup Wallabies.

O'Neill's action was drastic. But given the crisis the defeat at Pretoria had thrown Australian rugby into, he had few options. With only two seasons before the 1999 RWC tournament, the Wallabies had to start becoming a competitive team. The strategy of 'harsh measure for the great' seemed to be worth the risk. What Macqueen had in his favour was his past successes. Coaches come in all types. This is why it is so difficult to know beforehand whether a particular candidate for a coaching job will be successful or not. About the best test of a candidate is his previous record. Successful coaches tend to be successful throughout their careers. Success in the past presages, but does not guarantee, success in the future.

The gamble taken with the sacking of Greg Smith was a case, therefore, of 'Long Live Macqueen', or disaster for Australian rugby.

Fast-forward now to 6 November 1999 at Cardiff. The measure of the turn-around achieved by Rod Macqueen in his first two years as coach of the Wallabies was that 11 players who disgraced Australian rugby and themselves in front of 49,000 baying South Africans at Loftus Versfeld Stadium in 1997 were on the field at some time during the 1999 World Cup final in Cardiff.

Bad Start, Good Finish

The start of the Macqueen Era, though, was not encouraging.

Rod Macqueen inherited a team about to tour Argentina and Britain at the end of the 1997 season. Argentina was defeated 23–15 at Buenos Aires. The result was not comforting, for Argentina had conceded 90 points to the All Blacks earlier in the season. John Eales was the difference between the two sides, the Argentinian coach, Alex Wyllie, said. Then Argentina won the second Test 18–16.

This was the first loss by the Wallabies to a second-tier rugby nation in ten years. Greg Growden in the *Sydney Morning Herald* described the performance as 'spineless' and 'gutless'. Macqueen had brought to the Wallabies camp the open and inclusive coaching method he had developed with the ACT Brumbies. Several Brumbies players, however – only one of whom survived through to 1999 – got carried away by Macqueen's appointment and tried to run the practice sessions. Moreover, the Wallabies divided into Brumbies and anti-Brumbies groupings and this division was reflected on the field. On 15 November 1997, only two years away from the 1999 World Cup final, the Wallabies, making mistake after mistake, struggled to a 15–15 draw with England at Twickenham. This time it was Tim Horan, playing his best match for the Wallabies since coming back from a crippling knee injury suffered two years earlier, who saved the day for the team.

The inglorious season closed for the Wallabies with a 37–8 victory over Scotland at Murrayfield. The win was deceptive because the half-time score was 8–8. In the second half Stephen Larkham outplayed Scotland virtually on his own. His uncanny ability to beat player after player, by flitting through impossible gaps like a ghost through a wall, set up four tries for the Wallabies and 27 points in the second half.

The tour ended better than it started, and with Macqueen determined to prevent any repetition of a divided Wallaby camp.

Eye Witness, 15 October 1998

At a packed-out $100-a-head lunch to farewell the Wallabies before their European tour, a year after the disasters of the 1997 season and a year before the invasion of Britain for the 1999 World Cup, a spokesman for Vodafone, the major sponsor of the Wallabies, suddenly called for a moment's silence during his speech. Everyone sheepishly rose and bowed their heads. 'Thanks,' the Vodafone man said when they sat down. 'That was for all the teams the Wallabies are going to defeat next year.' The joke provoked applause. It was noticeable, too, that whenever the three-Test wipeout of the All Blacks was mentioned, the first since 1929, the suits growled their approval at the memory of what had been an historic result for Australian rugby . . .

At the lunch rugby officials made the point to me that in many ways it is harder to defeat the All Blacks three times in a row than win the World Cup tournament. After all, in 1991 the Wallabies only had to defeat the All Blacks once to win the William Webb Ellis trophy. The way the 1999 World Cup schedule works out, if the All Blacks stumble before the final, the Wallabies might not even have to face them to win the William Webb Ellis trophy . . .

There was one other significant incident at the farewell lunch. Before the speech of the Wallaby captain, John Eales, the gathering was asked to stand and sing 'Advance Australia Fair', the national anthem. A deep swelling chorus filled the large dining room and pictures of the Wallabies singing the anthem with great passion before one of their Tests with the All Blacks were shown on the huge screens behind the podium . . .

Turn On the Lights

The official programs produced by the organisers of the 1999 Rugby World Cup tournament listed the management officials of the Wallabies.

Team Manager	John McKay
Coach	Rod Macqueen
Assistant Coach	Tim Lane
Assistant Coach	Jeff Miller
Physical Conditioner	Steve Nance
Doctor	Dr John Best
Physio	Greg Craig
Physio	Cameron Lillicrap
Technical Adviser	Alex Evans
Video Analyst	Scott Harrison
Baggage Master	Ben Spindler
Team Media Liaison Officer	David Pembroke

This was the team within the team that coached, trained, counselled, advised, comforted and supported the players to get them ready to perform to the best of their physical and mental capacity during the World Cup tournament. One name was missing from the official list, John Muggleton.

Macqueen believed that rugby teams in general did not pay enough attention to the theory and technique of defence. Muggleton, a former rugby league international, was brought into the coaching squad to provide a rugby league perspective on defence. League players do not have to have the multiplicity of skills of union players. There are no lineouts, mauls, rucks, real scrums and contests at the breakdown for them to contend with. The league skills are those of defence, of ultra-fitness and of selecting shrewd angles to run on the ball from. Most importantly, the best league players are those who do not make mistakes with their basic skills.

This ethic of not making mistakes and knowing intimately the practice of defence was the knowledge Muggleton brought to the Wallabies. I saw him once drop-kick a goal from about 40 metres out at the SCG to force a win for Parramatta against St George right on time, a similar kick to that achieved by Stephen Larkham against the Springboks at Twickenham in the 1999 semi-final. Muggleton knew what teams had to do to win important matches. With tackling, he taught the Wallabies to drive with their shoulders and take one of their opponent's legs away while the shoulder drive was being completed. Players with the ball find it impossible to turn and set themselves as a target for their team-mates when they are trying to stand on one leg.

With this tackling trick the Wallabies rarely had to commit more than one player to the tackle. This meant that it was hard for oppositions to break their flat line of defence. As a player made a tackle, his team-mates moved one in or out, depending where the tackle was made. When there was the chance of a gang tackle, the players were drilled to break their line and complete the demolition of the ball carrier.

'We basically used a slightly compressed defence that moves straight up,' Muggleton explained after the RWC tournament, 'but which is able to drift when necessary. We compressed the defence because you have to be in a position to stop the maul.'

Muggleton's brief of making the Wallabies the world's best defensive team was achieved, with the side conceding only one try throughout the RWC tournament, and none once the finals section of the tournament began. The 1991 Wallabies had conceded only three tries in winning the William Webb Ellis trophy. Defence wins World Cups.

Muggleton's thinking complemented that of Rod Macqueen. Not long after Macqueen was given the coaching job with the ACT Brumbies he discussed with me his theories on defence. It was PhD stuff to my mind. He divided the field into zones, with the players expected to fill gaps according to a theory of defence for the various parts of the field. Depending on the situation, players would come up as a line or drift across the field. The calls among the players involved a number pattern that I found difficult to grasp. There was an additional point to this complexity, aside from its efficiency when carried out to the letter. Players had to be or become intelligent to understand this system, and to apply it in the tumult and the shouting of a rugby Test.

The system forced the Wallabies to be an intelligent team. They had to use their brains to apply the defensive system. This habit of thinking about play as events were swirling around them was applied to other facets of their game. In 1998 and 1999 rugby commentators frequently used the word 'composure' to describe the measured and calculated way the Wallabies went about the business of defeating their opponents.

It was not just composure, though, to my mind. Macqueen met me at a rugby function just before the start of the 1999 Test season and asked me what I thought the difference was between the Wallabies and the All Blacks. Based solely on the rugby talent of the two teams, the All Blacks had a better squad, I replied. 'But the Wallabies are a clever side,' I suggested, 'while the All Blacks are not a smart side.'

This cleverness was exposed in the multiple phases of play Macqueen devised and which the Wallabies practised endlessly at their camp at Caloundra. Rather than being a boring team, the Wallabies were a team for experts to savour. The two tries in the final against France were the first tries scored in a World Cup final since 1987. There was the subtlety of whisky rather than the directness of beer about their play. Once an attacking series was embarked on, the Wallabies varied their runners, presenting a different challenge to the defence with every tackle, depending on who was available and what forces the defence could muster. Australia's variety of movement and its intricate variation of plays, under pressure from a desperate defence, was the opposite to boring to anyone who understood the rugby game.

With Ben Tune's try against France, for instance, the winger came into the play twice, once at the beginning of the series and again at the end. Matt Burke, from the fullback position, was involved twice with his trademark dash through the middle of a ruck. George Gregan flipped a pass behind his back. He ran out of receivers towards the end of the series and scuttled through himself.

The Macqueen–Muggleton patterns of defence forced Macqueen to think deeply about attack, as well. He asked himself the question: How would his team cope with the sort of defence it was presenting to opponents? Macqueen looked to rugby league for ideas in this area, too. He told journalist Greg Growden at the beginning of the World Cup tournament that players had to be 'multiskilled' in the era of professionalism. The essence of attack was to have variations to moves rather than 'tricks up your sleeve'.

This philosophy fitted with the teaching of the ancient Chinese warrior-philosopher Sun-tzu whose book, *The Art of War*, has greatly influenced Macqueen's thinking. One of Sun-tzu's dictums is this: 'In planning, never a useless move: in strategy, no step taken in vain.'

Macqueen understood that about 70 per cent of rugby is played at the phases. 'That's why,' he told Growden, 'probably 80 per cent of our training is with forwards and backs together. Most other teams would struggle to train together for 25 per cent of the time.' He revealed, too, that for two years he had studied rugby league videos: 'You learn a lot. It again proves to you that the ideal situation is for the player to be instinctive and know what they have to do.' As Sun-tzu proclaimed: 'Know the enemy and know yourself: in a hundred battles you will never be in peril.'

In 1998 and 1999 the Wallabies prepared and practised in the quiet, slightly down-market resort of Caloundra, in Queensland. Steve Nance, the fitness coach Macqueen had poached from the Brisbane Broncos (the rugby league influence again, and Macqueen's smartest selection according to the Broncos' coach, Wayne Bennett), drove the players to a level of fitness they could not have ever envisioned reaching. The first training run in 1998 is now a legendary event. Players collapsed and were vomiting throughout the session. Not long after this Macqueen told me that Nance had raised the fitness levels of the Wallabies significantly but 'the real gains will come out in 1999'.

Lloyd Jones, a New Zealand writer, went to Caloundra to do a story on why the Wallabies had turned from a side that was a disgrace in 1997 into a team poised to defeat the All Blacks in three successive Tests in 1998. He found, as virtually every journalist has, a willingness on the part of the Wallaby management to explain what they were trying to do.

Jones went along with Jeff Miller to hear him address the Kawana Waters Chamber of Commerce on 'High Performance On and Off the Field'. Miller told the story of a small Italian village where motorists parked outside the shops all day, obstructing would-be shoppers. The village couldn't afford parking meters. What could it do? They rang up Edward de Bono. Within five minutes he had a lateral-thought solution. He told the village to order motorists to park with their lights on and ticket any parked car that didn't have its lights on.

Lloyd Jones then described Miller's spin on this story, as it applied to the Wallabies. What did we have to do, Miller asked, to return the Wallabies to 1991 when they were the best team in the world? 'We had some serious thinking to do,' he told his audience. 'Young players were being paid hundreds of thousands of dollars. They were living in five-star hotels. We were starting to think that these guys had gotten a bit soft in their preparation. Rod Macqueen recognised that something had to change. Out went the flashy hotels, city distractions and city living. In came Caloundra on the Sunshine Coast and flatmate conditions, a heavy dose of self-sufficiency, home cooking, performance criteria to meet, selection methodology and performance appraisal, and players understanding what was required for them to remain in the Wallaby team.'

To lift the darkness that had gathered in on the Wallabies at the end of the Greg Smith era, therefore, Macqueen had turned on the light of cleverness.

Eye Witness, 28 October 1999

A week before the Wallabies left home, coach Rod Macqueen gave me a long and detailed insight into his team's quest. He had an hour-by-hour schedule for the team from the beginning of the season, the first practice at Caloundra, up to 5.00 p.m. on 6 November when the Wallabies hope to be presented with the William Webb Ellis trophy by the Queen. He punched some commands into his laptop and showed me a play-by-play breakdown of a recent Test. Some more commands and up came an entire match in symbols for one player. Macqueen has devised and developed this system by himself . . . He has access to dozens of tapes on opposing sides, and special equipment can isolate an entire match played by one specified player, showing how he reacted in different situations . . .

Into the Pool

The pool rounds of the Rugby World Cup tournament are the most enjoyable for the players and coaching staff. With a team like the Wallabies, a place in the finals is certain. There is no fear, therefore, that after a match the team will have to pack up and leave for home early the next morning, as happens with the teams losing in the quarter-finals. If a team reaches the final it will have spent eight weeks in camp. There is plenty of time to fine-tune the training, drills and moves that have been gone over time after time at Caloundra before coming to Britain.

So after about 24 hours in the air, travelling in business class, the Wallabies arrived at their camp at Portmarnock, a village outside Dublin. The medical staff advised the players to stay up as long as possible, for those who played golf to have a game. The object was to set the body clock of the players from Australian time to British time. On the night before training was to begin in earnest, the entire squad of 40 – players and support staff – had a happy night in the team's pub enjoying the hospitality of the Guinness company, a sponsor of the RWC tournament. The drinks and the conversation flowed until the squad was bonded securely in its quest, as the ARU's advertising slogan had it, to 'Bring Back Bill'.

The first two matches played by the Wallabies in its group, E, were unimpressive. Belfast is a grim and unrelenting city with the grey ghosts of cranes on the waterfront, heavily fortified police stations and the city still divided into Protestant and Catholic sectors. A sense of being out-of-place affected the Wallabies. Although the scoreline against Romania looked healthy, at 57–9, the victory was not of a high quality.

The second pool match against Ireland – the key match of the round-robin for it decided which team would go straight through to the finals and which team would have to endure a midweek play-off – began with some gamesmanship from the New Zealand-born Irish coach, Warren Gatland. The winning team of Group E would play Wales in a quarter-final at the Millennium Stadium, if Wales won its group. But the team from Group E which won the play-off for second would probably play Argentina, at Dublin's Lansdowne Road, in a quarter-final. It could be in Ireland's interest – provided it won the play-off – to drop its match against the Wallabies.

Gatland made some suggestions to the media about this. Then he rejected the idea. But the way Ireland played against the Wallabies, going down 23–3, created the idea in the minds of some journalists that it was not unduly disturbed about losing. In its first World Cup match Ireland had played with the ball in hand as much as possible. Gatland had said that this was going to be the side's preferred style of play. Against the Wallabies, however, Ireland kicked continually. And it was not good kicking, either.

The most controversial aspect of the game was a ferocious fist fight between several Irish players, particularly Trevor Brennan, who seemed to be pumped up on jungle juice, and Toutai Kefu, normally a hard but fair player. Kefu, the best of the Wallaby forwards, was cited for punching and given a suspension which put him out of the tournament until the semi-final. Daniel Herbert was inexplicably cited, too. This charge was dropped.

There were more worries for the Wallabies during the match, as Phil Kearns damaged his ankle badly. The Wallabies had fixed up problems in the front row by bringing in Kearns' scrumming expertise; now they had to work out a solution once more. With Jeremy Paul, Kearns' replacement, being attended to after being smashed in another brawl, the Wallabies called for, and were given, several unopposed scrums until Paul came back on to the field.

One veteran out (Kearns) was matched by the returns of John Eales in the match against Romania and Stephen Larkham against Ireland. With Larkham at five-eighths, Tim Horan achieved the record at inside centre of playing alongside 10 different Test five-eighths. Larkham was rusty in his general play. His tackling was strong, though. He continued this throughout the tournament, achieving the most number of tackles, 26, brought off by a back. And there were glimpses of his deft passing and ghost-like running.

Horan told the *Sydney Morning Herald*'s Greg Growden about his pleasure at playing outside Larkham: 'He is a great talent. What marks him as different is that he's very well balanced on his feet, has a great step and fantastic vision.' Once Larkham came back into the five-eighths position and Horan moved out to inside centre, Horan started to establish himself as the player of the tournament.

Another lacklustre performance, against the United States, won 55–19, rounded out the pool section for the Wallabies. Only South Africa scored more points against the Wallabies than the USA did, while the USA's Juan Grobler scored the only try recorded against the Wallabies in about 500 minutes of World Cup rugby. A 15-point scoring spree with 11 minutes of play remaining gave the scoreboard an unwarranted respectability for the Wallabies.

Eye Witness, 20 October 1999

At 4.30 last Friday, the Italian players gathered in the foyer of their Huddersfield hotel before boarding a bus to take them back home and out of the Rugby World Cup tournament. The Italians had joined the All Blacks at a disco the night before, following their thrashing by the Kiwis, but now they have been told in the most brutal way that their RWC campaign is over . . . For the losing play-off teams, all sides that believe they should go further in the tournament, the firing squad at dawn experience will be one of the most traumatic ordeals they will ever endure. Matt Burke tells of arriving back in Perth in 1995 after the Wallabies were defeated by England in the quarter-finals. As the team was going through the terminal to its bus it saw about 200 Australian supporters waiting to fly out to South Africa. 'They thought we'd be still in the tournament,' Burke said. 'It was embarrassing for us. We ran out of the airport in case they saw us . . .'

The pundits were not impressed with the pool play of the Wallabies. Former Wallaby coach Alan Jones called on the Wallabies to stop being so complicated in their play. They had to unleash their talented backline if they wanted to win the Rugby World Cup. 'We're killing ourselves,' Jones said.

Mark Ella agreed. He picked New Zealand to win the World Cup and stated that the Wallabies were playing stupid rugby. 'They're not using their heads,' he said. 'For a side with our supposed intelligence, we play very stupidly.' He was not entirely impressed with New Zealand, however: 'New Zealand will want to play anyone but Australia. We've got their measure. The All Blacks are favourites, but if we make the final we can beat them.'

3 October 1999, at Belfast. Australia **57** (T. Kefu 3, J. Roff 2, T. Horan, J. Little, J. Paul, M. Burke tries; Burke 5, J. Eales conversions) defeated Romania **9** (P. Mitu 3 penalty goals)

10 October 1999, at Dublin. Australia **23** (T. Horan, B. Tune tries; M. Burke 2 conversions; Burke 2, J. Eales penalty goals) defeated Ireland **3** (D. Humphreys penalty goal)

15 October 1999, at Limerick. Australia **55** (S. Staniforth 2, S. Larkham, M. Foley, M. Burke, T. Strauss, C. Latham, C. Whitaker tries; Burke 6 conversions and a penalty goal) defeated USA **19** (J. Grobler try; K. Dalzell 3 penalty goals and 1 conversion; D. Nui 1 drop goal)

Improving Wallabies

It was thought by some leading British rugby writers that Wales would be the northern hemisphere's best hope to stop the southern hemisphere dominance of the Rugby World Cup tournament. New Zealand, Australia and then South Africa in 1995 (in that country's first attempt) had been the previous winners of the William Webb Ellis trophy.

Wales, however, had gone through a terrible period of rugby in these 12 years, when the heart and talent had gone out of the game. Throughout these campaigns, Wales, once one of the great Test sides, had been undisciplined on and off the field. On their last tour of Australia, for instance, Greg Growden, the *Sydney Morning Herald*'s rugby writer, had stayed back after a post-Test dinner and had witnessed Welsh players fighting with each other. Bob Dwyer, when he was coaching the Wallabies, complained bitterly after a fierce match against a Welsh club side that his players had been subjected to unrestrained 'bag-snatching', a tactic where a player's balls are grabbed instead of the match ball. But with the hiring of Graham Henry, a no-nonsense coach with a New Zealander's intuition about how rugby should be played, Wales had come back. Until Manu Samoa defeated Wales in the last pool match, a game that had no effect on the placing of the teams for the finals part of the World Cup tournament, Wales had equalled their best run of Test wins ever, with ten successive victories.

It was considered, too, that this resurgent Welsh side would be inspired by the new Millennium Stadium, an artefact especially built for rugby, with its vast stands rising steeply only metres away from the pitch. This was a true cathedral of rugby where Welsh *hywl* (that combination of patriotic fervour, spirit, talent and the joyfulness of ensemble rugby) would be revived against the unfortunate Wallabies. Or so it was thought.

The first ever Test between Wales and Australia, on 6 December 1908 at Cardiff, saw the Australians committed to playing a side that was the glory of British rugby. Wales was experienced (with Dicky Owen, a tiny halfback, making a record thirty-fifth appearance for his national side) and passionate. Then, as now, Welsh supporters demanded victory. Shopkeepers barricaded their stores in fear of a Welsh defeat and to protect the Christmas supplies they had in stock. The referee, Gil Evans, was clearly intimidated by the will to win of the crowd. He awarded Wales a try early on when the ball had not been grounded over the tryline. Then when the Wallabies equalised with a try he ruled against the conversion, even though the ball went through the posts before being blown away by a strong wind.

Ever since this match, Australia–Wales has always been a Test with passion embracing the play of both sides.

The Wallabies had emerged from the pool competition in the comfortable position of starting poorly and improving with each match. The most noticeable aspect of the improvement was the way the side had scored most of their points in the last quarter of their matches. Of the 135 points scored by the Wallabies in the pool matches, for instance, only 52 had come in the first half. Four tries were scored in the first quarter of play, three in the second, five in the third and seven in the last 20 minutes of play. Eight tries, therefore, were scored in the first half and 12 in the second half, with the greatest number of tries in the last quarter.

The fitness work organised by Steve Nance was clearly having a good effect. So were the impact players being sent on during the second half to raise the intensity of the Wallabies' play.

There was another point to these statistics, though, that was overlooked by the rugby experts in their reports on the RWC tournament. The statistics reveal that the players and the coaching staff were showing extreme cleverness in identifying the defensive weaknesses of opponents, and then devising the correct attacking response to capitalise on these discovered weaknesses. The instructions at half-time were accurate and were being carried out.

The Ferrari and the Bus

In the World Cup quarter-final the Wallabies, in a distorted replay of the 1908 Test, were helped significantly in their victory over Wales by two mistakes from the New Zealand referee, Colin Hawke.

George Gregan's first try came after he had kicked the ball back into the ruck. This offside was disregarded, as was a knock-on before the Wallabies cleared the ball to the blindside and let Gregan dash for the tryline. The last try of the quarter-final, scored by Gregan again, had another blatant knock-on, with Tim Horan being the undetected culprit of the mishandling.

In between these tries, towards the end of the Test, Stephen Larkham broke the deadlock of the Welsh defence by running the ball to the advantage line and then sliding a kick behind the scarlet jerseys. Ben Tune raced through, as if the spontaneous move had been rehearsed a hundred times, and skidded across the wet surface to touch down for the try.

After a strong start, when it looked as though the Wallabies would run away with the game by about 40 points, Wales had regrouped and with 11 minutes to go the score was 10–9 to the Wallabies. The discipline of the Wallabies was outstanding. Neil Jenkins, 'Jenkins the Boot', the recordholder for points scored in Test rugby, did not get one chance to kick at goal in the second half.

Wales, however, was shrewdly coached by Henry to kill the ball. The result was that the Wallabies could not get any continuity in their play. Wales won the rucks 38–33, the mauls 14–7, crossed the advantage line 28 times to 22 by the Wallabies, and made only five handling errors to 16. To a partisan, one-eyed spectator in the stands it seemed as though Wales might have done enough to win.

Referee Hawke, accordingly, was booed after the match as he made his way off the field.

Eye Witness, 1 November 1999

Wales is relying too much on imports – from coach Graham Henry down to the former Wallaby centre Jason Jones-Hughes. It was noticeable that the only Welsh player to rise to the challenge of the Wallabies in the World Cup quarter-final was Shane Howarth, a former All Black dropped from his national and provincial side because he was too slow. The fact that Howarth could become one of the stars of British rugby is a telling indictment on the quality of the players the British system is producing, and on the lack of intelligence being invested in the game there. David Campese was right when he accused the Welsh players of being too fat. The bulging bellies were obvious even though the Welsh management proclaimed that the team was the fittest Wales had ever sent on to the field.

All of the best play by Wales and all of the worst play by the Wallabies came after 15 minutes of play when the field, which was slightly slippery anyway, became treacherous after showers of rain pelted down through the open roof of the Millennium Stadium. Tim Horan made the quote of the 1999 RWC tournament: 'It was disappointing that they did not close the roof. It's a bit like having a Ferrari in your garage and going out to catch the bus. If it's there you should use it, because the weather probably spoilt the party a little today.'

---

23 October 1999, at Cardiff. Australia **24** (G. Gregan 2, B. Tune tries; M. Burke 3 conversions and a penalty goal) defeated Wales **3** (N. Jenkins penalty goal)

High Noon at Twickenham

The Springboks came into the semi-final of the 1999 RWC tournament against the Wallabies at Twickenham in a cocksure frame of mind. South Africans generally tend to be 'at your throat or at your feet' anyway and, despite their wayward form in the pool matches, the Springboks looked at the semi-final as a nuisance game they had to play before taking the All Blacks on in the World Cup final.

This cockiness is typical. After the conclusion of the 1991 Rugby World Cup tournament, from which the Springboks were barred because of the world sporting boycott imposed due to South Africa's apartheid policies, Louis Luyt, a senior South African rugby administrator, told journalists in London, 'We can field two teams that would defeat both World Cup finalists, one team playing at 1.30 and the other at 3.00.'

That disposition to arrogance was given a certain credibility in 1999 by the ten straight wins the Springboks had enjoyed in World Cup matches since coming into the RWC tournament in 1995. Those wins included a victory in the final in 1995 against New Zealand at the ground Louis Luyt virtually owns, Ellis Park.

The official press guide to the 1999 tournament put out by the South Africans played a hostage to fortune by suggesting that the Springboks would win every game. There were details about where the team would stay in Cardiff while preparing for the final at the Millennium Stadium. At Cardiff, the press guide said, the Springboks would train on Monday, Tuesday and Thursday (the day of the third place play-off). There would be a team photo taken on Friday. On Sunday the team and the William Webb Ellis trophy would head back to Johannesburg and the applause of a grateful nation.

There was an element of fun in all of this, amid the seriousness. The press guide, for instance, included a reference to the 'Springbok Media Code' which stated: 'Dealings between the Springboks team and the media should always be conducted in good humour. Professional rugby is a serious business but there should always be an opportunity to share lighter moments with the media. Good humour is important to a happy team environment.'

The Springboks' fun, however, was overshadowed by dark streaks of hubris. Their management simply could not envisage the South Africans being defeated by the Wallabies. This hubris, a fatal overweening ambition, allowed the Springboks' management to dismiss the evidence that their team was split between those players who felt that a sacred trust had been broken with the dropping of the long-serving captain Gary Teichmann and those rallying around the new captain, Joost van der Westhuizen. The pro-Teichmann clique tended to come from the coastal provinces, which were locked in a power struggle for control of the SARU with the veldt provinces. The new captain, the charismatic van der Westhuizen, was from the veldt province of Northern Transvaal.

Westhuizen's effectiveness as a runner had always been greatly enhanced when playing with Henry Honiball, a tall and robust player with the build and tackling and running instincts of a flanker. With Honiball at five-eighths, opposing sides had to try and cover two runners close to the ruck and maul. The consequence was that, from time to time, either Westhuizen or Honiball were presented with gaps to run through to score or set up tries. Honiball, too, was an enthusiastic and robust tackler. But Honiball, a key player in the 17 successive Test victories the Springboks had achieved in 1997 and 1998, was also a loyal friend of Teichmann.

With the dropping of Teichmann, Honiball's first inclination was to make himself unavailable for the World Cup squad. He had a genuine excuse – an injured knee. Teichmann talked him out of retiring from international rugby but Honiball's knee kept him out of the team up to the quarter-final against England at Paris. Jannie de Beer, his replacement, had filled the gap more than adequately, in terms of scoring points. He drop-kicked a record five goals, going back to the days of Bennie Osler in the 1920s who had won many Tests for South Africa with drop goals. The Springbok coach, Nick Mallett, explained to journalists that drop goals were impossible to defend against.

Mallett was unpleasant with the journalists, though, when he was questioned about divisions in the team. So much for the good humour in dealing with the media, according to the media guide. Mallett dared any one of the journalists to stand up and say that his team was not united. None did so. A South African journalist told me later that the Springboks had had a bonding session in the bars of Paris before the quarter-final and this had sealed with alcohol, for a time, the fractures in the squad. The journalists were prepared to give the Springboks the benefit of the doubt about their internal harmony, until they had evidence to the contrary. This is why none of them challenged Mallett.

But de Beer's success had given Mallett another excuse not to play Honiball. Honiball was now available for the semi-final and if Mallett had been able to disassociate him from his row with Teichmann, he should have been in the starting line-up for the semi-final against the Wallabies. But Mallett somehow could not bring himself to do the right thing.

Jannie de Beer was selected instead for the semi-final and the Springboks, as a consequence, were weaker than they should have been for the crucial match. Playing de Beer, who stood deep in the pocket rather than flat like Honiball, meant that the Springboks had to rely on van der Westhuizen for any attack with the ball in hand. This restriction made the defensive strategy of the Wallabies easy to devise. Watch van der Westhuizen and cover the kick. Against England, for instance, de Beer passed on only three occasions and kicked 16 times.

There was also the matter of de Beer's defence or, more accurately, his lack of defensive inclinations. Although he managed one strong tackle against England, de Beer liked to drop back as an extra fullback when the opposition had the ball. This habit meant that there was a gap inside the Springbok inside centre when the South African defensive line moved up. This was the gap Tim Horan exposed so relentlessly in the semi-final. The dropping-back habit of de Beer meant, too, that he was in no position to put pressure on Stephen Larkham if the latter decided to attempt a dropped goal. A photo taken at the moment of impact, when Larkham put his foot into the ball for the dropped goal of the RWC tournament, shows a desperate van der Westhuizen well on the inside trying to charge down, with Pieter Muller and Robbie Fleck coming up on the outside of Larkham. Jannie de Beer, who might have blocked Larkham's kicking line by running at him, is nowhere in the picture.

Eye Witness, 28 October 1999

Players and teams are creatures of habit. When the Springboks win a couple of quick rucks near the opposition's 22, halfback Joost van der Westhuizen instinctively chips over the top and races through to regather. The blindside defence will be on the alert and a chargedown by the Wallabies may result . . . The essence of the Wallaby game plan on defence against the Springboks will surely involve engaging their pack so robustly that Bobby Skinstad is forced to play in the forwards rather than roam wide in the backs . . . The Wallaby loose forwards, especially Toutai Kefu, will run at the five-eighth Jannie de Beer to squeeze him for space and upset his kicking. De Beer is an ordinary player and becomes even more ordinary when he is rattled . . . Rugby, a game that lends itself to cleverness, is all about centimetres: the centimetres between the ears. This battle of brainpower between Rod Macqueen and Nick Mallett will be a crucial factor in the outcome of the match . . .

While the Springboks were too complacent, the Wallabies had reached the stage in their preparation where they were confident but edgy. Game time had arrived. This was the first match of the RWC tournament where a defeat was a realistic outcome. The trick for the coaching staff was to get the players up but not so stressed that they would freeze on the big day. Jeff Miller told Greg Growden that some stress was inevitable. 'They know they are playing for sheep stations now,' he said.

But the stress was being managed well, with Rod Macqueen being unusually calm. The players, too, lightened the seriousness of their practices with the usual pranks and wheezes that take the monotony out of doing drills.

While Twickenham was slowly filling for the semi-final, the Wallabies went through some limbering-up exercises, followed by their defensive drills – which involved moving up in a line and moving sideways after each forward rush – about an hour before the match. The players appeared, from the distance of the press box, to be confident and full of energy.

The game itself turned out to be a classic high-noon contest, with both sides kicking what looked like decisive shots at goal. For the Springboks, de Beer kicked a long-range penalty from the sidelines well into injury time in the second half to equal the score and send the match into extra time. John Eales, who was used in the lineout constantly for the first time in the tournament, showed an inspired touch of captaincy by immediately running off the field to the dressing room as the kick soared over and the whistle was blown for the end of the second half. What this gesture demonstrated to his team-mates and the Springboks, it seemed to me, was that he was focused on working out how the extra time period was to be played. He was looking forward positively, in other words, rather than hanging back pessimistically in contemplation of what might have been.

During the break the Wallabies regrouped. Tim Lane casually mentioned to Stephen Larkham as he was going back on to the field that if he had a chance he should go for a dropped goal. Larkham had missed an easy shot earlier in the match. But the suggestion stuck in his mind. When he kicked his goal it gave the Wallabies a three-point advantage with time running out. This was significant because it meant that the Springboks then had to score a try to win the match because they had had a player ordered off during the RWC tournament, Brendon Venter against Uruguay. The RWC rules were that if the scores were level after extra time the team with fewest players ordered off in the tournament won the game. The Wallabies had had players cited but no one ordered off the field.

Eye Witness, 1 November 1999

Those who live by the kick can also perish by the kick. In one of rugby's great matches, the first tryless test between Australia and South Africa, the Wallabies defeated the Springboks and won their way into the World Cup final, booted to a six-point victory by a stunning Stephen Larkham drop kick. Minutes into the second half of extra time, Larkham ran wide and, from about 45 metres out, unleashed a tremendous drop goal, his first in Test rugby. It will go down in Wallaby mythology, to be enthused over with George Gregan's famous tackle and David Campese's overhead pass to Tim Horan that set up the winning try in the 1991 World Cup semi-final against the All Blacks.

The Wallabies have now established themselves as the World Cup giant-killers. The Springboks' defeat was their first loss in two tournaments. And it was the Wallabies who were the first team to defeat the All Blacks in the World Cup, too.

It was clear from the opening minutes of the match that the South Africans were going to rely on the kicking of Jannie de Beer. The risk in this strategy is that by favouring kicking rather than running with the ball, tries were disregarded as a way of scoring points. This is what happened with the Springboks. De Beer had five attempts at field goals, scoring with only one shot. This was a disastrous return. On several occasions the Springboks had over-laps when they were only about 30 metres from the Wallaby try-line. Still, only minutes from full-time and six points behind, they opted to kick for goal rather than go for touch to force a lineout near the Wallaby line. The kick was successful. And, right on time, after what seemed to be an eternity following the ground announcer's proclamation that only two minutes remained, Derek Bevan, the referee, awarded the Springboks a penalty on an acute angle about 40 metres out. De Beer kicked a beautiful goal, and the teams trotted off to prepare for extra time.

Hindsight provides easy scope for criticism but, even at the time, Joost van der Westhuizen's decision to go for goal, in the hope of winning a second penalty and equalising the score, looked to place excessive expectations on the validity of the kicking game.

To their credit, the Wallabies played with the ball in hand as much as possible, even in extra time, and moved it wide whenever *they could. The tactic tired the big Springbok pack, in the way a matador tires a charging bull. While Larkham played a balanced hand, kicking on 18 occasions and passing 23 times, de Beer kicked 28 times and passed only on four. Such was the Springboks' reliance on the boot that in the last play of the game, when they needed a converted try to snatch an unlikely victory, they resorted to a high kick to Matt Burke, which Burke caught securely . . .*

The outstanding player for the Wallabies, a team in which everyone played well, was Tim Horan. He repeatedly made breaks against a defence that had been secure throughout the tournament. The day before Horan had been struck down with gastric flu and had vomited for hours. He got out of bed on match day at 9.30 a.m. and said he was going to play despite his weakness. The medical team gave him the go-ahead. He ate two pieces of toast and played brilliantly until he was replaced for the extra-time period by Nathan Grey. Horan was still exhausted and barely able to move half an hour after the match ended, when Nick Mallett made his way into the dressing room and singled him out for the highest praise.

Before the semi-final Stephen Waugh, the captain of the world champion Australian cricket team, sent the Wallabies a prophetic goodwill message: 'There's only one thing better than beating the Springboks in a semi-final. That's tying with them and going through . . .'

---

30 October 1999, at Twickenham. Australia **27** (M. Burke 8 penalty goals; S. Larkham 1 drop goal) defeated South Africa **21** (J. de Beer 6 penalty goals and 1 drop goal)

Disdain for the Wallabies

The day after the 'high noon at Twickenham' first semi-final, on Sunday, the second semi-final between France and New Zealand was played. The talk of the journalists from the southern hemisphere gathered in the huge newsroom underneath the stands at Twickenham before this match was the bizarre, bad-tempered and uninformed article written by a doyen of the British rugby media, Stephen Jones, in the influential broadsheet paper, the *Sunday Times*. Journalists discussed the article and shook their heads in bewilderment at the opinions Jones had expressed. The drama of the Wallabies–Springboks match would be remembered, Jones wrote, 'when the poor quality of the match itself is forgotten'. Stephen Larkham's drop goal was 'an event of heavy irony' because he had 'almost throttled his own team with a heavyfooted display'. Wales and England would be disappointed with the realisation that 'they had somehow managed to lose to this lot'. Australia 'had little to offer bar the boot of Burke, their own excellent defending and the foothold given to them by their scrummaging'. There was very little on show in the first semifinal 'to shake the conviction that New Zealand are now favourites for the World Cup by an overwhelming margin'.

That prediction by Jones proved to be as flatulent as his demeaning comments about the performance of the Wallabies.

Later on in the afternoon the unpredictable French, after being 24–10 behind some minutes into the second half, piled on 33 unanswered points against the All Blacks in about 30 minutes. The British journalists in the press section pumped their arms in the air at the pleasure of seeing a southern hemisphere upstart put in its place by a northern hemisphere side. There were hugs, huge smiles and high excitement as it became increasingly clear that the northern hemisphere would have a team in the World Cup final at Cardiff.

A letter to *The Times*, though, pointed to a local difficulty for British supporters, and a resolution of the problem: 'Sir, an estimated 50,000 Englishmen and women cheered France on at Twickenham. What possible reason can Lionel Joslin have for not doing the same for British beef?'

An editorial in *The Times* on the morning of the World Cup

final, titled 'Whom To Shout For?', summed up the dilemma for the British rugby fan: 'He cherishes stereotypes for both finalists, frogs and Foster's, onion johnnies and kangaroos. Brigitte Bardot and Edna Everage . . . The French have flair, panache and the bite of the underdog . . . The Australians have the advantage of power, professionalism and discipline. The British are both jealous of and admire their sporting success.'

Despite the typical even-handed approach espoused in *The Times*'s editorial, it was clear in talking about the match and its prospects with British journalists. Most of their articles expressed that the British rugby establishment — the Rugbyocracy — desperately wanted France, as the champion of the northern hemisphere's supposed hegemony over rugby, to defeat the Wallabies.

Enter the Rugbyocracy

With Stephen Jones's article we get the authentic, braying voice of the Rugbyocracy, stridently anti-southern hemisphere, stridently partisan in favour of the so-called 'Home' unions and dogmatically and infallibly ignorant about what constitutes successful and attractive rugby.

The Rugbyocracy is a loose confederation of officials from the Home unions (with the implication that these unions are the true home of rugby), some members of the International Rugby Board, some influential journalists, former British players and men of influence — or wanting influence. In rugby's northern hemisphere and southern hemisphere split, the Rugbyocracy continually works to ensure the domination of the northern hemisphere interests.

The Rugbyocracy will stoop to any tactic, including racist insults, to get its way; it is obsessed with the necessity of maintaining its control over the laws of rugby and the practice and structure of the game; it retains Imperial delusions; it hates professionalism and modern rugby; and it is officious and obnoxious.

The parts of the confederation often wrangle among themselves. The influential journalists will criticise the officials. But they come together, like lemmings racing towards the cliff face, to assault the ambitions of the southern hemisphere unions, who want to make rugby an athletic, entertaining and democratically organised world game.

This attitude is firmly entrenched. During the first Test played between England and Wales in 1881, the England captain, Leonard Stokes, threw a 'colossal' cut-out pass which set up an easy try. The officials running the game decided that the try wouldn't be allowed because long passes were not part of rugby. This hostility to 'passing' rugby has been a mark of the Rugbyocracy ever since. So, too, has been its contempt for the former colonial unions like the ARU.

The Lion and the Kangaroo

The denigration of the way Australians play rugby began with the Rev. Mullineux in 1899, when he brought a touring team to Australia. It was intensified by the Rugbyocracy during the first tour of Britain by the Wallabies in 1908 and has been maintained throughout the twentieth century up to the 1999 World Cup tournament.

How do we explain this persistent hostility?

D.H. Lawrence, arriving in Australia in the early 1920s, knew instinctively that it was a place that was 'absolutely and flatly democratic'. The absence of deference offended his English sensibilities. 'In Australia authority was at a discount,' he wrote. The sensibilities of the Rugbyocracy have been similarly offended. The Rugbyocracy has attacked Australian rugby because it resents the lack of deference shown to its demands for authority over the game.

Accusations of cheating by the Wallabies and their use of foul and over-rough play were so persistent as far back as 1908, for instance, that Dr Herbert Moran, the Wallaby captain and a natural gentleman on and off the field, felt impelled to write an article in the *Daily Mail* answering the criticisms. He carefully went through the way the Wallabies played, showing that the protection of the halfback and the ball by the 'swinging out of our backrow' was 'no particular vice'. The problem with the way the Wallabies were being 'penalised so frequently' was due, he argued, to the Wallabies playing specialist forwards, unlike the British.

Dr Moran insisted that the Wallabies were cleverer and more systematic than their British opponents (as they are today when compared with British teams) and the referees mistook their robust, athletic tactics for rough play. 'This Rugby game is a strenuous struggle between physical giants,' Dr Moran concluded, 'and we must not refer to gentle ladies for a decision on what constitutes rough play.'

In identifying supposed rough play and a hypocritical boringness as marks of Australian rugby, the Rugbyocracy was – and is, with its continuing attacks – making a general criticism of the Australian character. It is in this area that the racism of the Rugbyocracy comes through. The sociological context of the Rugbyocracy's hostility to Australian rugby is that Australians are marked by the convict stain, making them by nature undisciplined, unmannered, unruly, lawless, hard to control, devious and difficult to civilise. A typical expression of this notion occurred when the Australian Prime Minister, John Curtin, complained to Winston Churchill during the Second World War that he had not been consulted on the secret decision taken by Churchill and President Roosevelt to concentrate on beating Hitler first, even if this meant a Japanese invasion of Australia. Churchill explained to colleagues that Curtin's bitter reaction could be expected of Australians because they came from 'bad stock'.

The British Establishment, of which Churchill was a leading figure, gave itself the task of somehow trying to civilise the Australians. This has been a long-standing ambition. Governor

Carrington told an assembly at Sydney University on 21 April 1888, commemorating 100 years of colonial rule in Australia: 'I consider that the position which I have the honour to hold is not simply that of an Imperial official sent here to represent English ideas and English views of Australia.' There was a civilising role, he suggested, of taming the wild Australian beast. The *Bulletin*, a republican magazine, mocked Governor Carrington's mission to civilise with a cartoon of a lion that had the bottom half of a kangaroo, with Governor Carrington in its pouch. 'The Kanga-lion, or Lion-garoo. A curious animal lately discovered by Lord Carrington', the *Bulletin* caption read.

It was the *Bulletin*, too, that explained, using the example of rugby Tests, the ambiguous relationship Australians have experienced with Britain and things British from the convict days: 'When Australian rugby teams play British teams migrants and native-born alike are British in their love of the game, and Australian in their hope that the colonial side will win.' As the popular toast at political and sporting gatherings in the nineteenth century expressed it, 'The land, boys, we live in!'

The Rugbyocracy is the British Establishment in rugby boots. It has attempted to exploit this vision that Australia is a new Britannia on the edge of the world. When Australians are more lion than kangaroo, the Establishment and the Rugbyocracy embrace them. But when Australians are kangaroo, like the Wallabies throughout the twentieth century, rather than lion, the slurs and criticisms are unleashed.

'I Am a Wallaby'

My case is that the Rugbyocracy is wrong about rugby and wrong about Australians. It is an insidious institution, too, that works against the real interests of rugby.

Australians are not lawless, poorly bred or hypocritical. They have rather, as Robert Hughes argues, an aversion to pomposity. They will not kowtow to self-proclaimed leaders. This is connected with the convict past, for it liberated the Australian spirit. It did not subjugate it. It is the convict past that makes Australians a great and unique people. The land was 'designed to punish', Hughes points out, but 'it was renamed with the sign of freedom'. Freedom from the leg-irons of the British class system and its manifestations in every area of life, including sport.

This democratic instinct towards what the historian Dr Inga Clendinnen calls Australia's 'obstinately horizontal view of society' was reinforced by the dynamics of migration. Rather than the 'bad stock' of Churchill's jaundiced view, the Australian type is the product of the best genes of nations around the world. Migrants bring variety to the nation's gene pool. Migration acts, too, as a selection process. The bravest, the most optimistic, those who want to get on for themselves and their children, the risk-takers, the desperate and people with a determination to make good no matter how hard the battle become migrants. Migrants make the best stock, not the worst stock.

And this best stock has enriched the Wallabies. Many of the players have an Anglo–Celtic background but others are more varied. John Eales, like David Campese, has an Italian background. Eales's face in repose resembles a portrait of a Medici prince, and he has the same leadership quality of quiet hardness and sense of the excellent as the Medicis. There is George Gregan, too, whose mother comes from Zambia. Jeremy Paul is Maori. And Toutai Kefu has Tongan parents.

There is also the matter of temperament. Throughout the 1999 RWC tournament the rugby journalists remarked on the 'composure' of the Wallabies. Australians react well to pressure. An explanation for this comes from Dr Peter Hay, a lecturer in geography and the environment at the University of Tasmania, who sees a 'natural optimism' and 'sunniness' as part of the Australian character.

These strong mental advantages are complemented by an environment that allows Australians to fulfil the Greek ideal of a healthy mind in a healthy body. Historian Dr Timothy Coughlan claims that at the turn of the century the average Australian's diet generated far more energy than the diet of the Germans, French, Americans and British. Meat was eaten three times a day. But where once, before the coming of the eight-hour working day, the energy created by this high-protein diet had been dissipated in back-breaking toil, by the time Australia played its first rugby Test in 1899 it had been redirected to the sports field.

A feminist at the turn of the century, Jessie Ackermann, observed child-rearing practices in Australia, especially noting the way children were allowed to play endless and unsupervised games by themselves. This led to her acute observation: 'This form of child-rearing spells out in very large letters the beginning of independence of the children of Australia.'

A high-protein diet and the chance to play outdoors all year from early childhood creates the sociological explanation for the superior speed, energy and stamina of Australian rugby teams. The influence of the bush in toughening the Australian type, in mind and body, shouldn't be overlooked, either. In Henry Lawson's story 'Going Blind', a man from the bush comes into the city to get his eyes fixed. But he has left it too long and his sight is rapidly going on him. He talks stoically, in the manner of a man from the bush, about how he will cope as a blind man trying to earn his living. His brother comes down to Sydney to take him home. 'I felt their grip on my hand,' the narrator of the story says, 'for five minutes after they had gone.'

The mental and physical strength of Australians – the equivalent of the bushman's grip – comes out in games, and in the most deadly of all games, warfare. One of the British commanders on Gallipoli noted 'the radiant force of camaraderie in action' when the Australians defended their bridgehead. Compton Mackenzie, the Scottish novelist, who was also at Gallipoli, observed a toughness mixed with touchiness in the way the Australians, giant men stripped to the waist under the burning sun, refused to salute their British superiors. Mackenzie was impressed with the quality of these Australians. 'There was not one I saw who might not have been Ajax or Diomed, Hector or Achilles,' he wrote later.

The real secret of the 1999 world champion Wallabies, therefore, was that the team was the epitome of the Australian type and the Australian lifestyle. At its best this Australian type tends to exhibit, even under extreme pressure, 'the radiant force of camaraderie in action'.

And this is what the Wallabies did at Cardiff in the World Cup final.

Preparing for French Dirty Play

The fundamental coaching problem faced by Rod Macqueen and his team in the week's preparation for the RWC final at Cardiff was how to prepare the Wallabies to cope with the foul and dangerous play of the French.

The eye-gouging, the biting, the scratching and the bagsnatching of the French had somehow been allowed to go on against the All Blacks by the Scots referee, Jim Fleming. Fleming is a noted laws pedant but he could not control the maniacal French, who got away with foul play that should have had several of their players sent from the field. Instead of playing with a man or two down, the French prospered with their fouling tactics. The All Blacks, believing they were not being protected by the referee, cracked under the physical violations being inflicted on them.

All Black Josh Kronfeld's father has lost an eye and his son was fearful that the same fate was going to happen to him after being eye-gouged twice at the bottom of the ruck by French forwards. As it was, he was forced to play much of the match in a blur. Back in New Zealand, Kronfeld explained, 'Eyes are very important in our family, and so I was disappointed the referee did not pick the eye-gouging up.'

Taine Randell was bitten by the prop Franck Tournaire. The television microphone picked up Randell shouting out as the teeth sank into him, 'He's biting me! He's biting me!' Another All Black can be heard complaining to Fleming, 'He's chewing him.'

The French play the most exquisite rugby of any nation. A collection of the greatest tries in Test rugby would probably have about half of them scored by French teams. This is Le Rugby Champagne. But there is another side: Sean Smith, a rugby historian, in a letter to the *Daily Telegraph*, published on the day of the World Cup final, wrote that he had discovered in his research that a player had been kicked to death on the pitch during a notorious game between Perpignan and Quillan in 1927. Smith blamed the 'fearsome competition' of the national club championship, with rivalries resulting in too much bad blood, for the foul play in French rugby.

This is the dark side of French rugby that prospered against the All Blacks. Macqueen realised from Jim Fleming's inadequate handling of the French foul tactics against the All Blacks that the Wallabies could expect more of the same during the final. They had to devise systems to ensure that they were not rattled as the All Blacks had been. The answer was to prepare the players not to accept the foul play. 'We have spoken about this issue a lot over the last two years,' Macqueen told journalists, 'and we want to ensure that no one intimidates this side. My instructions before they run out will be that it is crucial for us to impose ourselves on them, rather than worrying about them. That is what has to happen.'

But this was only a small part of the preparation. Just before the start of the Year 2000 rugby season I chatted to Rod Macqueen about how he had prepared his Wallabies for their greatest challenge. This is what he told me.

He watched the semi-final between New Zealand and France in the Wallabies' hotel at Cardiff. The entire squad, players and management, gathered around the television set as the dramatic game unfolded. There were shouts of amazement from the Wallabies as the French produced their magical 30 minutes of play in the second half.

But as the game came to its end, Macqueen realised that he had a coaching crisis on his hands. All the preparations before and during the tournament had been based on the premise that the Wallabies would play the All Blacks in the World Cup final. During the tournament the Wallabies had tried some moves they wanted to play against the All Blacks, to test them under match conditions. Moreover, Macqueen and his players knew the All Blacks' game almost as intimately as the All Blacks knew it themselves. This knowledge gave them the confidence to believe that they would defeat the All Blacks in the final.

Macqueen took the team's video expert, Scott Harrison, aside when the second semi-final was over. 'You're in for a busy night,' he told him. First thing the next morning, he wanted all the French lineouts and scrums on a CD.

The positive aspect of playing a surprise opponent in the World Cup final was that it gave the team a wake-up call. The preparation for a final against New Zealand would have involved a predictable strategic plan and rehearsing moves that had been rehearsed a hundred times before. But now Macqueen, his coaching staff and the players had to do some new thinking.

After studying the video of the French play during the RWC tournament they decided that two French sides had been on display. There was an unimpressive, B-quality side at the beginning of the RWC tournament. This, however, had been transformed into an A-quality side that had played impressively against Argentina and brilliantly against the All Blacks.

The A-quality French side, though, was a reactive team. The Wallabies agreed that the key to victory was to impose their muscular and passionate game on the French, rather than worry too much about how the French would play. 'In our discussions,' Macqueen told me, 'with myself, Jeff Miller, Tim Lane, John Eales and George Gregan, we decided we had to be careful about turnovers. We wanted to neutralise Olivier Magne, who was having a sensational tournament on the side of the scrum. We planned to use Toutai Kefu coming inside Tim Horan to run at Magne. Early on, too, Horan would be used as a dummy runner as the loose forwards aimed at taking Magne out of the game. After 15 minutes Magne had broken his nose and his impact was diminished, anyway, by all the tackling he had to do.'

It was important that the Wallabies were psyched up for the final. They could not afford to be complacent in the way the Springboks had been. So minutes before the match began Macqueen read out to the team an inspiring fax from the head of the Australian forces in East Timor, Major-General Peter Cosgrove. The fax compared the sacrifices and dedication the Wallabies had endured to reach the final in the name of Australia with what the young soldiers were experiencing in East Timor.

The Wallabies had visited Villers-Bretonneux, the site of a crucial battle in November 1918, on Remembrance Day during their 1998 tour of Europe. The experience had been profoundly moving for the young Wallabies, as they wandered through the memorial cemetery with its graves of Australians who had died so young. Macqueen now followed Major-General Cosgrove's inspirational fax with a reading from the diary of a young Australian soldier who had been in charge of a machine-gun company during the battle of Villers-Bretonneux. The young officer had been given instructions that his position had to be held, no matter what the cost was. Conscious that these might be the last words of his diary, he wrote: 'If the section cannot remain here alive, it will remain here dead, but in any case it will remain.'

With these words resonating in their minds and souls, the

Wallabies made their way on to the Millennium Stadium for the great rugby battle of their lives.

The Welsh Rugby Union had given the Wallabies (and their Welsh counterparts) an enclosed box at the stadium for the World Cup quarter-final between Australia and Wales. But for the final the WRU gave the Wallabies and the French seats in an open section of the main stand. At half-time Macqueen and the coaching staff made their way to the lift to take them to the Australian dressing room. There was no attendant present and they waited, with the French entourage, for the lift to arrive, both coaching staffs being forced to travel together. This provided an awkward interlude. The lift stopped at the first level to allow a drunken Frenchman to be taken to the ambulance room. The Frenchman was vomiting, without much regard for the sensibilities of those jammed in the lift with him. Macqueen says that he felt like vomiting himself by the time he made his way into the Australian dressing room, white-faced from this nasty episode.

The Wallabies followed their usual half-time rituals. First, Dr John Best went through the injury list and reported that everyone could play on. Then John Eales gave his views on what had happened in the first half. He talked about how the Wallabies had to be patient and how he was sure the breaks would come. George Gregan followed, making similar points to those expressed by the captain.

Then the players divided into the forwards and the backs for more detailed instructions. The backs were told to bring the wingers and Matt Burke closer in to the centre of the field, to force the smaller French centres to make front-on tackles. The forwards were told to start opting for longer lineouts in the last 20 minutes when the forwards and backs could expect to punch holes in a tiring French defence. And that was it. The players moved towards the tunnel and the start of the second half.

All the coaching by Rod Macqueen was over.

The French Are Flattened

Before the RWC final, Australia and France had met 28 times since their first rugby encounter in 1928. The series was remarkably balanced, with each side winning 13 times. There had been two draws. France had scored 481 points from 57 tries, 33 conversions, 48 penalty goals and 17 dropped goals. Australia had scored 498 points from 46 tries, 29 conversions, 75 penalty goals and 9 dropped goals. The last four Tests between the two sides had resulted in comfortable victories to the Wallabies.

The World Cup final started with a series of galvanic scrums, as the Wallaby front row buckled like chunks of earth being thrown up after an earthquake. Then the quiet and informed instruction from Alex Evans, who had been specially drafted into the coaching squad to prepare the front row, came into play. The Wallaby front row concentrated on shutting down the gap at impact, keeping its shoulders square, eyes steady, back straight and a low crouch. The disaster of a fractured scrum was avoided. Towards the end of the final it was the Wallaby pack that was shoving the French back.

Midway through the second half the television microphones picked up John Eales saying to Andre Watson, the referee, 'If this keeps up, I'm going to take my players off the field.' Eales had been poked in the right eye.

The two tries scored by the Wallabies revealed the different strengths of the side: first, the power of its combinations, and second, the individual strength and determination of each player. The first try came when Ben Tune dived through a mass of French defenders, after a long and intricate build-up. The superior fitness of the Wallabies was revealed once again when Owen Finegan scored a memorable individual try. 'I decided I wanted a bit of the action,' Finegan said later. 'So I told Jeremy Paul to throw deep to me . . . When I received the ball, a huge gap opened in front of me. I began looking for support but when the tacklers held off, obviously expecting me to pass, I decided to be selfish and keep going.'

Finegan's call had over-ridden an earlier lineout call to Michael Foley to throw short. Before he could make the short throw, Foley had been substituted by Paul. Macqueen, loyal to a team that had been loyal to him, made sure everyone on the bench actually took the field during the final. Chris Whitaker, George Gregan's backup at halfback for two seasons, raced out with seconds remaining in the match. Afterwards, he found he had a new nickname, '29 Seconds Whitaker'.

Eye Witness, 7 November 1999

A soufflé doesn't rise twice. The Wallabies won the world championship of rugby, the William Webb Ellis trophy, by the overwhelming margin of 35–12, by ensuring that France could not rise to the greatness of the occasion, as they had the previous week at Twickenham. For most of the week the experts mulled over the possibility of a second helping of the magic that destroyed the All Blacks. But aside from a few dazzling moments, one of them heart-stoppingly in the first minutes of the match, when the blue jerseys flashed down the touchline, France spent the match grimly, and occasionally viciously, defending.

The Wallabies had a simple but shrewdly executed game plan. The tricky plays were eliminated in favour of the KISS formula: Keep It Simple, Stupid. The Wallabies also ensured that once they gained possession they made the French tackle, tackle and tackle again . . . By forcing the French backs and forwards to make numerous tackles, the Wallabies took the legs away from the French fliers. On the rare occasions when they did have a chance to run, the French backs tried and failed to make breaks on tired legs . . .

France looked like scoring only once in the final but a knock-on saved the Wallabies. So the Wallabies conceded only one try throughout the tournament. This definitive defensive record represents triumph for the entire coaching staff. It is also a triumph for

the discipline and strength (both mental and physical) of the play-
ers and the quality of mateship unbeatable teams have, when every
player subordinates his ego and his body for the cause of the team.

The defensive game-plan devised by Macqueen, though, essen-
tially stood or fell on the kicking form of Matthew Burke. For the
Wallabies to win, Burke had to kick the goals. Goal-kicking, like
putting in golf, is sometimes the easiest or the most difficult of
tasks. Hundreds of players can kick goals from 40 metres out. But
only the most talented and the most nerveless of kickers can make
a shot when a stadium holding 72,000 spectators, most of them
hostile to you, is resounding with roars of outrage against the ref-
eree and the goalkicker. Burke kicked nine from 11 shots under
the most intense pressure, one of them a conversion from the side-
line, to put the Wallabies three scores in front and ensure victory.
He did it elegantly, too, in keeping with Hemingway's dictum that
style is 'grace under pressure'.

As Burke calmly kicked the Wallabies to glory my mind was
taken back to the fabled fields at Hunters Hill where I saw him
play many games for St Joseph's at a time when John Eales, Tim
Horan and Jason Little (so effective when he replaced the injured
Daniel Herbert) were stars of the 1991 world champion
Wallabies.

Many have contributed to Saturday's famous victory. All the
teachers and the boys who have played rugby in the schools around
Australia since the youngsters at Sydney University decided to
give the game a crack in the 1860s. And all the Test players going
back to 1899, when Frank 'Banger' Row captained the first
Australian rugby team. So, too, all the stalwarts, like Norbert
Byrne, the Queensland official who carried a large part of the
administration of rugby in his state during the dark days of the
1970s. And Peter Crittle, David Brockhoff, and thousands of
officials over the years are part of the triumph. John O'Neill, the
chief executive of the ARU, who has led the revival in Australian
rugby since the turmoil of 1995, summed up the passion invested

in Australian rugby, telling everyone he saw during the tense week leading up to the final to 'keep the faith'.

The great strength of Australian rugby is the faith of its supporters, the famous and the unknown. Before the final I saw the great Wallaby number 8 Tim Gavin, as craggy as ever, Wallaby cap on his head, climbing unobtrusively to the highest levels of the steep west face of the Millennium Stadium to join a group of friends. Earlier in the World Cup tournament I made a train journey back to London from Twickenham with a raucous group of Petersham Rugby Club supporters who were following the Wallabies, playing social matches and drinking Britain dry, though not necessarily in that order. This World Cup is their World Cup, too.

After the presentations by the Queen, the Wallabies made a slow walk around the ground. They stopped in front of various groups of supporters and assembled so team photos could be taken. It seemed to me as the crowd at the Millennium Stadium hung around, unwilling to leave the scene of the great occasion, that it was fitting that the Wallabies, now world champions for the second time out of four tournaments, were not presenting themselves as heroes or as a group apart from their supporters, but were enjoying with them a golden moment for the Australian rugby tribe . . .

The Wallabies played as definitively and as accurately as any team could in the tenseness of a world championship final. The game statistics indicate this: penalties conceded, Australia 12, France 16; rucks won, A 58, F 42; mauls won, A 6, F 5; balls won in open play, A 64, F 47; set piece ball won, A 35, F 32; gain line crossed, A 29, F 28; handling errors, A 7, F 13; turnovers won, A 8, F 3; first-half possession time, A 14 m 12 s, F 7 m 8 s; second-half possession time, A 12 m 23 s, F 9 m 27 s.

6 November 1999, at Cardiff. Australia **35** (B. Tune, O. Finegan tries; M. Burke 7 penalty goals and 2 conversions) defeated France **12** (C. Lamaison 4 penalty goals)

ARU Fury

The line of players, support staff and officials inching towards the Queen seemed to be unending. Strath Gordon, the affable and unflappable media manager for the Australian Rugby Union, decided to share in the historic moment. He went to the end of the line and made his slow progress to the medal table. When he came to Princess Anne, he gazed sideways along the line of players and officials shuffling ahead of him towards the Queen and said: 'Geez, there's a lot of us, isn't there?'

The tart-tongued Princess Anne replied: 'Have you all got jobs?'

Back, finally, in the changing room, the Wallabies were exultant and feisty. They revived a chant first heard after the 1991 World Cup final when a player had suddenly cried out, 'Nick Farr-Jones, world champion!' That cry had bursted into an instant explosion of sound as all the players received their accolade. The ultra-modern dressing room at the Millennium Stadium now rang to the 1999 version of the Wallaby World Cup chant: 'Steve Larkham, world champion! Matt Cockbain, world champion! Tim Horan, DOUBLE WORLD CHAMPION! Jason Little, DOUBLE WORLD CHAMPION!'

John O'Neill, the forceful and brainy chief executive of the Australian Rugby Union, came into the changing room. Before the World Cup tournament he had been in a stiff negotiation with the Players' Union over the size of a bonus if Australia won the World Cup. The players spotted O'Neill's entry. They dropped their chanting and took up a new cry: 'We want a double bonus. We want a DOUBLE BONUS!' O'Neill took the needle with good grace. He smiled at the players and told them, 'Well done.'

But inwardly he was seething: during the presentations he had heard a British rugby official say sarcastically: 'This should go down as the first Creatine World Cup.'

Throughout the World Cup tournament many of the British

rugby writers had commented on the size of the Wallaby outside backs. Players like Daniel Herbert, Ben Tune and Matt
Burke, they reckoned, were bulkier than some of the British forwards. Creatine is a substance that is supposed to aid athletes to
bulk up. It was used and advertised by Mark McGwire, baseball's
most prolific home-run hitter, in the season he smashed Babe
Ruth's long-standing record for hits out of the park. It has been
used, too, by rugby players around the world. Used – as far as any
Australian player is concerned – is a word in the past tense,
though. Dr John Best, the Wallaby doctor, has insisted that the
substance not be taken by any Wallabies. His instruction has
been followed. Incensed at the accusation that the Wallabies had
used a dubious performance-enhancing substance to win the
World Cup, O'Neill challenged the official to say out loud what
he had muttered. He wanted to expose the lie publicly.

There was a sullen silence in response.

A particular reason for O'Neill's fury was that the ARU has
taken a leadership position in ensuring that rugby is a clean
game with none of the allegations of illegal drug use that have
dogged, say, Olympic sports. To this end he authorised, before
the start of the 1998 rugby season, a press statement detailing a
three-year anti-doping agreement the ARU had signed with the
Australian Sports Drug Agency. The agreement significantly
increased 'out of competition' testing for players at every level of
Australian rugby. It maintained 'high' anti-doping testings at
home and abroad. And it confirmed the ARU's continued
lobbying for consistent drug testing throughout the rugby
world. The ASDA praised the ARU: 'We believe Australian
rugby is providing a very good example to all rugby playing
nations.'

The world champion Wallabies had been tested before their
rugby season began. They had been subjected to tests during the
Super 12 tournament. And they were tested after international
matches. ASDA has a justified reputation for efficiency and

fairness, too. No Wallaby has ever produced a positive result to illegal drug use.

But a second World Cup for the Wallabies, out of three RWC tournaments, clearly rattled the Rugbyocracy. Every effort was made, therefore, to demean the achievement. This envy is behind the muttered drug allegations. And there was what amounted to a campaign intended to deny the world champion status of the Wallabies.

Simon Barnes, for instance, writing for *The Times*, accused the Wallabies of winning the World Cup with 'boring, defensive' rugby. 'My God, they were dull,' he wrote. 'They are dullness incarnate.' But he was unable to leave his criticism at just the playing style of the Wallabies. Part of the Rugbyocracy's world view is that there are character flaws in the rugby men of the southern hemisphere that impose a virtuous duty on the Rugbyocracy to tame and modify. Australian rugby, Barnes insisted, leads a 'double life, pretending to be stylish and creative and beautiful but really being boring all the time'.

The Wallabies, he asserted, are hypocrites, 'and that is what I can't stand'.

Australia's World Cup

The Rugby World Cup victory was a golden moment for the Australian rugby tribe, and the Australian nation. For 1999 was an annus mirabilis, a year of marvels, for Australian sport. Competition after competition turned to gold for Australian athletes.

When a Davis Cup victory over France followed the defeat of France in the World Cup final, newspapers took to publishing lists of the many Australian triumphs around the world. The *Sun Herald*, under the headline 'Good On Ya, Sport', produced this list of sports in which Australians were number one in the world: athletics, baseball, boxing, cricket, equestrianism, golf, hockey, indoor cricket, kayaking, lawn bowls, mountain biking, netball, Paralympic events, rowing, rugby league, rugby union, sailing, shooting, skiing, skydiving, squash, surfing, surf life-saving, swimming, tennis, tenpin bowling, triathlon, waterski-jumping and windsurfing.

A national discussion erupted with various experts trying to pinpoint the reasons for this remarkable list of achievements. The influence of the 2000 Olympics in Sydney in energising the aspirations of Australian athletes was cited. So, too, was the work of the Australian Institute of Sport in providing the facilities and expertise in sports science for players and coaches. A number of the 1999 world champion Wallabies are graduates of the AIS.

But is there something special about Australians that allows them to be successful? And if this is so, what are the special factors?

On a hot January day, I went to the Mitchell Library in Macquarie Street, a short walk away from the central business district of Sydney, to do some research on the 1908 Wallabies. There was a delay of about 30 minutes for the documents I wanted to be brought up from the stacks. In the Dixson Room enclosure of the main reading room I glanced through a shelf of books and came across *Sport And Pastime In Australia* written by Gordon Inglis and published by Methuen in 1912. As I flicked through its pages, the book exuded the mothy smell of paper that had not been exposed to light for decades. Inglis, an Englishman, had written a straightforward account of most of the sports practised in Australia, when they had started up and who the leading practitioners were. The title to the opening chapter, though, caught my attention, 'Why Australians Have Excelled'.

Inglis said he was amazed that a population of four and a half million Australians could achieve 'such good results' in so many different sports. He listed the sports, many of which are on the *Sun Herald* list: cricket, football (four kinds), lawn tennis, rowing, sculling, yachting, sailing, swimming, surfing, lacrosse, bowls, hockey, athletics, boxing, billiards, golf, shooting, baseball, cycling and skating. 'Then there is Horse-racing,' he continued, 'and those other sports in which the thoroughbred is used, Polo and Hunting.'

An interesting aspect of this list is that the 1911 census, reflecting 50 years of reform and nation-building, revealed that for the first time there were more native-born people than immigrants over 40. All the 1908 Wallabies, for instance, were native born. This was not surprising, as the number of younger native-born Australians had surpassed young immigrants for most of the nineteenth century. The Australia of 1912 was truly Australian, and not an offshore station of Britain.

To discover 'whether there were any outstanding reasons' for this success of Australians, Inglis went to see Professor T.P. Anderson Stuart, who had been Dean of the Medical School at Sydney University for 30 years. Professor Stuart insisted that 'the spirit that was necessary to enable people to carve out their fortunes in a new country, to triumph over difficulties in a new country, to ultimately achieve, must inevitably be reflected in their descendants'. These migrants were 'the most fit of their kind, and it was only to be expected that they left behind them children and grandchildren equipped with more than ordinary "virtue" '.

Professor Stuart, therefore, demolished the Churchill 'bad stock' allegation and suggested instead that Australians are of a superior stock. 'I have had the unique opportunity for nearly 30 years of seeing young men of the community in one of the most impressionable periods of life,' he told Inglis, 'and my experience of the young men of the Australian Universities is that they are both mentally and physically of the highest order . . . Now let us go to another class of the community, the working man, the artisan. The Australian working man is given shorter hours and a more adequate reward for his labour, but at the same time responds by putting in a great deal more work in the time than does his brother overseas.'

Being a professor at Sydney University at the turn of the twentieth century, Professor Stuart was probably a rugby man, for Sydney University was a rugby powerhouse at the time. I like to surmise that he watched the first Test between Australia and England at the SCG in 1899. He certainly taught Dr Herbert Moran, the inspirational captain of the 1908 Wallabies, when Moran was a medical student.

With these possibilities in my mind as I read Professor Stuart's measured reasoning, I formed the notion that Australia, of all the countries in the world, most closely approximates the blessed utilitarian state propounded by the nineteenth-century philosopher, Jeremy Bentham, of a community that provides 'the greatest good for the greatest number of people'.

Of course, there are stains and rips on the national fabric of society. The treatment of Aborigines since 1788 has involved too many disgraceful episodes. There is too much poverty, domestic violence, unemployment, youth suicide, anti-intellectualism, racism, gambling, drug addiction, violent crime and damage to the environment. Yet, despite all these social evils, Australia has a social harmony and a comparative contentment. It is a nation, as the historian Dr John Tregenza has argued, that is 'unusually free from violence and deep social antagonism'.

By any criterion, Australia is a successful society. Australians believe in the Australian Dream of egalitarianism, mateship, going hard at things, even at pleasure, where any Bill or Bob can aspire to the job and lifestyle of a William or a Robert. They believe in the Australian Dream because in their lives or the lives of their children or their neighbours the Dream has been achieved.

Sport is one of the many ways the Australian Dream has been transmuted into real living. Sport, perhaps more than success in other areas of human activity, defines the national identity. This is because it is prominent and it can be measured. Measurement leads to a sense of worth.

The 1999 world champion Wallabies arrived back in Sydney on flight QF2 a few days after the final. They were greeted in the airport terminal by about a thousand wildly enthusiastic supporters waving Australian flags and wearing green and gold. 'Advance Australia Fair' and 'Waltzing Matilda' reverberated around the terminal. Journalists could not recall a more boisterous homecoming for an Australian sporting team.

John Eales emerged with his team-mates from Customs with the William Webb Ellis trophy perched precariously on top of his luggage trolley. There was a rapturous ovation. Eales, with a bloodied eye that had been almost closed by a jabbing French finger, held the golden cup aloft amid the gold and green streamers. Arms were punched into the air. There was a volley of yells.

As usual Eales found the right words to express the deep significance of the golden moment. 'Australians have high expectations of their sporting teams, and that's a good thing,' he told the throng of well-wishers. 'This World Cup is Australia's World Cup.'

The sentiment was unmistakably that of 'Bill Is Back!'

PART II: 1991 World Cup Triumph

'Kick It to the Shithouse!'

5 August 1991

The Test season so far has been promising. Wales and England have been thrashed, the All Blacks defeated well in Sydney, 21–12, and lost to narrowly in Auckland, 6–3. The Wallabies selectors have, finally, worked out the squad for the Rugby World Cup challenge. Now they have to work out a World Cup winning team. The Wallaby team, in fact, will be harder to select than the squad.

Marty Roebuck should be (and deserves to be) the fullback. There has been some criticism of his play in Auckland, but aside from running away from his winger in a thrilling dash from his 22 (after a David Campese break), Roebuck was sound, especially under the high ball. The notion of playing Campese at fullback has surely been ruled out after his weak attempt to tackle the rampaging Michael Brial on Saturday for Randwick against Easts. The selectors have to reconcile themselves to the fact that while Campese is the most devastating broken-field runner the code has seen, he can't tackle anyone running hard at him, and this rules him out for fullback.

There is a question mark over Rob Egerton as well. Egerton has delighted and surprised rugby supporters this year. But the two Tests against the All Blacks revealed that enthusiastic following up, gutsy tackling and stalwart running can't cover up his lack of real speed or the run-through-a-brick-wall toughness of his opponent, John Kirwan. The enthusiasm shown to get John Flett into the Wallabies squad for the Bledisloe Cup game, despite his lack of match play, indicates that the selectors want him in the Test side. He may be slightly weaker on the tackle than Egerton but he is certainly more dangerous with the ball in his hands, as he demonstrated on Saturday against Easts.

In the pack, the front five should be unchanged, although Tony Daly has been surprisingly humiliated by Easts. There seems to be a desire to shift John Eales to number 8, a position he has played from time to time. But there is no reason to believe that a McCall–Cutler–Eales tall timber partnership will provide the drive the Wallabies have been applying this season in the scrums and mauls.

Getting the correct combination of loose forwards is the real challenge facing the selectors. With Tim Gavin in such masterful form driving and covering, the Wallabies could afford to carry Willie Ofahengaue on the side of the scrum as an impact player. Without Gavin, though, the balance is all wrong. The Eden Park test, for instance, exposed Ofahengaue's inability to provide coverage away from the scrums and mauls. The All Blacks are clearly going to play a fast game at Dublin in the semi-final (presuming they beat England) and the Wallabies will have to match this speed in the loose.

This is not an argument for Ofahengaue to be dropped, however. The Test against England showed how valuable he is with his bell-ringing tackles and his unstoppable charges near the line. No forward in the world has the ability to change the course of a match with one tackle or a ferocious charge as much as Willie Ofahengaue, and for this reason it would be folly to discard him.

He played his rugby in New Zealand as a number 8 and has always appeared to be better suited to this position than on the side of the scrum. Simon Poidevin, with his tackling and his fierce competitiveness in the mauls, will be one flanker – if the selectors are really precise, the blind-side flanker. On the open side, there is the choice of Brendan Nasser or Jeff Miller, depending on whether the selectors want drive (Nasser) or more field coverage (Miller).

This is a team that can win the World Cup with one proviso: the tactics have to be right. After the start-whistle-stop Test at Eden Park, Wallabies coach Bob Dwyer remarked, 'We'll have to adjust our thinking to a more static pattern of play.' The point is that when the referees are being nitpickers, as they are in the

United Kingdom, there is less phase ball. When there is a second or third phase, a team has to make the most of it.

3 October 1991

Geography and the circadian rhythms are pulsing in favour of the Wallabies in their quest for the World Cup. The Wallabies play their first match tomorrow against what should be the weakest team in their pool, Argentina, at Llanelli. It isn't until October 12 that the Wallabies come up against Wales, which should be their hardest pool match, at Cardiff Arms Park. Three days earlier they play Manu (Warrior) Samoa at Pontypool.

The grounds at both Pontypool and Llanelli are tightly encased within the spectator seating. This atmosphere of being crowded in, which creates the illusion that the field itself is narrower than it really is, should help the forward-bullying style that coach Bob Dwyer has created for the 1991 Wallabies. At one of his press conferences, Dwyer told the media not to expect 'entertainment' from the Wallabies.

The circadian rhythms of the equation relate to the fact that by the time the Wallabies play Wales, the team will be well over the jet lag induced by flying halfway around the world. Jet lag, of course, affects the daily (circadian) rhythms of the body.

The Wallabies have the New Zealand referee, David Bishop, to keep the Argentinians within the rules for their first game. Against Manu Samoa they have Fred Howard, the English referee. As the Wallabies will want to play a set-piece match against the athletic Samoans, a referee who is reluctant to play the advantage might suit them. Against Wales, in the sometimes overpowering atmosphere of Cardiff Arms Park, the Wallabies will have the impressive New Zealand referee, Keith Lawrence, controlling the match.

Who will win the trophy? The bookmakers initially made the All Blacks favourites for the World Cup. Then they established the All Blacks and the Wallabies as joint favourites. After watching the Wallabies train, they made them favourites. But after watching the All Blacks train, the bookmakers restored them to favourites' odds. The bookmakers then made the Wallabies and the All Blacks joint favourites. Now, after further training sessions, the Wallabies are the favourites again.

7 October 1991

After an impressive start, the Wallabies were rescued from possible defeat against an unexpectedly resilient Argentina side by the rugby genius of David Campese. Watching the winger beat three Argentinians to score his first try, then burst through explosively for a second and finally set up centre Tim Horan for a try after retrieving a lobbed pass from number 8 John Eales, I was reminded of Kenneth Tynan's tribute to the beauty of Greta Garbo: 'What men see in some women when they are drunk, they see in Garbo when they are sober.'

This can be paraphrased into rugby terms along these lines: 'What good players fantasise, when they are drunk, of doing on the rugby field just once in their lifetime, David Campese does every time he plays.'

It is customary to criticise Campese's reluctance to tackle. Against Argentina, for instance, his opposite player stepped inside him to continue an attack with the ease of a person going through his own front door. But the Wallabies have to adjust to Campese's defensive weaknesses the way cricket teams reconciled themselves to the fact that Sir Donald Bradman wasn't much of a bowler.

'Campo' has now scored 42 tries for the Wallabies in Tests (a Bradman-like record) and this knack of getting across the line, together with his skill in setting up tries, is one of the great, and still unacknowledged, strengths of the Wallabies.

The match against Argentina also revealed that without hooker Phil Kearns, the pack goes back about 20 per cent in effectiveness. The third revelation of the match was that the

Wallaby second and back rows are not working well and need different players. On this evidence there is perhaps a need for Bob Dwyer to re-assess his 'might is right' philosophy. Putting the ball more through the backs, instead of a relying on smashing through continually in the forwards, and deliberately using Campese as a match-winner, might be better tactics for the Wallabies for the rest of the tournament.

---

4 October 1991, at Llanelli. Australia **32** (D. Campese 2, T. Horan 2, P. Kearns tries; M. Lynagh 3 conversions and 2 penalty goals) defeated Argentina **19** (M. Teran 2 tries; G. Castillo 1 conversion and 1 penalty goal; L. Arbizu 2 drop goals)

---

11 October 1991

The Western Samoan High Commissioner, Feesago Fepuleai, rang me some weeks ago to discuss how the Manu Samoa team would go in the World Cup. He also had a complaint to make. 'Why did Alan Jones have to call our team "head-hunters"?' he asked.

In their sensational 16–13 defeat of Wales, Manu Samoa were penalised once for a high tackle, a decision that was ridiculous. Throughout the match, the Samoans turned on a display of bone-shattering, literally, tackling of a ferocity and technical excellence I have not seen in decades of watching rugby. The muscularity of the tackling had a noticeable effect on the Welsh players. Virtually all of them, except one or two of the braver forwards, were reluctant to run with the ball or went to ground when confronted by a Samoan defender. The Welsh, despite the fact they regarded the match as the most important in their rugby history, lost their nerve. Even more impressive than the tackling of Manu Samoa, though, was the team's composure and mental integrity.

According to traditional belief, Samoa is the centre of the universe and Samoan chiefs are descendants of the gods. Samoans tend to be inward-looking. Contact with the non-Samoan outside world in the early part of the century was kept to a minimum. They are intensely religious. The great Samoan–New Zealand breakaway, Michael Jones, for instance, will not play rugby on Sundays, even when a World Cup semi-final is scheduled.

After Manu Samoa's match against Wales, I was so hyped up I couldn't sleep. I pulled out from the bookcase the short story collection *Flying Fox in a Freedom Tree*, written by the Samoan writer and current Professor of Literature at Auckland University, Albert Wendt, to try to understand, in a sociological sense, what the Samoans had just achieved. In one of the stories, 'Declaration of Independence', a woman is found guilty by a New Zealand judge of premeditated murder. 'To have blown out his unfaithful brains with a shotgun was extremely fitting; to have given herself up to the police, and confessed all, was truly grand, heroic and Christian.' The story explains the thinking of the people of Apia.

Manu Samoa exemplified this Biblical 'eye-for-an-eye' spirit against Wales. And against Australia tonight, the team will surely carry their uncompromising approach on to the field again. This will ensure the Australian players will have to work hard and suffer some physical pain for their victory, no matter what the scoreline suggests.

---

9 October 1991, at Pontypool. Australia 9 (M. Lynagh 3 penalty goals) defeated Manu Samoa 3 (M. Vaea penalty goal)

---

10 October 1991

The struggling Wallabies have two major problems to solve before the quarter-finals of the World Cup: the best back five in the forwards remains to be selected and the game plan of 'all power to the forwards' isn't working.

Wallaby coach Bob Dwyer's solution to the back five problem has been to restore Rod McCall and John Eales to the second row, and play Simon Poidevin and Jeff Miller on the side, with

Willie Ofahengaue to play the Shelford-type role as number 8.

Dwyer has given away just about all his lineout, except for Eales. The justification is probably that the tall timber of Troy Coker and Stephen Cutler did not fare too well against the shorter Samoans. This new lineup lacks height at the end of the lineout. But Poidevin and Ofahengaue can win ball, and should ensure the Wallabies win their own, provided Phil Kearns can throw in accurately to Eales.

More importantly, this back three should be more competitive in the loose than anything the Wallabies have shown in the World Cup so far. The problem with playing Poidevin as the main loose forward has been that he is most effective closer to the rucks and mauls. Miller should be able to play the more traditional open side breakaway game. Mobility in the loose is necessary, as the Samoans have shown, because the tournament has been, and will continue to be, blighted by whistle-happy referees. Ed Morrison, the referee in the Wallabies–Manu Samoa match, frequently blew up play when the ball was just coming out of a maul. Sometimes he blew play up when the ball was out.

It is clear that the referees (and more importantly the referee supervisors) don't want any second- or third-phase play. The traditional response to this is to do what the Wallabies have been doing, concentrate on the first-phase game. This approach only works when the penalties forced from the first-phase pressure can be kicked, but the World Cup ball is hard to kick accurately. Michael Lynagh missed two easy penalties and the Samoans also missed several kickable shots. Argentine kickers converted only one in eight penalty kicks at goal against Wales. Pressure, in other words, isn't easily converted into points from penalties.

I have in my files an extract from a fine book on rugby that deals with British referees. Here are some of the comments: 'Rugby in Britain, in our honest opinion, is being strangled by referees . . . undoubtedly, Rugby in Britain, on the lines on which it is guided at present by referees, is not by any means so attractive as it might be . . . The British referee is a very slow man, and he seems to like a slow game. At all events, he takes care that it is slow . . . British referees are undoubtedly far too fond of the scrum. They will insist on calling a scrum for the most trifling infringements, which do not affect either side, and which might very well, in the interests of the game, be allowed to let go . . . In Britain, the referees are very loath to allow the advantage which accrues to a player from an opponent's knock-on, and when such a thing is done they generally whistle for a scrum.' The authors of those comments were David Gallaher and Billy Stead, the captain and the vice-captain of the 1905 All Blacks. Their book, *The Complete Rugby Footballer*, was published in 1906.

Nothing, apparently, has changed in 85 years. British referees, on the evidence from the tournament so far, remain whistle-happy and scrum-obsessed. It will have to be the Wallabies, therefore, who must change and adapt their game to this stifling British tradition of the nitpicking, intrusive referee.

14 October 1991

Wallaby coach Bob Dwyer is a 'Perils of Pauline' expert. Just when it looks as though an onrushing train of critics is going to run over him, the Wallabies play superbly, and with one bound, Dwyer is free.

After the first two matches in the World Cup tournament, the lacklustre forward-power-obsessed play by the Wallabies focused attention once more on the coach. But the result of the match against Wales, and, more particularly, the way the Wallabies played, has released Dwyer from his critics once more. In the second half the Wallabies played as well as a team can in a Test match, where the passion and intensity of the opposition (as Scotland found against Ireland) can cover a multitude of weaknesses for a time.

The quibbles first, though. In the first half, the Wallabies were unable to convert their dominance of possession into points. Michael Lynagh couldn't kick goals with the erratic ball being used in the World Cup tournament, that was one reason. But, perhaps more significantly, the Wallabies were obsessed with smashing through in the forwards, and Wales were able to just hold them out.

When a team is on the back foot, as Wales were with their meagre supply of ball, it can stay in the match if the opposition that is winning all the possession relies solely on forward power. In a sense, for most of the first half the 15 Welsh players had only to contain the eight Wallabies in the pack and Peter Slattery, the halfback. The one time the Wallabies brought winger David Campese into the play, he set up a try. The rest of the half, however, the pack played to the 'might is right' doctrine. Wales were battered all around the paddock . . . but not on the scoreboard.

After the match against Western Samoa, I asked a friend who knows something about rugby why the Wallabies weren't running the ball in the backs and why the emphasis was on smashing through continually in the forwards. 'Bob's got a new toy,' he said, referring to the giant pack he had put on the field for the first two matches. Against the Samoans, for instance, the Wallabies walked their opposition scrum about 20 metres at one point, and then didn't release the ball. The point of driving forward, which is to get across the advantage line and scatter the opposition, is lost if the ball is not delivered to the backs.

In the second half against Wales, the Wallabies, at last, got the balance right between driving and releasing. The result was a perfect half of rugby. The backs were able to run all the correct lines. The forwards were released to set up second-phase, third-phase and (can it be believed in this tournament blighted by whistle-happy referees?) fourth-phase ball.

The resulting ensemble play was marvellous, and the

Wallabies can go into the finals series with a renewed confidence in their ability to win the tournament. The Australian players rose to the occasion, in the end giving Wales their biggest defeat ever at Cardiff Arms Park.

---

12 October 1991, at Cardiff. Australia **38** (M. Roebuck 2, D. Campese, T. Horan, M. Lynagh, P. Slattery tries; M. Lynagh 4 conversions and 2 penalty goals) defeated Wales **3** (M. Ring 1 penalty goal)

---

19 October 1991

Damon Runyon once reckoned 'all of life is six to five against'. What, then, are we to make of the bookie odds making the Wallabies virtually unbackable favourites to beat Ireland tomorrow night in the quarter-finals of the Rugby World Cup? If the scribe of Broadway is right, the Irish have a chance on the grounds that odds should never be prohibitive. They also have a remote chance because they have a gifted lineout forward in Neil Francis and, against Scotland at least, a strong scrum. Backing up these forward skills is a determined, hard-running winger, Simon Geoghegan, and one of the better goalkickers in the tournament, Ralph Keyes.

There is the smallest of fears, though, that Wales might have been so appalling that a false impression of the Wallabies' skills could have been created. The lineout count, for instance, was 28–2 to the Wallabies. And this was achieved without a lineout jumper in the back three (the only real weakness in the Wallaby team). In all the years I have watched rugby, at venues as different as cow paddocks in New Zealand to high school grounds in Sydney and legendary venues like Cardiff Arms Park, I can't recall coming across such a one-sided lineout count as the one in the Wallabies–Wales match.

The virtual certainty of the Wallabies winning every lineout (thereby defying Runyon's odds) meant fullback Marty Roebuck could camp himself among the three-quarters. This meant, in turn, that the Wallabies had the numbers whenever they moved the ball wide. It's unlikely that Francis will allow the Wallabies to achieve a similar overwhelming advantage in the lineouts on Sunday.

And Ireland will show more grit and enthusiasm than Wales. The Ireland Rugby XV is a unique sporting team. It has no anthem because it represents an ideal, not a country. It is the only sporting team where men from the North and the South come together on a national basis. This sense of somehow representing the best of Irish life comes through in the resolute way Ireland play, especially at Lansdowne Road in Dublin.

Despite all this, the bookmakers' odds seem to be a better indication of a final result in favour of the Wallabies than Damon Runyon's odds.

22 October 1991

The sign of a great side is how it lifts itself to a great deed when it is playing poorly. If that sounds a bit Irish, it was the Wallabies' last-gasp try against Ireland in the quarter-final at Dublin that demonstrated once again the truth of this adage.

Are the Wallabies perhaps fated now to win the Rugby World Cup tournament?

No other rugby side in the world could have come back after Ireland's spectacular try, as the Wallabies did, and score a match-winning try with only minutes of play left. The Wallabies kept their nerve (one of the toughest challenges in sport) when everything seemed lost.

And just as importantly their captain, Michael Lynagh, made a series of critical decisions, all of which came off. From the kick-off, should the Wallabies kick short (and try to win the ball back) or long (and strike from the next lineout, if possible)? Lynagh kicked long, knowing that a good catch and a raking kick would virtually finish off the Wallabies. Then, when the scrum was forced, Lynagh had to decide whether to keep the ball close from the scrum and play one of the now famous back-row moves, or run the ball in the backs. He had to consider, also, whether the Irish would second-guess the Wallabies and anticipate a backline movement.

The danger with the back-row move was that Ireland had a strong scrum, and Willie Ofahengaue hasn't been explosive from the back of the scrum so far in the tournament. But if the ball was run in the backs, surely the Irish would get their defensive screen right at last? And which of the backline cut-out moves should be run, given that the simple ploy of cutting out Jason Little in the centres and passing flat and long to Marty Roebuck coming in from fullback had worked three times before?

Could it work a fourth time?

All these decisions had to be taken in a matter of moments, with the crowd screaming and the Wallabies realising that one mistake would have them on the plane back home. An intriguing thought: would Nick Farr-Jones have come to the same decisions as the calm, confident Lynagh?

Cut now to the Irish. All through the match, they had played their defensive screen in the backs as poorly as I've seen it played. Could they get it right this one time? Did they even try to get it right? The theory of defence in the backs is that you play either a drift system, with each back guarding a zone and then drifting across the field as the ball is moved out wider, or a man-on-man defensive pattern is used. The man-on-man requires the fullback to play in the line to cover his opposite number, with the blindside winger acting as a surrogate fullback. But throughout the match, the Irish had used man-on-man without the fullback in the line – the equivalent, in a way, of having a fence but leaving the gate open.

This meant that every time Marty Roebuck came into the line from fullback he was unmarked. Faced with this last scrum, would it now occur to the Irish backs to use a drift defence and force Campese into touch?

As it happened, the Irish backs kept to the man-on-man system and continued to leave their fullback out of the line. Why they didn't present a long line of defenders and force a kick-and-chase from the Wallabies is beyond belief.

And for Wallabies supporters, beyond relief.

> **20 October 1991, at Dublin.** Australia **19** (D. Campese 2, M. Lynagh tries; M. Lynagh 2 conversions and 1 penalty goal) defeated Ireland **18** (G. Hamilton 1 try; R. Keyes 1 conversion, 3 penalty goals, 1 drop goal)

28 October 1991

England has won its way into the Rugby World Cup final by playing an almost perfect game of 'Wazzaball'.

In the late 1980s, the great rugby league coach Warren Ryan developed a style of play based on strong-arm defence, kicking for position and then converting the pressure into goals. The perfect 'Wazzaball' game was a 1–0 win (a dropped goal to nothing from the opposition).

By my reckoning, England lapsed only twice from their 'Wazzaball' game-plan of winning through kicking, both times in the second half when perhaps some mental and physical tiredness was setting in. On one occasion, a series of attacks were launched near Scotland's goal line. It seemed in this sequence that England were actually attempting to score a try. The scrum following these attacks yielded a penalty, which was kicked. Then winger Rory Underwood was given a chance to run down the line which he almost turned into a try. Several scrums later Rob Andrew finally dropped the winning goal.

Aside from these lapses, England – despite their glut of perfect possession from lineouts, mauls and scrums – did not dare to cross Scotland's line. In a sense, the English have taken the game back 120 years to when the first rules were drafted and a try did not count on the scorebook until it was converted with a goal.

Given the fact that Scotland played without an effective tight five (they lost the first eight lineouts, for instance, and their scrum seemed to have five reverse gears), England really made hard work for themselves in winning the match.

Some of the fire went out of Scotland when fullback Gavin Hastings, the outstanding player of the match, missed a shot right in front in the sixty-second minute. The significance of this miss was that Scotland would have taken the lead in the last quarter of the match. England, instead of taking the easy option of the dropped goal 11 minutes later, might have been tempted to take a bite from the forbidden apple and actually try to score a try.

Next Saturday, therefore, in the final at Twickenham, England will pose the curious challenge of being hard to beat but hard to lose to. England's supporters, in sympathy with their team's uncompromising, win-at-all-costs approach, have adopted the notorious Millwall soccer club chant: 'No-one likes us, we don't care!'

29 October 1991

It's the end of the All Blacks' era and the beginning, perhaps, of a new world rugby order of Wallaby power.

The Wallabies did the tackling and the All Blacks controlled (and too often fumbled) the ball for long periods of play. But it was the rugby genius of David Campese, the outstanding player of the World Cup tournament, that turned the Dublin semi-final Australia's way again. Without Campese, the Wallabies would have struggled to find a way through a swarming and dedicated defence. While some of the most gifted running backs in world rugby, on both sides, found it virtually impossible to breach even the first line of defence, Campese took the All Blacks on three times, scored one try, set up Tim Horan for the decisive try of the match and almost got away for another.

That third time it was only a desperate ankle tap by Grant

Fox that sent Campese sprawling before he could set Rob Egerton free. Even then, Campese's brilliant passing skills enabled him to get rid of the ball while he was hurtling through the air.

It's common practice to criticise Campese for his defensive fragility, although he wrapped up John Timu every time the All Blacks' winger tried to run through him. The inference is that Campese lacks heart. The criticism is unfair. It takes more courage in fact to run with the ball on a rugby field than to make punishing tackles. With the Horan try, Campese had to accept the inevitable pain of being thrown hard on his shoulder by Graeme Bachop to allow Horan time to position himself for the dash to the goal line.

A colleague has described Campese as 'the rugby incarnation of quantum physics: he's there, he's not there, he's atomic'.

In three Tests against the Wallabies this year the All Blacks only managed one try and that was a fluky one from a high kick at Sydney. The New Zealand backs in the Dublin semi-final played as if they had never met each other before. Passes went to ground, or were thrown behind a support player. Except for John Kirwan, no one looked capable of breaking the defensive line. With hindsight, we can see the All Blacks had been kept together a year too long. But the great team from the 1987 Rugby World Cup had lost only three Tests (including yesterday's defeat) and drawn once in nearly 30 Tests, which made it difficult for the selectors to take out the axe. All those losses and the draw, though, were to the Wallabies.

While the All Blacks were ageing, the Wallabies were maturing. A victory against England, a team that plays with the courage of its restrictions, in the World Cup final on Saturday will be the definitive test of the greatness of this Wallaby side.

---

27 October 1991, at Dublin. Australia **16** (D. Campese, T. Horan tries; M. Lynagh 1 conversion and 2 penalty goals) defeated New Zealand **6** (G. Fox 2 penalty goals)

1 November 1991

One doesn't like to be the ghost at the banquet but it won't be a matter of the Wallabies singing 'Advance Australia Fair' and then piling on the points easily against England to win the Rugby World Cup final.

When the performance of the Wallabies throughout the World Cup tournament is scrutinised, several unsettling points emerge. Manu Samoa, for instance, almost held the Wallabies on a slippery, windy field (the conditions which could prevail at Twickenham if the weather forecasts are accurate). And Ireland, with a relatively small pack and only one lineout jumper, got enough ball to nearly steal an unexpected win.

England have approached the tournament not as a series of one-off matches but as a competition in which the only result that really counts is a victory in the final. The side, I suspect, wasn't greatly upset about losing to the All Blacks in the opening match. The restrictive, eight-man method used against France made sense because it's now accepted that if you keep the ball behind the French forwards they'll give away enough penalties to lose several matches. Why the restrictive method against Scotland, though – a side the All Blacks exposed as having virtually no scrum and not much of a lineout?

The answer is that this was the one match in the tournament England couldn't bear to lose. John Jeffreys, the Scots flanker, said before that match, 'If Scotland can't win the World Cup, I don't care who else does, as long as it isn't England.' The England players felt the same way about Scotland.

Despite all this, England's restrictive method should come unstuck against the Wallabies in a match that has to be won rather than not lost. England's approach has been very much like the negative attitude of Argentina in the last soccer World Cup. But the Argentinians found in the final that their style of playing not to lose wasn't flexible enough against an attack-minded and stylish West Germany.

The Wallabies are the West Germans of this World Cup Rugby tournament. They also have the best balanced team. England are fragile at fullback where Jonathan Webb appears unable to control his nerves on occasions. The England pack is good in the set pieces, especially the lineouts, but slowish around the field. The Wallabies demonstrated in Sydney, too, that the ponderousness of the England flankers and number 8 can be punished with adroit back-row moves from the scrum.

The final sign of a Wallaby victory has nothing to do with reason. Just before mystics achieve the victory of total spirituality they endure 'the dark night of the soul' when their character and all their beliefs are tested to the limit. Those minutes behind the goal-posts contemplating Ireland's try four minutes before full-time in the quarter-final were the 'dark night' for the Wallabies.

Once Michael Lynagh scored the match-winning try, though, it was as if the Fates had decided the Wallabies, having passed their great test of character and faith, were destined to be the world champions.

2 November 1991

Bob Dwyer's 1991 Wallabies are now, deservedly, immortal.

The Rugby World Cup triumph (which has saved commentator Chris Handy from walking to Toowoomba in a bowler hat – and only a bowler hat?) was achieved using all the best qualities of Australian rugby, an eye for a try, resilience, a trust in youth, courage (mental and physical) and a confidence to attack and protect the tryline.

What has distinguished the world champion Wallabies from the rest of the teams in the tournament is an awareness of the tryline, in attack and defence. Fifteen of the 17 tries scored by the Wallabies in the tournament were by the backs, with David Campese and Tim Horan contributing ten of them. Near the tryline, the Wallabies, of all the teams, were prepared to go for tries. For this reason alone the Wallabies deserved to win the World Cup tournament. Towards the end of the final the Wallabies were still trying to keep the ball in hand and set up tries. Even within their own half. Bob Dwyer got so frustrated with this recklessness that in despair he cried out, as if he were at Coogee Oval and not at Twickenham with a po-faced Queen Elizabeth II sitting a couple of rows in front of him: 'Kick it to the SHITHOUSE!'

Although it was the Daly–McKenzie front-row machine which scored the only try of the final, the significance of the try was the ruthless way the Wallabies capitalised on a gut-wrenching run out of defence from Tim Horan. The bulky England back-rowers were still trying to gather their breath after a hectic chase, and they allowed Willie Ofahengaue a free jump for the lineout ball.

And the one time David Campese got the ball with a little bit of room, he almost created a try by kicking past the fullback and chasing on. Only an erratic bounce prevented Campese or Ofahengaue from scoring.

On their own tryline the Wallabies were just as fearless and committed. Just as in the All Blacks game, the match hinged, coming up to half-time, on a series of scrums and driving mauls near the Australian line. In the three finals (and despite being beaten for possession in two of them), the Wallabies conceded only one try, and that was the marvellous sweeping movement from Ireland.

Throughout the week I've had a number of letters from England supporters berating me for my attitude to England's negative style of play. 'It is clearly obvious that Mr Zavos has no idea what the game of rugby is all about, assuming that to run with the ball is the be-all and end-all,' was one of the kinder comments. All these kickomaniacs missed the point. My argument was that England could win their matches more easily if they kept the ball in their hands. The way the England side played in the final, mounting attack after attack of running play, proved my case, in that the England game plan for their most crucial match was clearly based on mounting pressure by running and passing rather than kicking the ball.

In 1978, I chatted at Cardiff Arms Park with a man with a resonant voice, vivid blue eyes, a huge head and a look that was vaguely familiar. Afterwards I was told he was 'Richard Burton's brother'. Something had gone out of Welsh rugby, he told me, when ticket prices had soared so high 'the man who runs the sideline in the rain every Saturday afternoon can't afford to go to the internationals'. Wales would pay the price, he insisted, for neglecting their grassroots.

This mustn't be allowed to happen with Australian rugby. The Wallabies are world champions because the grassroots of Australian rugby are world championship quality. The victory of the Wallabies was a victory for Australian rugby and for all the players who turn out week after week, many of them in the bush travelling hundreds of kilometres for a match. The Australian rugby community is a tribe which has its roots in time past, and is aware of the generations yet unborn. The Twickenham triumph was the tribe's greatest moment, so far.

> **2 November 1991, at Twickenham.** Australia **12** (A. Daly 1 try; M. Lynagh 1 conversion and 2 penalty goals) defeated England **6** (J. Webb 2 penalty goals)

4 November 1991

By a special alchemy that can be observed but not really explained, the almost woeful Wallabies of the early part of the 1990 season transformed themselves into the wonderful Wallabies, the world champions of rugby in 1991.

The team personnel was not much different in the two seasons but the team was. It was a team that had no weaknesses and a number of the gifted players were at the peak of their powers. Eighteen months after a fumbling, maul-shy performance against the All Blacks in Christchurch, the world champion Wallabies comfortably resisted an increasingly feverish series of attacks by the All Blacks in Dublin in the semi-final.

A week later, an England side that was pampered and prepared with all the ingenuity and largesse that a wealthy code could devise, was swept off its feet in the early part of the match and then tackled behind the advantage line with bone-jarring ferocity when its backs tried to run at the Wallabies.

In the 1980s the Wallabies, mainly through the passing magic of Mark Ella, revolutionised back play by adopting rugby league passing techniques. In 1991, rugby league expertise was used again, but this time for defence. Bob Dwyer called on the experience of the Manly and Kangaroo second-rower and renowned 'hit-man' Terry Randall, one of the most feared tacklers in rugby league. Randall devised a series of exercises for the Wallabies to indoctrinate them into the techniques of the offensive tackle. The result was that although in both the semi-final and the final the Wallabies were starved of second-phase ball, their tackling was so aggressive that running the ball at them became a poor option. This tackling practice, and the fierce drills devised to inculcate the necessary contempt for pain that aggressive tackling requires, had another spin-off for the Wallabies. They were not only fitter than their opponents, they were harder.

This is unusual for Wallaby sides. But the 1991 Wallabies were as tough as gum trees. There was a memorable moment in the final at Twickenham when Simon Poidevin took the ball on the burst and ran straight into a braced and ready Mike Teague. Teague wears his jersey collar tucked into his shirt like a rugby league heavy. He is powerful and ruthless. He put his shoulder into the charging, unsuspecting Poidevin. The physical collision was tremendous and Poidevin was sent sprawling. But he retained the ball and was able to bounce to his feet immediately for the ensuing scrum.

There is no doubt that the Wallabies were superbly prepared by the coaching and support staff. The players had their first conditioning sessions in January 1991 and from then there was a military precision about the preparations for Operation Twickenham. That great rugby character and enthusiast, David Brockhoff, repeatedly rang me during the year to point out how methodical and intelligent the planning and the practices were. His point was – and it was an integral part of the final success – that all the resources of Australian rugby were being put to the task of preparing a world championship side.

Everything, however, finally rested on the last four minutes of the quarter-final against Ireland at Dublin. Ireland had scored the try of the tournament, against the run of play, to snatch an unexpected lead. Peter FitzSimons – who nearly made the final Wallaby squad and took his cutting with grace and good humour – has a theory that the way a team huddles after a try is indicative of its resolve: if the team spreads out, its morale is down, but if the huddle is tight, the resolve is still high. The Wallabies huddled tight.

The acting captain, Michael Lynagh, told his players he'd kick deep for position and when they got the ball back to keep it in the hand. David Campese, not noted for his aggressive mauling, got caught in a maul on the Irish tryline. Despite the fierce attention of the Irish forwards he kept hold of the ball and ensured a Wallaby put-in to the scrum. A five-yard scrum was forced and again Lynagh showed superlative leadership by calling for a backline movement to score a try and win the game, rather than go for a drop goal and a draw.

It's history that Lynagh backed up outside David Campese, in the manner of Mark Ella, to score the crucial try.

A team that could show such resolve, confidence, execution and flair when confronting its most desperate situation deserved to win the world championship. It was as if the acid had been poured on the ore and the gold was exposed.

By my reckoning, ten of the side would be candidates for a best-ever Wallaby side in the modern era: David Campese, Tim Horan, Michael Lynagh (although he could never displace Mark Ella), Nick Farr-Jones, Willie Ofahengaue, Simon Poidevin, John Eales, Tony Daly, Phil Kearns and Ewen McKenzie. The other five players, Marty Roebuck, Rob Egerton, Jason Little, Troy Coker and Rod McCall, all played well in the tournament.

There was one moment in the final against England that summed up the team. The Wallabies were under sustained pressure when Phil Kearns, the hooker, broke from a maul where he had been vigorously contesting for the ball and ran hard across the field, positioned himself in the defensive line and then went forward to make a crunching tackle on an England back. Having this sort of courage to make the extra, gut-wrenching effort to be a winner was what made the 1991 Wallabies such a wonderful side.

10 December 1999

There was a birthday party for Bob Jones last night in an apartment overlooking Elizabeth Bay. A violent storm had smashed through Sydney earlier in the afternoon, but by the time the guests started arriving for the party in the fading light the night air was still. The details of the bay, with its fingernail of pumpkin-yellow sand and the apartments almost on the waterline and the office buildings of the CBD standing like giants as they gazed over the shoulder of the hill leading down to the water, were set out as if in an enhanced photograph. In this opulent and serene setting conversation was friendly and intimate.

Bob and I met when we were at university in Wellington and boxed in the 'varsity team. We stayed friendly over the decades. He became a powerful figure in New Zealand and Australian business life. He started a political party in New Zealand that was responsible for bringing the Labour Party into government in 1983. He wrote a number of best-selling books. He is an expert on boxing and opera. He ran a popular radio talkback program for a time. He is a man who has used his money to widen his horizons with travel and study. He has a knack of friendship with interesting and successful people.

He gave Michael Lynagh a job in his Australian operations, for instance, when he was captain of the Wallabies. Later, he had Nick Farr-Jones, another Wallaby captain, appointed to the board of his Australian company. Through these connections he had come to know a number of the Wallabies and developed a fondness for the team.

Around 8.30 Nick Farr-Jones came into the main room. He had just returned from the funeral in Brisbane of the stalwart Queensland and Australian rugby identity, Bob Templeton. The funeral, he said, had been a moving and fun (if the circumstances were understood) occasion.

'Tempo' was a great mate to anyone in the rugby community. Old players had recounted many memorable stories connected with him. There was his '6 Ps' theory, for instance: 'Proper Preparation Prevents Piss-Poor Performance.' The players remembered, too, how on the 1991 World Cup campaign Bob Templeton would sit in front of a fire in the lounge of the team's hotel with a whisky in hand and anyone who wanted a chat about life, his problems or anything else on his mind could join him in conversation while the embers glowed.

He worried so much before big matches that he found it hard to go to sleep. He'd go to bed late and get up early. On the morning of the semi-final against the All Blacks he was up earlier than usual and was sitting quietly in the lounge when he spied David Knox creeping up the stairs to his room. Knox had obviously been partying, something that was not offensive to the management because Knox was not listed in the run-on team or the reserves.

Templeton waited for about 30 minutes, until he felt sure that Knox would just be easing himself into sleep. He rang

Knox's room number. There was a delay and then an indistinct reply. 'Knoxie,' a concerned Templeton said, 'I'm sorry to wake you so early but Noddie [Michael Lynagh] has been crook all night. He won't be playing.'

Knox mumbled something. Templeton pressed on. 'We wanted to make sure everything is alright with you. No problems, boy? You're not only in the team, you'll be wearing the number 10 jersey. Are you up to it, boy?'

Some seconds passed before Knox replied, 'Give me about four hours more sleep, and I'm your man.'

Templeton waited for another hour, when he was sure that Knox would be in a profound and satisfying slumber, before ringing him again to tell him of the prank he'd played on him.

Someone at the party yelled across to Nick while he, Bob and I were talking about these things and about politics and why journalists like myself had such a hostile attitude to politicians. 'Nick, what was the best Wallaby team you played for?' the questioner asked.

Nick Farr-Jones was lucky enough (like all great players he made his own luck, too) to play for three great Wallaby sides: the 1984 Grand Slam Wallabies; the 1986 Wallabies, which won the Bledisloe Cup in New Zealand for the first time since 1949 and only the second time ever in New Zealand; and the 1991–92 Wallabies, the winners of the RWC tournament and unbeatable the next year.

After some thought Nick said he believed the 1991–92 side was probably the best.

Bob Jones told a couple of stories to back up his assessment that great teams were also smart teams. While the Wallabies were in Dublin in 1991, he said, Michael Lynagh organised a group of them to go to Trinity College to have a look at the historic *Book of Kells*, a masterpiece of early medieval drawing and penmanship. 'Can you imagine the All Blacks,' he asked, 'especially those oafs who wear their dark glasses in the middle of the night and

have earphones on all the time playing crap music, even knowing what the *Book of Kells* is, let alone having the intelligence to
go and have a look at it?'

He told another story about going jogging in Dublin at
about 5.30 in the morning of the 1991 RWC semi-final ('real
final, in fact') between Australia and New Zealand. He saw a
senior Wallaby in his track suit walking quickly away from his
hotel. They stopped and had a chat. The Wallaby said he was
going to visit his girlfriend to indulge in some conjugal activity.

'Can you imagine it?' Bob said. 'On the morning of the most
important game of the tournament this senior player was
relaxed enough to trot off to his girlfriend's place for a cuddle.'

Nick Farr-Jones has a manner that is informal and confiden-
tial. There is a famous story about him luxuriating in a huge
bath at Twickenham after the 1991 World Cup victory, a cigar in
his mouth, when the British Prime Minister, John Major, came
into the room to congratulate the Wallabies. Nick stood up out
of the bath. 'Gidday John, how are you?' he said, with the water
dripping down his naked body.

He grasped my arm and seized on Bob Jones's stories to make
the point that the best teams, like the 1991 Wallabies, allow their
players to see rugby as a game, a game they had to win but without cutting the players off from their real life. You trained really
hard, he said, 'and you know, I couldn't have been fitter during
my career.' But the players shouldn't be made one-dimensional
by a coaching staff that wanted to monitor everything they did
away from training. He said he suspected that this was what happened to the All Blacks in the 1999 RWC tournament.

Then, linking his great 1991–92 Wallabies with the other
great Australian side of the 1990s, the 1999 world champions of
rugby, he said, 'Rod Macqueen learned to loosen up a bit and
the players responded to being treated like adults.' Management
and players had to enjoy the challenge of trying to become
world champions. They had to avoid being ground down by the

seriousness of it all. This sense of the necessity of having fun was brought home to him by a story he'd heard told at Bob Templeton's funeral, of how 'Tempo' had threatened to streak across the Millennium Stadium at Cardiff if the Wallabies won the 1999 World Cup. His bad knees, though, prevented this exhibition from taking place.

When I was going through a massive file of newspaper clippings on the 1999 World Cup tournament I came across this quote from Rod Macqueen which I hadn't read when it was first printed. He was explaining why his team had not cracked under the strain of high expectations, as England and New Zealand had. 'We don't seem to feel the pressure that much. Perhaps that's because we see rugby as a sport and not life and death.'

But this attitude did not prevent the Wallabies from playing the Rugby World Cup tournaments in 1991 and 1999 as if they were life or death experiences, and enjoying coming up against the best that the rest of the rugby world could throw at them.

PART III: Golden Wallabies

1908 Olympic Gold Medal

Rugby Rules, OK!

During the 1880s it was common for three football codes – rugby, soccer and what was called at the time Victorian Rules – to be played on the restricted spaces of Moore Park, some way out of the city of Sydney. Crowds of spectators following the various games often spilled on to the areas of the competing sports.

A game of Victorian Rules had been played between the University of Sydney and Newington College in 1869. This was only a few years after the students at Sydney University had begun to play the new fad game from Britain called rugby football, a tough, rough game involving collisions and chasing a pumped-up leather ball according to laws that had been worked out over several decades at Rugby School.

You had to have ticker to play rugby in those days. In the 1860s, in fact, there was an attempt in the NSW Parliament to ban the game on the grounds that it was far too rough. The *Sydney Sunday Times* observed: 'Footballers are a howling, brutal set of cads – the game makes them so – they should be put down accordingly.' The *Bulletin* was similarly blunt, describing rugby as 'the undertaker's friend'. Snowy Baker, a sportsman who has claims to being Australia's greatest athlete, played rugby for NSW in 1904 when he was 19. His Hollywood good looks were marred by a magnificent cauliflower ear, a legacy he reckoned of a vicious kick to his head by a clergyman in a game of rugby.

You had to be tough, too, to cope with the hard grounds. Mosman Oval, one of the better grounds around Sydney, was described in the 1890s as 'a downhill ground of loose gravel and innumerable tree stumps, which caused many injuries on collision'.

The later decades of the nineteenth century were marked in Australia by what could be called the 'football war', a struggle between different groups of players in different states to establish their code of football as the Authorised Version of Football. Association football (soccer) became popular in Sydney in the

1880s when many parents, like modern soccer mums, became fearful of the brutality of rugby. But by the end of the last century, it was rugby that had won the day in NSW. Rugby was the dominant football code in Sydney until 1908. Then there was a civil war within the rugby community and the professional rugby game, rugby league, established its dominance, which it maintains into the twenty-first century.

Why did soccer fail in Australia when it succeeded in becoming the major winter sport throughout most of the rest of the world?

The answer, probably, is that soccer was dismissed by the young Sydney bloods of the late nineteenth century as being 'too British'. We have an ironic situation here. Soccer was the people's game in Britain. Rugby was a game invented by public school boys who were reluctant in Britain to allow the lower classes to play it. But the Sydney young bloods thought soccer was too British for their taste. This notion probably came from the practice of the British military playing soccer against the locals at places around the world.

Rugby, too, with its roughness and emphasis on collisions between players, appealed to young men in a new country who worked hard and expected to play hard. Soccer, of course, had the body contact element taken out of it. The game, therefore, was seen by Australian youths as an unmanly activity with the additional disadvantage, for a generation pushing for an Australian federation, of being too associated with connotations of Britain as 'Home'. Soccer players were called 'Homies'.

Why this same construct was not applied to cricket is not clear. Perhaps lawn tennis, the main alternative to cricket as a summer sport, could not arouse the same interest and passion in young Australian men as rugby clearly did.

There is the final point, too, that rugby (in Australia) is a democratic game in its ethic and its requirements of the players. All shapes and sizes, from the lanky lineout forwards to the squat props, to the nippy halves and the strong three-quarters, are needed in the ideal rugby team. This inclusive element in rugby appealed to an egalitarian society where you saluted no one, no matter how highly placed the other person might be.

Victorian Rules was also a democratic and inclusive game. But it had the overwhelming disadvantage in Sydney of being regarded as a Melbourne game. There was a reluctance, too, on the part of officials involved with Victorian Rules to encourage touring. An invitation to a Melbourne side to tour Queensland, for instance, was rejected because it was too expensive. Ian Diehm, in *Red! Red! Red!: The Story of Queensland Rugby*, claims that this rejection by some Victorian Rules officials led to a meeting in downtown Brisbane at the Exchange Hotel on 2 November 1883. The agenda of the meeting was to decide whether or not a rugby union should be formed in Queensland. Over the stern objections of several passionate supporters of Victorian Rules, who wanted players banned from playing rugby, it was decided 'the formation of a Rugby Union will advance the interests of football'.

The meeting was mindful of the fact that the previous year the rugby authorities in Sydney had offered the young bloods a tour of New Zealand, which took place in the middle of 1882. The *Sydney Mail* reported that two customs officials examined the belongings of the NSW players. 'They found nothing contraband,' the reporter noted, 'save and except a tiny revolver which a heroic Woollahra man brought to overawe the Maoris.' A rugby team from New Zealand crossed the Tasman two years later and the Australian connection with the New Zealand rugby community was engaged.

And in 1882, too, the first NSW–Queensland rugby contest took place. The secretary of the Brisbane Wallaroo club wrote to his Sydney counterpart suggesting a challenge match. It came down to a bidding war between the Victorian Rules, soccer and rugby administrators. The Southern Rugby Union (NSW) offered to pay all the expenses of the Queenslanders, provided only rugby was played on the tour.

The Queenslanders were softened up, after their rough two-day voyage down the coast, with some extreme hospitality on their arrival. 'All assembled,' the *Queenslander* reported, 'and the sparkling fluid was handed around.' Twelve of the Queenslanders, moreover, were Victorian Rules players. Hardly surprisingly, NSW won comfortably – either 26–4 or 28–4, depending on how the points were computed, or how much amber fluid was consumed by whom, perhaps.

The return match in Brisbane, on a ground described as 'hard as stone and as slippery as glass', resulted in a win for the locals. This victory made rugby the main winter game in Queensland and set up the uncompromising and ferocious inter-state rivalry that has retained its intensity into the twenty-first century. In 1883 Queensland recorded its first victory in Sydney with tactics that seem very familiar to this day. 'Don't pass, boys,' the Queensland captain instructed his players. 'The ball is wet.' Wet or dry, though, Queensland has continued with the 'don't pass' tactics to the present day.

So rugby, with its touring options, became the game of Sydney University and of the private schools (in Sydney and Brisbane) which later became the Greater Public Schools (GPS). The significance of these allegiances is that Sydney University and the private schools were the only institutions in Sydney that had sports grounds.

A further significance was the problem of getting grounds in Sydney: its hilly topography finally killed off Australian Rules (as Victorian Rules became) in Sydney as a major sport for a hundred years. Australian Rules is one of the few sports codes where the measurements of the field are not standardised. The game requires a large oval, however, and last century the fields were sometimes marked out at over 800 metres in length. With the limited open spaces in the public domain available in

Sydney (as opposed to the vast open spaces of flat Melbourne), the Australian Rules game, literally, had no space where it could be played.

Thomas Hickie, in his masterly account of the early days of rugby in Australia, *They Ran with the Ball*, points to the recommendations of the NSW Parliament Select Committee Report of 1861 as being crucial in shutting Victorian (Australian) Rules out of Sydney in the 1880s. The report recommended that the fence around the Domain's cricket area and a football area in winter be taken down and the land be used for general public recreation. The decision, Hickie claims, 'was a victory for passive recreation over organised sport concerning the use of public lands'.

The smaller field required for rugby meant that rugby games could be played more easily (but obviously with some problems) on this public domain than the Victorian Rules game. Nevertheless, rugby teams that toured Australia in the last decades of the nineteenth century generally went down to Melbourne and played matches under the Victorian Rules format. This was part of the skirmishing tactics in the football war. The 1888–89 New Zealand Natives side, for instance – the team that pioneered the extensive international tour – played 74 matches in Britain and on its way back to New Zealand played 13 games of Victorian Rules throughout Victoria.

At the turn of the century there were 100 teams in New Zealand playing the Victorian game. A jubilee carnival marking the first 50 years of Australian Rules was held at the MCG in 1908. New Zealand sent a team to the carnival. This team defeated New South Wales and Queensland but was defeated by the Victorians and the West Australians.

The attempt to internationalise Australian Rules did not succeed with this jubilee, however. And this was a fatal impediment to the game becoming entrenched in NSW and Queensland. Rugby was already international, and this made it attractive to the young bloods. While the Australian Rules carnival at the

MCG was taking place in 1908 the grandest of all sporting tours, a rugby tour of Britain, the United States and Canada, was in preparation.

That touring side became known as the 1908 Wallabies. The tour was a six-month adventure. Players were paid 3 shillings a day in expenses. There were Tests against Wales, Ireland and England, and the chance to win a gold medal for rugby at the 1908 London Olympic Games.

'The Honours of Australian Footer Look a Bit Dickey'
A cryptic cable

At 12.25 in the afternoon on 15 Feburary 1899 the Reverend Matthew Mullineux, a teaching fellow at St John's College, Cambridge University, received a cryptic, reply-paid cablegram from Sydney, Australia: 'Newspapers here report your Abarataron Tamsomente all aerofobo Widerhakerr sebacica Marzauilla have a team aboloris desabozar. Rand'

This cable was followed a few days later with a letter from the British Post Office giving a full transcript of the message. The use of an elaborate code was clearly intended to prevent the urgent message in the cablegram being passed on to other sports organisations in Australia.

A well-informed person about sport in Sydney, for instance, might have guessed that 'Rand' was A.W. Rand, the masterful secretary of the New South Wales Rugby Union. But what could 'Newspapers here report your . . .' mean? Someone knowledgeable about rugby might remember small items in the *Sydney Mail* and the *Sydney Morning Herald* noting that difficulties had cropped up over the proposed rugby tour by an English team to be led and organised by Rev. Mullineux.

Whether these obstacles were known in the wider community must remain moot. But the fact that the tour was in doubt was the centre of a discussion at a council meeting of the NSWRU held at its rooms at 109 Pitt Street, in the heart of the central business district, on Tuesday 14 February 1899. The motion for discussion was what the NSWRU should do about press reports 'that English Team's visit has been abandoned'.

It was decided after a vigorous debate that the cablegram be sent to England asking Rev. Mullineux if 'the question of terms' was the problem. The meeting agreed, too, that Rev. Mullineux needed to know that the NSWRU 'must have' the team and that it would be a 'serious detriment' to rugby if the tour were cancelled.

Mullineux's offer

The inspiration for the 1899 tour had come from a letter to the NSWRU, literally out of the blue, from Mullineux. The letter, which exhibited a mixture of boldness and optimistic misinformation, was dated August 1897 although it was received in April 1898: 'I should be glad to know if a visit of British footballers to Australia would be welcomed next year. The South African tour of last year was a great success and there is a desire among prominent footballers to visit Australia next year. If you think such a visit would be a success, I would be glad to get together a strong team to leave England next year.

'The team would be drawn largely from my own University and that of Oxford and from the Internationals from outside the Universities. We would leave in June and play some 16 to 20 matches before leaving the land again. The financial aspect of the visit we can consider if you decide to send me the invitation to get the team together. Kindly let me know soon. I am sending a similar letter to Melbourne in case Sydney is not one of the centres of Rugby Union.'

Only whispers

A month later (4 May 1898) the *Referee* explained to its readers why the rugby tour had been called off until 1899: 'The reason, Mr A.W. Rand, Hon. Sec. of the New South Wales Rugby

Union. tells us, is that the gentleman manipulating the strings at
the antipodean end could not quite fix things up as he desired in
time to reach Australia in time for this football season.'

Specifically what was holding matters up was Rev. Mullineux's shrewd and less-than-honest attempts to keep the
NSWRU on hold while he tried to put in place a follow-up
tour to the successful South African tour he had organised in
1896. The dark clouds of the gathering storm of the Boer War,
however, made it obvious that a rugby tour of South Africa by a
team of British players, at the same time as troops around the
Empire were being sent to that country to put the Boers in their
place, was not possible. The Australian tour, therefore, was
rushed back into preparation.

The gossip writer for the *Referee* went on to note that 'someone whispers that Mr Molyneux, of Cambridge, paused in his
organising efforts, and pondered deeply over the fate of his
brother sportsmen who play cricket. Then, rather than come
along to take the kangaroo down a peg at Rugby with a team of
doubtful strength, he discreetly postponed the venture. But this
is only a whisper.'

Mullineux's men

On 20 May 1899, the *Sydney Mail*, in a sports section devoted to
Football Notes, listed the team that had finally been put
together by Rev. Mullineux. The writer 'Fullback' said that
'it adds much interest to the team to know that it contains the
best men hailing from England, Scotland, Ireland and Wales'.

The team was: E. Martelli (Dublin University), C.E.K.
Thompson (Lancashire), E. Gwyn Nicholls (Cardiff), A.B.
Timms (Edinburgh University), G.P. Doran (Lansdowne), A.M.
Bucher (Edinburgh Academicals), E.T. Nicholson (Birkenhead
Park), Rev. M. Mullineux (Blackheath: Captain and Manager),
G. Cookson (Manchester), C.Y. Adamson (Durham), F.M. Stout
(Gloucester), J.W. Jarman (Bristol), H.G.S. Gray (Scottish Trials),

G.R. Gibson (Northern), W. Judkins (Coventry), F.C. Belson (Bath), J.S. Francombe (Manchester), B.I. Swannell (North-ampton), E.V. Evers (Moseley), T.M. McGown (North of Ireland), A. Ayres-Smith (Guy's Hospital).

Eight of the players were internationals at the time (Nicholls, Timms, Doran, Bucher, Nicholson, Stout, Gibson and McGown). Jarman later represented England and Swannell, described by Jack Pollard in his *Australian Rugby: The Game and the Players* as 'a tough, courageous English-born forward with outspoken opinions' represented Australia on the first tour of New Zealand in 1905.

The liniment of memory might have softened opinions, but rugby writers decades later insisted that Rev. Mullineux's side was one of the best to ever tour Australia. The team's record – of played 21; won 18; lost 3; points for 333; against 90 – is impressive.

Before Mullineux's team had even played a match, the newspapers expressed the perpetual fear that the colonials could not match the British mother race on the sports field. The *Truth* cast its worried eye over Mullineux's team and then made a defeatist prophecy: '*Truth* can safely say the safety of the honours of Australian footer look a bit dickey. And it is more than likely they will be carted to England for a longish period of time.'

The English are here – all systems go

The first sighting of Rev. Mullineux's team in Sydney confirmed that they were 'a fine athletic-looking lot of men'. Reporters, though, were struck by their lack of heft and bulk: 'The visitors do not strike Australians as especially big men.' The feeling was that the weights given for the forwards, who were claimed to have an average weight of 13 stones, were greatly exaggerated. But while the English players were not as beefy as their publicity suggested, 'they are all big limbed and powerful, as is natural when it is reflected that to secure county, university, and international honours, each man is the pick of a host of athletes'.

The precedent for selecting the first national Australian rugby team was set by the cricket authorities who had developed a strategy of loading the selection panel with locals, depending where the cricket Test was played. The Test side in Sydney played in Waratah blue and the second Test side at Brisbane played in Queensland maroon.

The selection panel of one Queenslander and two New South Wales officials announced their team on the Monday before the first Test:

Fullback: R. McGown (Queensland)
Three-quarters: A. Spragg (NSW), F. Row (NSW), C. White (NSW)
Five-eighths: P. Ward (NSW), W.T. Evans (Q)
Half: A. Gralton (Q)
Forwards: J. Carson (NSW), W.H. Tanner (Q), W. Davis (NSW), H. Marks (NSW), P. Carew (Q), A. Colton (Q), A. Kelly (NSW), C. Ellis (NSW).

The Australian forwards lined out as they were named, in a 2–3–3 formation, with James 'Jum' Carson and William 'Doey' Tanner being the hookers. The team trained at the Sydney Cricket Ground at 3.30 on the afternoons leading up to the Test under the supervision of W. Warbrick, one of the great men of New Zealand and later Australian rugby.

Australian rugby experts before and after the Test rated this first national team as possibly the best side Australian rugby produced up to the First World War. Bob McGown at fullback was regarded as the 'finest produced' in Queensland. Stocky and dynamic, he was 'fast, very clever in handling, kicking, and passing the ball, and tackles well'. In an era when the fullback was regarded as a custodian, McGown was modern in his concept of what the position required: 'Indeed, he possessed in a high degree the essentials of a crack three-quarter.'

The team's crack three-quarter, the winger Alfonso 'Lonnie' Spragg, was the prototype of the brilliant outside back that has been one of the enduring glories of Australian rugby from Dally Messenger, Cyril Towers, Charlie Eastes, Trevor Allan, through to the moderns like David Campese, Tim Horan and Ben Tune. Spragg was a natural. He did not start playing rugby until he was about 17 and two years later was a Test player. As a youngster bursting into senior rugby, Spragg was described as 'possessing rare gifts, denoting a special aptitude for the game . . . He is as fast as, if not actually faster than S. Wickham, dodges like the old Wallaroo winger, yet unlike him, too, he dodges both ways. Spragg is a splendid kick, either place or drop, and is eager and capable on defence.'

Holding the pack together was the formidable front rower 'Jum' Carson and the backrower Charlie Ellis. Carson was regarded as 'the best all-round forward in Australia . . . In the pack, in the loose and on the lineout, he is equally good.' The highest praise that was lavished on Carson was the acknowledgment by New Zealanders that he was as good as any forward in that country.

England v. Australia

The *Sydney Mail* of 1 July 1899 carried a series of photographs that give a certain resonance of the great occasion. There is a team photograph, with the players in their Test caps, taken shortly before the match. The shinpads on A. Colton are exposed. P. Ward marks his Test debut by wearing a colourful sash around his waist to hold his shorts up. The captain, F. Row, is grim-faced and sitting in the middle of the middle rank with a fat leather ball resting on his knee. Seven of the players, most of them the more experienced members of the team, including the captain, C. Ellis and J. Carson, wear military-style moustaches that infer they are officer material. The younger members of the side, A. Spragg and A. Colton, have a baby-faced toughness about them that does not augur well for their opponents.

The referee, the Christchurch-based W.G. Gerrard, is in the middle of the back row, moustached and wearing the standard white outfit of the referee. Gerrard was so determined to maintain a fairness throughout the game that he sometimes fed the scrum himself.

A controversial first try

The early part of the Test featured 'dashing' play by England. England 'returned to the attack with vim', a journalist reported. A break by G. Cookson was followed with another 'brilliant run that reached almost to the Australian line'. England were playing with the panache that was later adopted by British Lions sides. The game 'became extraordinarily fast and things for the moment looked bad for the Australians'. Then came the moment that defined Australian rugby history. The first try in a Test by an Australian side turned the tide of the match and enabled Australia to win a famous victory.

Here is the eye-witness account of what happened written by the rugby writer for the *Sydney Morning Herald*: 'Back again was the ball worked, until in front of the goal Gralton secured and passed back to Evans, who took a flying shot for goal. The ball went high, failed to score, dropped in front of Martelli, who allowed it to bounce, and Kelly and Colton came with a rush. The former jostled the English fullback, secured the ball, and scored a try. Several of the Englishmen appealed for two reasons – for offside and for illegal interference – but the referee allowed the try. From the press table, in the balcony of the members' pavilion, the interference appeared to be simply a jostle, but it seemed hard to come to any other conclusion than that Kelly and Colton were offside. There was great excitement amongst the spectators. Spragg took the kick, but failed to add to the extra points.'

Rev. Mullineux's sermon

The *Australian Field* published a controversial interview with Mullineux at the end of the tour, in which he was quoted as objecting to the incipient professionalism he observed throughout Australia. Although Rev. Mullineux claimed he had been misquoted, the quotations were extensive, which raises the question of whether they could have been invented to this extent.

Mullineux was arguing from an English perspective, where amateurism was regarded as part of the natural order of life and a bulwark of the class system. Amateurism, as it applied to reinforcing the strict class system, was, for Mullineux and others of his class, God's work. This divine order of life was applied by leaders in the Rugbyocracy to the organisation of rugby. While the tour was being put into place, for instance, there was the news that the famous James brothers, the inventors of the half-back formation, had defected from Welsh rugby and had 'gone over to the Northern League and professionalism'.

The behaviour of such professionals was seen as an offence against the proper order of society. The only response to this type of attack on amateur rugby and good order in society, therefore, was to contain an outbreak of the plague with total isolation and ostracism. One of the touring conditions for the players in Mullineux's team was that 'they must be amateur'.

But this was not what was happening in Australia. The egalitarianism of ordinary life was accepted as appropriate for rugby, as well. Because the game appealed across the community, from lawyers, doctors and students through to men who worked with their hands – when they could get a job – there was no objection to talented rugby players getting financial rewards for their skills. The belief was that being good at rugby was a skill that deserved recognition as much as being able to read a commercial document.

This belief was sustained by the influx of New Zealanders to

NSW and Queensland who had, from the beginning of rugby in that country in 1870, accepted that the game should provide some financial rewards to the players. There was a depression in New Zealand throughout the 1890s and many players and former players looked to Australia and rugby in Australia, particularly, as a way of earning their keep until better times arrived. The *Rockhampton Bulletin* was moved to issue this warning in 1892: 'One has only to note the many famous players who have migrated to Charters Towers during the past 12 months to see if professionalism does not exist there, appearances are exceedingly deceptive.'

There is an item in the minutes of the NSWRU of 30 August 1897 that appears to confirm this suspicion: 'It was decided that the railway fares of Roberts (the New Zealand player) to Queensland be borne by this union, and that the N. Zealand Union be informed.'

This incident suggests that Australian authorities were putting in place a professional code of rugby, along the lines of cricket. And by 1899 this professional ethic was becoming ingrained in Australian rugby. Players were being paid to move from their country (New Zealand in most cases, but some British players migrated with their rugby boots to Australia, too), from one state to another, and from club to club. Clubs were being paid, as well, to hire professional trainers. Costs from injuries were also being were covered by the NSWRU.

The minutes of the NSWRU's meeting of 6 February 1899, when details of the tour by Rev. Mullineux's team were being finalised, carried this item under 'Correspondence': 'Letter from Kelly – re Medical Expenses amounting to 2 pounds, 11 shillings and 6 pence incurred through being injured whilst playing football. Mr Henderson moved and seconded by Mr Lane that account be paid.'

Truth reported accurately, therefore, in May 1899: 'By slow degree the old order of things has changed, and in the new regime, controlled and managed by young men of up to date ideas, every senior club is entitled to a grant of 10 pounds for the purpose of defraying the costs of a trainer. This to the old hands sounds suspiciously like professionalism, but it is nothing like what will come . . . Clubs have the permission of the Union to arrange matches among themselves, the gatetakings of which they divide equally. It must be obvious that contests played under these conditions are not for sport but for monetary gain – that those engaging in it are doing so not for the love of it but what they can get out of it. In other words, the real issue of the game is not so much the object of achievement as that the club coffers will respond to the ring of the shekels.'

The article went on to criticise the fact that intercolonial players received 'pay' from their local union of the substantial amount of 5 shillings a day. This allowance was 'ostensibly a wine bill expense'. But as the *Truth* of May 1899 fearlessly pointed out, the wine bill expense was exclusive of travelling expenses. It was paid to players whether they drank wine or water. One player with private means refused his expenses but was told that if he did not accept them someone else would. He took the money.

Truth then articulated the arguments against this virus of professionalism that Rev. Mullineux was to make so emphatically at the end of England's tour: 'To those who know anything about Rugby football in the old countryland, the acceptance of this money constitutes a distinct breach of the rules, and any player who is proved to have done so is regarded as a professional . . . Once let it get its hold of NSW football and the game will become not one of pleasure but of business. And we in Australia know by past experience that when a sport becomes a matter of business the results in the main are decided by pounds, shillings and pence.'

By 1907, however, the NSWRU had embedded the culture of amateurism. Rugby in NSW, particularly, had taken on the attitudes and sensibilities of rugby in England. There was a conscious attempt to make it an exclusive game for the middle and upper classes. When a row over injury payments broke out in Sydney in 1907, the NSWRU took the same position as the RFU had in 1895, when it voted against professionalism.

This circle of rugby evolving into a professional game and then being administered into an enforced and restrictive amateurism was completed in May 1995 when the NSWRU issued a statement headed 'Rugby Is No Longer Amateur'. The statement made the obvious point that 'the rugby world has been remunerating players and coaches in various ways for a very long time . . . Amateurism as a concept is outmoded and should be dispensed with in the modern game.'

This historic statement, which was inspired by News Ltd's raid on rugby league to set up Super League, which in turn was threatening to cannibalise rugby union for its players, was the breakthrough that led to the News Ltd deal made during the 1995 Rugby World Cup tournament – to finance rugby by buying the television rights for the game in South Africa, New Zealand and Australia. This deal forced the hand of the International Rugby Board (IRB) which agreed, a century after the Great Split, that rugby union was no longer an amateur game but that it had become an 'open' game, professional to whatever level the administrators wanted to make their payments.

Australia's team

On the Monday before the first Test, the *Sydney Morning Herald* editorialised on the joy of rugby: 'The strenuous struggles of the opposing parties, the quickness and readiness of the players, the breeziness of the atmosphere in which all games are played – all stimulates the interest of the onlookers.' Mullineux was complimented for bringing a team to Australia that was 'utterly indifferent' to gatetakings: 'They have come here for the love of the game, and some of them . . . are really losing money on the tour.'

But as Dr Thomas V. Hickie points out in his history of sub-urban club rugby in Sydney, *The Game for the Game Itself!*, the tour provided a tremendous fillip for rugby throughout Australia: 'Crowds for Brisbane and Sydney premiership matches leapt to hitherto unknown levels with 15,000 for needle games not uncommon.' The NSWRU pushed ahead with its restructuring of the Sydney club system, which had been discussed throughout the 1890s and had been held back by the England tour. In 1900 the inaugural district premiership competition was launched. This competition is still in place. One of its effects – of tying players to the team in the district they lived in – was to make buying players to change clubs very difficult to operate.

'The Cause of Australian Union'

Federation of the states into a country, Australia, did not occur until 1901. An Australian rugby team contested Test matches against England, therefore, at a time when Australia as a consti-tutional entity did not actually exist. There was no Australian anthem and no Australian flag in 1899. The concept of a distinct Australian citizenship did not come into force until Australia Day, 1949. Australia as a nation only existed when the national rugby or cricket side became Australia's team.

Thus it was in sport, essentially, that the sense of being some-thing other than British developed in Australia. Sport released the national identity. General William Booth, the founder of the Salvation Army, reported after his visit to Australia in 1892: 'The hilarity and vigour of youth leads to a love of excitement, with all its consequent dangers. One manifestation of this is to be found in the terrible hold which gambling has on Australians . . . Another manifestation of the same thing is the tremendous passion for outdoor sports.'

It is a truism of sociology that sport and culture are like Siamese twins. But as Chris Laidlaw, an All Black and Rhodes Scholar, points out, these twins are often in denial with each other. Cultural groups in Australia at the end of the nineteenth century looked to England. Sport looked within Australia. The national identity, therefore, was forged by the national sporting teams.

The first rugby Test between Australia and England actually coincided with the vote in NSW on federation. 107,274 people in NSW voted for the Federation Bill; 82,707 voted against. The majority of 24,567 was regarded as a handsome one by the political class. Did the prospect of 30,000 people at the Sydney Cricket Ground cheering on a national rugby team and the patriotic excitement that a victory over the tourists would generate convince many of them to vote for the future of a united but federated nation?

The opening sentence of the editorial in the *Maitland Daily Mercury* celebrating the Federation Bill victory was quoted in the *Sydney Morning Herald* directly beside that newspaper's report of Australia's victory in the first rugby Test. The sentence could have represented both results: 'The cause of Australian union has triumphed gloriously in New South Wales.'

The joy of rugby

As Australia moved into nationhood, rugby and the joy that the game provides for players and supporters grew in popularity. The catalyst for the rugby side of this equation was the tour of Rev. Mullineux's team. Unlike England sides of later generations, this side played exhilarating rugby. The passing game based around strong-running three-quarters – what has become the traditional Wallaby style – was given a stimulus from the example provided by the England side. The science of rugby was exposed by England as the winning way, where Australians had previously seen the game as a battle of brawn.

Young players flocked to grounds to play rugby. Huge crowds gathered to watch significant matches. Jack Pollard put the 1899 tour in this context: 'The visit . . . excited great public interest, and gave rugby a clear advantage over its rival codes. For almost a decade, public support for international and interstate games made rugby the pre-eminent winter game in NSW and Queensland . . . From the turn of the century, the influence of the GPS schools spread to Catholic colleges, associated schools and public high schools. Thousands of young men started playing the game, at first with no thought of playing for their state or for Australia. A lot of them played the game for fun after they left school, believing in the concepts of amateurism and sportsman-like behaviour they had learnt at school.'

This last comment makes an important point. Australian rugby suffered at the highest level from the adoption of the amateur ethic, following Mullineux's forceful and continual arguments for a lilywhite game. The England team was scheduled to go on to New Zealand but the NSWRU refused to pay the cost for the journey across the Tasman. This proved to be a godsend for New Zealand rugby. Without the sermonising of Rev. Mullineux, New Zealand rugby officials allowed their game to become quasi-professional.

The irony was that when the split between the rugby codes came in Australasia in 1907, a New Zealand rugby league team was put together to tour Britain with Dally Messenger, Australian rugby's superstar at the time, included in the side as an honorary New Zealander. There is a photograph of Messenger in the black jersey with the silver fern emblem. But while rugby league displaced rugby union as the main rugby code in NSW and Queensland, it was beaten into marginalisation in New Zealand. New Zealand was saved by the fact that there was no real reason for the better rugby players to make the switch, as they were already making money out of playing the game.

Toasting the future

This history, however, was well into the future. On the evening of the last Test the English footballers were entertained by the

NSWRU at Tattersall's Hotel. About 160 men were present. The evening began with a series of toasts. J.J. Calvert, the president of the NSWRU, proposing a toast to 'The English team and the Rev. Matthew Mullineux', said that the English players could forget the 'little pinpricks' they had suffered during their tour after their splendid victory earlier in the day. 'If you are unable to carry the ashes,' he said,' you have to take the mud.'

The Test had been played on a wet SCG and this remark was greeted with laughter. The toast was concluded amid 'great cheering'. Rev. Mullineux was asked to stand on a chair so that he could be seen at the back of the room as he made his reply. He was out here as a representative of English rugby football, he said, and he felt he had a duty to speak against anything that was not conducive to the game being played in a sportsmanlike manner. As a clergyman, he should denounce anything in the game that was 'unmanly'. What he said should not be seen as 'carping'. He objected to the Australian trick of holding a man back when coming away from the scrum: 'I am told that the Australian remedy is to bite the hand, but we have not mastered the art of cannibalism.' Shouting to an opponent for a pass was the lowest thing he had heard of: 'Please blot these things from your football, for instead of developing all that is manly they bring forth all that is unmanly.' (Cheers.) The trip was now virtually over but he wished to say that it had been one of 'joy and delight', a remark that brought forth further effusions of cheers.

The toasts were honoured in Royal Maximum Champagne.

The 1908 Olympic Champion Wallabies

The 1899 tour by Rev. Mullineux's team globalised Australian rugby. The money that poured into the coffers of the NSWRU was used to bring the first New Zealand national side to Australia in 1903. This was the beginning of one of rugby's greatest rivalries, with over 100 Tests between the Wallabies and the All Blacks being played by 1999. The success of this tour, in turn, provided the funds for the first tour of Britain by a national Australian rugby side, in 1908. This side won an Olympic Gold Medal for rugby and became known as the Wallabies.

Here we are at the Waldorf Hotel, Aldwych, London, on 11 November 1908, at a dinner for the touring Wallaby rugby side which is being hosted by the London Rugby Football Union to commemorate the Wallabies winning the rugby competition at the London Olympics. The players are to receive their gold medals later in the evening.

The food – soups, entrees, several meat dishes, the main course, desserts – follow each other in a stomach-stretching parade. The air is foggy and eye-wateringly sharp with cigarette and cigar smoke. There is a constant chatter of conversation.

The Wallabies have played one of the oldest clubs, Blackheath, repesenting London, that day, for another win (24–3) on what is turning out to be a successful tour. So far 15 matches have been played for 14 wins and a loss, to Llanelli (3–8). The main cause of this loss was the curious decision by the Welsh referee to penalise the Wallabies for knocking the ball back from their lineouts. When Dr Herbert Moran, the astute Wallaby captain, asked the reason behind the ruling, the referee said he preferred to discuss the matter after the match. Dr Moran had his bags rifled and his boots stolen after the match to add to the pain of the loss. 'Up until then,' he wrote later, 'I had thought this a purely Australian habit.'

Despite the loss to Llanelli, it had been a happy tour for the Wallabies. Skylarking and storytelling filled in the hours spent on the seemingly endless train journeys and in the hotel bars at night with their fires blazing. Fair ladies had been chatted up. A photograph of the Wallabies leaving their hotel on a huge charabanc revealed a couple of servant girls at the hotel door and at a first-floor window there is another servant girl casting, perhaps, a longing look at the departing players.

A glass is tinkled in the banquet hall. Silence slowly falls around the room. And the toast, 'To the King!' is made and drunk to. 'To the King!' booms around the room in a loud, deep intonation. Now Rowland Hill, past president of the Rugby Football Union, rises laboriously to his feet to speak to the toast. He welcomes the distinguished quests, the Rev. R.S. de Courey Laffan (the honorary secretary of the British Olympic Council), the representatives of the RFU and the Welsh Rugby Union, the management of the Wallabies and the players from both sides, Australia and Cornwall, which competed in the Olympic Games rugby final.

Throughout the tour the British press, ever partisan, has been critical of the alleged over-rough play, bordering on deliberate illegality, perpetrated by the Wallabies. Journalists have dubbed the Wallabies, 'the foulest set of players imaginable'. Hill opens his speech by rejecting the allegations. 'The fact is,' he says, 'the great Australian side plays the game according to the best traditions of British sport.' (Applause.) The rugby union game, he continues, is 'safe and sound' in the cause of amateurism. Finally, he refers to the 'sporting manner' in which the Australian team entered for the Olympic Games. 'Of course,' he says in anticipation of a laugh, 'they are desirous of taking back to Australia some little memento of their tour.'

The toast is received with enthusiasm.

Rev. de Courey Laffan presents an Olympic gold medal to each of the successful Australians. He expresses the wish of the Olympic Games organisers that Australia 'takes a place in connection with the Games among the nations of the world'.

Dr Herbert Moran, the captain of the Wallabies, replies to the toast. The Australians, he says, 'deeply regretted' that the side they played in the Olympic final was not 'thoroughly represenative' of the United Kingdom. 'When we decided to enter we hoped to conquer or be conquered by the best team in the world,' he states. Nevertheless, they are honoured by the presentation 'here in the citadel of rugby where amateurism is impregnable'.

Dr Moran's speech was typically forthright and thoughtful, for in 1908 he set the standard of intelligence, excellent play and leadership, on and off the field, that has created the template of a Wallaby captain throughout the twentieth century. John Eales, the Wallaby captain at the beginning of the twenty-first century, is essentially a taller version of the small, tigerish (on the field), thoughtful and inspiring Wallaby captain type created by Dr Moran a hundred years ago.

If you look up 'Dr Herbert Moran' in the card index of the Mitchell Library in Sydney you will find a list of entries that reveal the character of the man. In 1917 he published *Some Points in the Treatment of Septic Compound Fractures* and *A Doctor Sahib in Mesopotamia*. *Plan of Campaign Against Cancer* was published in 1923; *Radium Therapy in the Treatment of the Nose, Larynx and Oesophagus Problems* in 1930; and *Beyond the Hills Lies China* in 1945.

His finest book, however, was an autobiography, *Viewless Winds: Being the Reflections and Digressions of an Australian Surgeon*, which was published in 1939. The book is an Australian classic, different in its meditative and opinionated style when compared to Albert Facey's *A Fortunate Life*, but as memorable.

Dr Moran's story is an inspiring Australian tale of a brilliant and successful second-generation son building on the hard work of his battling and successful first-generation father. His father came to Sydney in 1876 'with little money and the most elementary knowledge of farming'. After saving hard for three years Moran's father put his savings into a little bakery business in Chippendale, an inner suburb of Sydney. His partner suddenly disappeared, leaving Moran senior heavily encumbered with debts. But 'forty years later,' Dr Moran proudly notes, 'he had the largest private business of its kind in the State.' Dr Moran tells, too, how his father in his pomp made a journey back to Ireland but returned to Australia in 'joyfulness'. He realised that 'this was his home'.

Dr Moran, therefore, was the product of a loving and financially secure family that had made good in Australia. The family, despite its habit of calling each generation of Morans 'Paddy', identified strongly as Australian. During tense moments in rugby matches on the 1908 tour Dr Moran would make the call 'Australia! Australia!' and the Wallabies would respond with an extra effort.

Dr Moran was educated at the two Sydney powerhouses of Catholicism, St Aloysius' College and St Joseph's College at Hunters Hill, where there was an emphasis on the 4Rs – reading, writing, arithmetic and rugby. Dr Moran, though, did not play rugby at either college. At 15 he entered Sydney University to study medicine. He was clearly an intellectually precocious student. He says in his biography he was interested in playing rugby but the system prevented him from getting a game, possibly because he was small and lightly built. He was chided, in his third year at university, for his slackness at being a mere onlooker.

'I was a miserable, stooped, poring, introspective sort of fellow,' Dr Moran writes. When his accuser offered him a game of rugby, he accepted it. 'Five years later I captained the first Australian Amateur Rugby team which visited England.'

At the time of his selection, Dr Moran had not represented Australia. He was working as a doctor at Newcastle Hospital, so was not playing grade rugby in Sydney at the time. The decision to put him in charge of a tour that could make or break the reputation of Australian rugby was, therefore, a bold stroke. Dr Moran's leadership, though, fully justified the faith invested in him.

As captain of Australia, he was determined to maintain rugby's inclusive ethic. He hid behind the ranks of the other Wallabies when they did their Aboriginal dance before matches, for instance. The dance was forced on the team by the Australian rugby authorities, who wanted a 'native' dance from the

Wallabies like the haka that had been popularised by the All Blacks in 1905. Dr Moran believed that the treatment of Aborigines was so disgraceful he forced the abolition of the dance from the Wallabies' pre-match repertoire on later tours.

Dr Moran had a view, too, that rugby was a game of brains as well as brawn. 'Cleverness,' he insisted, 'was a great thing but perfectly useless without a considerable admixture of hard virility.' Rugby was, therefore, a manly game. 'The hard code,' he insisted, 'was not without its chivalries. In the decalogue of our Rugby there are two commandments . . . "Thou shalt not squib it" and again "Thou shalt not squeal".'

On the long sea voyage to Britain Dr Moran introduced the practice of having team meetings that were part lecture and part brainstorming. Players were encouraged to provide ideas on how the team's performances could be improved. Dr Moran, standing at a blackboard, lectured to the players in the manner of an academic. His hope was to instil a sense of cleverness and skill in players who had previously 'never thought of rugby as a game of chess'. When Dr Moran first proposed discussing plays and tactics with the use of a blackboard the players yelped with derision at the stupidity of the idea.

This notion of rugby as a clever game clearly came from Dr Moran's experience as a student and his disposition to think deeply about matters that concerned him. It was a product, too, of the fact that he was slightly built and to hold his own in the rough and tumble of forward play, he had to mix cleverness and shrewdness with hard play to make his game effective.

Dr Moran's description of the Wallabies' rugby gold medal triumph at the 1908 London Olympics is again typically forthright. 'Cornwall, the champion county, was nominated to represent England in the Rugby Competition, included amongst the Olympic games, then being held,' he wrote. 'We had already defeated this team in our third match, but our opponents were hopeful of turning the tables because, in the meantime, they had been reinforced by two internationals who had been absent in the previous match. It was the first match after my injury and I was, for the first time, an onlooker. Our team played magnificent football, chiefly due to the fact that McKivat was at last in his proper position at half and MacCabe was at five-eighths. We were leading easily when an important official in the Cornish side came to me to lay a complaint that our men were using running spikes: at half time they had found some scratches on the body of one of their players . . . A moment's reflection would have convinced anyone of the folly of using running spikes in Rugby, but somebody's mortification at being so severely defeated had to find an outlet. I insisted at once on an examination of boots of all the players as they came off the field at full time, and I nominated an English doctor to carry out the task. In due course he reported that some of the sprigs on both sides were worn down, but that on the whole the boots of Cornish players were in the worse condition. There was not a trace of a spike! In such circumstances I expected at least a graceful withdrawal of the accusation. Nothing of the kind happened.'

Harry Gordon, in his magnificent history *Australia and the Olympic Games*, says that the 1908 Olympics 'simultaneously set new standards for organisation and for acrimony'. The organisation related to the way rule books were prepared in French, German and English for the competitors in 26 different sports which took place over six months. The acrimony, according to Gordon, related to the way 'adjudications and much general behaviour of the host officials at times led to a succession of protests from the United States, Sweden, Finland, Italy, Canada and France'. And, he might have added, Australia.

For the sleazy accusation by the British official that the Wallabies wore spikes to win the Olympic final fits into this pattern of partisanship. It is linked, through the rugby connection, to the equally sleazy accusation made to John O'Neill that the

Wallabies had bulked up on illegal drugs to win the 1999 Rugby World Cup. The irony of the spikes accusation against the Wallabies, moreover, is that the British Olympic officials allowed a British tug-of-war team to win the gold medal against the Americans by permitting them to wear 'monstrous' ground-gripping boots to give them a strong grip on the ground.

The interest in the 1908 Olympic rugby final was 'only luke-warm', according to the Official Report of the Games. There were several reasons for this. The final was held in the last week of a Games that had taken place over six months. A number of European sides, including France and Germany, withdrew from the rugby tournament at the last moment after saying they would be playing. England refused to play its national side, a decision that downgraded the importance of the occasion. Neither the Springboks nor the All Blacks, teams that had established their credentials on their tours to the United Kingdom in 1905 and 1906 as the best sides in the world, entered a team.

There was also the curious fact that the Wallabies technically, at least, represented Australasia and not Australia. As Harry Gordon points out, the 1908 Olympics was 'the first time Australasia competed as a team . . . So the all-male, shoe-string team arrived in London at assorted times: twelve Australians — four of them already working or travelling in Britain — who either swam, boxed, dived (or, in the case of Reginald "Snowy" Baker, did all three), ran, walked, jumped or shot a rifle, and two New Zealand track and field men . . . The initial fourteen, who had not had to contend with selection trials, were joined numerically the following October by fifteen members of the rugby union Wallabies, who had begun their 1908–9 tour of the British Isles. One date on the football itinerary — 26 October 1908 — was allocated to what was called the Olympic rugby tournament, and the players chosen for it became Olympians for a day. The Australasian Olympic team thus totalled twenty-nine . . .'

Dr Moran did not include the Olympic triumph as one of

the achievements of the 1908 tour. 'What worried me,' he wrote in 'Men, Rough Men and Rugby', Chapter 2 of *Viewless Winds*, 'during those first weeks on board ship was that some of our players might fall by the wayside and contract venereal disease . . . There was indeed a surprising ignorance about the subject even among the more lascivious of the team.' One of the first rules on the tour, promulgated after Dr Moran had required players to attend lectures on the subject and look at some graphic pictures of what the disease could do to affected private parts, was that any players who contracted a venereal disease would be sent home immediately. No player was subjected to this punishment. 'I count this as a real achievement for both them and for me,' Dr Moran concluded.

His achievement, however, was more substantial than this. Before Rev. Mullineux's team toured Australia in 1899 a number of officials argued that the Australian rugby community could not field a competitive team. They suggested a combined side with New Zealand, along the lines of the athletic teams that would later be presented for the Olympics in 1908 and 1912. The 1908 Wallabies proved that Australian rugby was equal to that anywhere in the world. Their success provided enough impetus for Australian rugby to survive a mass defection, with the exception of Dr Moran and a couple of other 1908 Wallabies, to rugby league in 1909.

Major Trevor, in his match report of the Olympic Games final for the *Daily Telegraph*, emphasised the way the Wallabies had risen to the great occasion. This report can be read now virtually as an account of the 1999 Rugby World Cup final against France. For the methods used by the 1999 Wallabies, and their steadiness under pressure, indicate that there is a golden link between the contemporary game and the standards set by Dr Moran's side.

'The Australians beat Cornwall, representing the United Kingdom, very badly indeed at the Stadium by 32–3, and the victory was a remarkable one for several reasons,' wrote Major Trevor. 'It will be remembered that less than a month ago there was a match played between Australia and Cornwall at Camborne, and although the Australians also won on that occasion, the beaten side then played, on the whole, a very good game. Yesterday the champion England county was practically at full strength, but from start to finish they were outplayed. The methods by which this victory was gained were even more creditable to the winners than the completeness of the victory itself, and it is only fair to the Australians to speak of their play in terms of unqualified praise. The ground was very slippery and very heavy, and as a result of several hours of continuous rain the ball was very greasy. The continued excellence of the play of the Australian backs therefore surprised the spectators agreeably. They gave a display of football which would have done credit to a Welsh international side, at its best. They scored eight tries, and so good was the play leading up to each of them that it would be hard to say which was the best.'

Ernest 'General' Booth, a former All Black, covered the 1908 Wallabies for Sydney's leading sporting newspaper, the *Referee*. Booth had trouble getting into the stadium before the Olympic final, as his badge was not recognised by one of the officials. This difficulty was finally removed and Booth was able to see the historic match. Booth praised the way the Wallabies 'seized and utilised every opportunity'. The Wallabies, he wrote, showed 'plenty of vim and went out to win'. Cornwall was outclassed. 'Their style of play,' Booth claimed, 'was slow and the backs were sadly lacking in pace . . . Coo-ees echoed across the ground through the fog as the Blues' score totted up.'

Possibly Cornwall was put off its game by the abnormal setting – the London Olympic complex at Shepherds Bush. John Mulford at the ARU Archives has researched the ground the Olympic final was played on, a ground, he says, which was 'unparalleled' in international rugby: 'The match was played on an area alongside the Olympic Games swimming pool, which measured 110 yards in length, the same length as a rugby field. Along the side of the "noted 110 yard cement swimming bath" was placed a long line of netting to catch flying balls and maybe, stray players sent tumbling into touch. The netting almost bordered the touchline. Large mattresses were spread along the rim of the bath or pool to prevent injuries to falling players. Two men with long poles on which there were attached nets fished successfully for numerous balls which went over the top of the netting. Was this the only time in the history of rugby that we had "water ball boys"?'

Our appreciation of the robust manner in which the Wallabies ran the ball at every opportunity during this first Olympic rugby final gains in strength from the understanding that a successful tackle from a Cornwall cover-defender could have had a Wallaby runner sprawling into the netting, or even through the netting into the swimming pool. To risk a ducking or an injury by playing the running game provides evidence of a strong commitment to the clever, ball-in-hand game that Dr Moran demanded of his players.

The tour record of the 1908 Wallabies was 21 wins, 4 losses and a draw. They scored 377 points and had only 123 scored against them.

The team and its captain, therefore, set the standard for future Wallaby teams. The tour was a triumph for the vigorous, tough game propounded by Moran, a game that allowed backs with flair to run in tries from every part of the field. If one person can be given the accolade for shaping a destiny for Australian rugby, Dr Moran is that person. Photographs of him show a serious face, austere glasses, an unsmiling but confident face, a man who looked older than his years with a pugnacious jaw and a steely look.

Dr Moran created the role of the Wallaby captain. The captain was apart from the team (he still has his own room on tour) but he had a pastoral concern for the team's welfare, on and off the field. It is a job that involves the highest sporting and ethical standards. It is a job that forces the best out of players.

Early in 1998 Rod Macqueen was thinking about taking the captaincy of the Wallabies away from John Eales and giving it to George Gregan. John O'Neill, the ARU's chief executive, had a game of golf with Eales. Towards the end of the round O'Neill started to talk about the Wallaby captaincy and how the job had to be handled. Without consciously doing so, O'Neill went back to Dr Moran's handling of the job to point out to Eales how the captain sometimes had to be tough on players for the good of the team. 'Do you really want to be the Wallaby captain?' he asked.

'It's the only thing I want to do,' Eales replied.

Dr Moran was a great captain and a great Australian. The bedrock of his beliefs and methods was his pride in being Australian. Here he is writing about the last minutes of the titanic struggle against Wales: 'We wanted the ball very badly from the scrum in those last moments. Each time as we settled down to push, I would mutter one single word "Australia", and each time those forwards responded magnificently. I could feel their muscles grow taut. The weight came surely on, slowly our opponents were shoved back, and the ball came cleanly through.'

He was angry, too, at the way the Rugbyocracy attributed the alleged dirty play of the Wallabies to their convict ancestry. 'There were many in England,' he wrote, 'who believed that our misconduct was due to the old original sin breaking out like some hereditary disease. It is a curse of modern conditions that good fellows earning their living as journalists should think it necessary to make their readers addicts perpetually craving for a new sensation.'

It was being an Australian that counted with Dr Moran. Australians accepted that rugby should be 'vigorous and a little dangerous', like life itself in a pioneering country. If people in Britain did not understand this they did not understand

Australians, Dr Moran believed. That was their problem, not a problem for the Wallabies. He concluded his chapter on his rugby experiences with this resonant paragraph: 'There are two memorable dates in the story of the game; that first one when a player, suddenly inspired, picked up the ball and ran with it, and a second when at Loos in a hard match an Irish battalion dribbled the ball towards the enemy lines. My people, too, joined in that rush, forming up again and again in their drive to the goal. There was then no prig who dared to shout out of a self-righteous crowd: "Play the game, Australia".'

Daniel Carroll: Rugby's Greatest Olympian

Shirley de la Hunty (née Strickland), the brainy, brilliant athlete from Western Australia, has been acclaimed as the first Australian athlete, male or female, to win a gold medal at successive Olympic Games. She won the 80 metres hurdles at Helsinki in 1952 and then at Melbourne in 1956, adding another gold medal in the 4 × 100 metres relay at Melbourne. She was the first female athlete in Olympic Games history to win a gold medal at successive Games. Dawn Fraser was chosen by the International Olympic Committee in 1999 as its female swimmer of the century for winning the 100 metre freestyle swimming event for women in three successive Olympics, 1956, 1960 and 1964.

The eminence and honours, rightly, piled on Shirley de la Hunty and Dawn Fraser provide an appropriate context in which to measure the Olympic exploits of Daniel Carroll, rugby's greatest Olympian and one of the great, if unfortunately almost unknown, figures of the early decades of the Olympic movement.

Like Shirley de la Hunty, Daniel Carroll won an Olympic gold medal in the successive Games in which his sport of rugby was presented. And like Dawn Fraser, Carroll was involved in gold medal triumphs in three Olympics.

Daniel Carroll's first Olympic experience was in 1908 as a member of the successful Wallaby side that defeated Cornwall for the gold medal at the London Olympics. In the eight-try rout of their opponents, Carroll, a fast-as-a-flash winger, a 'good finisher' we would call him these days, scored two tries, both of them runaways. That gold medal won by the Wallabies was the only gold medal won by the Australasian side in the 1908 Games.

When rugby was on the Olympic competition list again in 1920 at Antwerp, Daniel Carroll won his second gold medal as a player–coach for the successful American team. Harry Gordon, in his book *Australia and the Olympic Games*, says that 'ironically, the only Australian to carry away a gold medal from the 1920 Olympics was Dan Carroll, the playing coach of the American rugby team and a former winger with the Wallabies'. Then in 1924, at the Paris Olympics, Carroll coached the successful American rugby team.

Daniel Carroll won two gold medals, therefore, like Shirley de la Hunty, and almost emulated Dawn Fraser's achievement of gold medals at three different Olympics. Coaches were not given gold medals with their successful team in 1924. This expression of the amateur ethic – where athletes are supposedly required to prepare themselves from their own resources for Olympic competition, and where participation rather than winning is the ideal – prevails in theory today. Successful coaches still do not receive Olympic medals along with their teams. If the film *Chariots of Fire* is historically accurate, as it probably is, it reflects the official thinking in the Olympic movement that coaches are equated with a professional approach to sport that is somehow unacceptable to the Olympic ethic.

However, other premier sports events – like the English FA Cup final and the Rugby World Cup tournament – now honour coaches with a gold medal along with the winning side.

So Carroll came as close as someone could come to winning

three gold medals at three different Olympics and reaching the Dawn Fraser class of Olympic achievement. Daniel Carroll's gold medal achievements need to be put into the context, too, that rugby has only been played at four Olympics, 1900 (when Carroll was 12 years old), 1908, 1920 and 1924.

The 1908 Games was the first properly organised Olympics. The British experience of hosting touring sides, running a national cricket and soccer competition and an annual international rugby tournament, was used to present the first well-run Olympics. The 1900 Games at Paris, on the other hand, were disorganised and chaotic. A combined British rugby side was surprised to find, for instance, that its match against France was part of the Olympic program. The British thought they were attending the Paris Universal Exposition. They accepted their third placing, though, when they later found out they had actually competed in the Olympic rugby competition. France played Germany (a team from Frankfurt) in the final, winning 27–17.

Australia did not defend its rugby Olympic gold medal won at London in 1908 at the 1920 Antwerp Games. The USA was represented by a team from California (made up of players from the universities of Stanford, Santa Clara and California) which defeated France 8–0 in the only rugby match of the Games. The British rugby unions refused to send teams as it was out of their season. Romania and Czechoslavkia offered teams and then withdrew after being thrashed by France in the continental championship. Daniel Carroll coached and played for the Americans.

Carroll came back to Paris in 1924 as coach of another successful gold medal American side. The Romanians entered this tournament but were defeated by France 61–3 and by the USA 39–0. In the final the Americans shocked a full-strength France with a 17–3 defeat. The French chauvinistic crowd at Colombes Stadium took the loss badly, giving the Americans a hostile reception. An American reporter noted: 'If the team representing the Stars and Stripes is going to be hissed every time it wins an Olympic title, it would be better for the Americans to return home and concern themselves no longer with international athletics.'

As far as rugby as an Olympic sport was concerned, this is what happened: 1924 was the last time rugby featured at the Olympics. The disgraceful behaviour by the French crowd, which was an affront to the Olympic spirit, was the deathblow to rugby as an Olympic sport. In four Olympics, anyway, there had never been more than three countries competing and only two national sides, Australia and France, actually took part. The international aspect of the rugby competitions at these Olympics was slight, at its best.

This should not detract from Daniel Carroll's gold medal achievements, however. As the old sports adage has it: 'You can only defeat the opposition in front of you.' Jack Pollard, the rugby historian, claims of Carroll that 'his record in Olympic Games rugby will never be surpassed'.

It all started for Daniel Carroll at St Aloysius' College in Sydney, where rugby was a passion among the boys and their teachers. Carroll then went on to Sydney University, another hotbed of rugby, where he studied dentistry. After strong performances for NSW against Queensland and an Anglo–Welsh side, he was selected for the 1908 touring Wallabies. He was the youngest player in the team.

On the way back to Australia the Wallabies travelled across America before taking a ship at San Francisco back to Australia. They played several matches against American sides, with Carroll being an outstanding player.

Most of the 1908 Wallabies, with the notable exception of Dr Moran who went to Edinburgh to get his qualifications as a surgeon, defected to the new rugby league code which started in Sydney in 1908. Daniel Carroll was another exception. He stayed with rugby, even though he was overlooked by the

Australian selectors for the three Tests against New Zealand in 1910. He was back in the Wallabies in 1912, being selected for the Australian side which toured California and defeated All-America 12–8. The aura of Olympic gold still surrounded this Australian side, even though Carroll was its only Olympian. The team was dubbed by the American newspapers as 'the world champions of rugby', a reference to the 1908 Olympic victory.

The Test against America at Berkeley looked like being an upset victory to the locals with them leading 8–0 with only 12 minutes of play remaining. The Wallabies scored two quick tries: 6–8. Then, according to an American report, 'the Australian backs were playing like a set of demons and from hand to hand the ball went until Carroll planted it over the line': 9–8. On time the Wallabies kicked a penalty to give them a hard-earned victory, 12–8.

Daniel Carroll remained in California, enrolling at Stanford University where he took a degree in geology in 1920. He played for America in 1913 against the All Blacks in a Test won by New Zealand 51–3. He served as a lieutenant in the American army in the First World War and was wounded in 1918. He recovered sufficiently from his wounds to play for the Australian Army side in the King's Cup tournament in 1919.

Why did Daniel Carroll go back to the United States at the end of 1919 and not return to Australia?

Harry Gordon refers to Carroll being the financial backer of a Hollywood film in which 'Snowy' Baker starred. There is a certain charm in this story as Baker competed successfully in 29 sports, five of them internationally, with one of those international sports being rugby. Baker represented Australia against a touring British rugby side in two Tests in 1904 and in 1908 Baker competed in the Olympic Games as a boxer. The Wallabies watched this contest, so Carroll may well have watched as Baker out-fought J.W.H.T. Douglas, later a Test cricketer, in a final only to lose the referee's decision. A number of newspaper reports claimed that the referee was Douglas' father. 'Snowy' Baker later went to Hollywood, where he starred in silent movies and became a director of the Riviera Country Club at Santa Monica. Daniel Carroll lived out his life in the USA, too, after 1919.

But Harry Gordon's connection between the two men is a case of Homer nodding. It is a good story. It is a story that should be correct, given the sporting history of the two men. Unfortunately, it is a furphy. There was a Dan Carroll who bank-rolled several Hollywood movies of 'Snowy' Baker and there are, in fact, a number of references to this 'Movie' Dan Carroll in the files of the *Sydney Morning Herald*. 'Movie' Dan Carroll died, aged 63, in 1959 at St Luke's Hospital, Sydney. This would have made him 12 in 1908. His obituary described him as a 'leading entre-preneur'. He was, the obituary noted, 'an early producer of motion pictures in Australia, including *The Sentimental Bloke, On Our Selection*, and the Snowy Baker series'.

Clearly 'Movie' Dan Carroll was not 'Rugby' Daniel Carroll. 'Rugby' Daniel Carroll went to California to extend his academic credentials and did not become involved with the movie industry.

It is only a surmise, but I think the amateur nature of American rugby probably had a great appeal for him. This, together with the chance of studying at an American university, led him to Stanford. He was probably aghast at the way most of his fellow Wallabies on the 1908 tour had 'converted' to the professional game. This is further guesswork, but probably this mass defection to rugby league turned him away from rugby in Australia. But not from his love of amateur rugby. He was sufficiently in love with playing rugby (as opposed to playing rugby in Sydney) to play for the AIF in 1919, after all. I would further surmise that the influence of Dr Moran, an apostle of amateurism in rugby, was important in creating this mindset for Carroll.

Daniel Carroll was the youngest member of the 1908 Wallabies. He went to the same school and the same university as Moran. It is not fanciful to claim, therefore, that Dr Moran's strong views on the necessity of amateurism in rugby influenced Carroll's thinking on the issue.

The ARU Archives has several documents on Daniel Carroll. There are photographs of his Olympic gold medal. There is the original card from the President and Council of the NSWRU inviting D.B. Carroll Esq. to a function at the Sydney Town Hall on Friday 31 July 1908, to celebrate the farewell of the Wallabies before their tour of Britain and the United States. There are several newspaper clippings. One of them, with a photograph, highlights his successes as a student at St Aloysius' College, where he was timed to do the 100 yards 'in a shade over evens'.

Another clipping from an Irish newspaper published in 1992, written by David Guiney, goes through the familiar details of Carroll's rugby career. At the end of the article comes the punchline, however. Guiney quotes the research of Dr Bill Mallon, of North Carolina, 'the most meticulous of America's Olympic historians', who states categorically that Daniel Brendan Carroll was born on 17 February 1892. Guiney points out that Carroll's birthday is usually given as 17 November 1888, the date given by the rugby historian Jack Pollard. But Dr Mallon's 'emphatic finding' is based on records preserved at Stanford University and US Olympic records.

David Guiney concludes his fascinating piece: 'Which means, if you care to check it out, that Daniel Brendan Carroll was 16 years and 286 days when he won his first cap for Australia against Wales on Saturday, 12 December 1908. That not only makes him the youngest man to be capped for Australia but also the youngest to win an international cap in the long history of rugby.'

The ARU Archives, though, has a birth certificate of Carroll which gives 1887 as the year of his birth and Flemington, Melbourne, as the place.

A newspaper clipping from the local Stanford paper published 21 November 1935 with the headline, 'Danny Carroll Here', provides some further but scant information about Carroll's life in the United States. The article talks about 'the old grads' coming 'from far away to see the California–Stanford Big Game . . . Danny Carroll of Great Falls pulled in yesterday, for the first time in five years.' The article said that Carroll 'played four years of Rugby at Stanford and one year of American football at Stanford. He won his letter in Rugby in 1913, 1914 and 1915. He broke his shoulder a week before the big game in 1916 and did not play, so he did not get a letter for that year.'

The article says that he 'played his last game of rugby in 1921, when a pick up team visited British Columbia'. Carroll, therefore, remained a rugby missionary to the last. And a successful missionary at that, for British Columbia has become the heartland of Canadian rugby.

Other documents in the ARU Archives on Daniel Carroll relate to some correspondence conducted by Carroll's niece, Patricia Doohan of Five Dock in Sydney, in January 1998, to the US Army Reserve Personnel Command, concerning the whereabouts of the Distinguished Service Cross won by Carroll during the First World War. The letter noted that Carroll married Helen Warden from Great Falls, Montana, in 1927. The couple had one son, Daniel, who is deceased. Helen Warden Carroll died in 1941.

The notes end with the sad sentences about an athlete who should be remembered and honoured as one of Australia's greatest Olympians: 'We believe D.B. Carroll remarried and lived in San Bernardino. However the family in Australia had his last known address in New Orleans. Date of death 1956/7(?).'

'The Greatest Band of Sportsmen': the 1927–28 Waratahs

Dr Moran's Wallaby side of 1908 did not play Tests against

Scotland or Ireland on its pioneering tour. The Scotland Rugby Union was having a row with the Rugby Football Union (the England union). And it was still trying to recover from the shock of refusing to share expenses and profits with the 1905 All Blacks, allowing that team to make a massive profit from the 21,000 spectators who turned up to watch the Test at Inverleith, Edinburgh. Scottish intransigence about doing the right thing for the worldwide rugby community still prevails, unfortunately. But in 1927, the SRU agreed with the other British unions to play a Test against the touring NSW Waratahs side, a side that for practical purposes represented the best team available in Australia.

This magnificent side played 31 official matches, for 24 wins, two draws and five losses. In an era when try-scoring was difficult, the Waratahs averaged four tries a match. All but one player came from just eight Sydney clubs – the quicksilver halfback Syd Malcolm from Newcastle was the only outsider.

Peter Crittle, a fine all-round forward for the Wallabies in the 1960s, later a leading official with the NSWRU and a devoted scholar of rugby history, paid the highest possible tribute to this team: 'The 1927/28 Waratahs changed forever the style of Australian rugby . . . Under the inspired captaincy and coaching of A.C. "Johnnie" Wallace, they dazzled the British and the French with displays of 15-man rugby, which had rarely been seen in Europe . . . Whenever possible defence was to be turned into attack. When danger threatened the ball was not to be kicked into touch, but thrown about until the opposition rush was stemmed. Counter attack was to be the order of the day.'

This running game and the notion that attack is the best defence, whether with the ball in hand or tackling, became the trademark of Australian rugby. Peter Fenton has written a loving account of this historic tour, and from his researches he created a poem that is often read out to rugby audiences, to their great pleasure:

The Waratahs who packed their bags in 1927
And sailed away to play the running game
Spent six weeks on the high seas
As they made their way to Devon
With neither thought of riches nor of fame
But they were meant for greatness,
It was somehow pre-ordained,
They thrilled the crowds at every rugby ground,
They played the game with passion
And the glory they attained
Is tribute to the legends that abound . . .
Now when you see a team
That plays the game they play in heaven
A team that you would love to call your own
You're looking at the Waratahs of 1927:
The finest team of sportsmen we have known.

By the time of the Test against England on 7 January 1928, the Waratahs were tired men. They had been on tour for six months. Ireland had been defeated 5–3. Then Wales more comfortably, 18–8. In the bitter cold of Edinburgh, with ice making the field as slippery as a skating rink, Scotland held out to defeat the Waratahs 10–8. Johnnie Wallace made a dash for the Scottish tryline with only minutes of play left, but he slithered on the ice as he tried to steady himself for a diving try. Scotland held out.

The England selectors made their now-traditional selectorial blunder. For the Test against the Waratahs they left out W. W. Wakefield, the greatest forward of his era and a devotee of the athletic southern hemisphere rugby style. The British press noted that England had not been successful at home against a southern hemisphere side since they had defeated the New Zealand Native side, aided by doubtful hometown refereeing decisions, in 1889. The northern hemisphere inferiority to southern hemisphere rugby is not, therefore, a construct of the 1990s.

A crowd of 62,000 packed Twickenham so tightly that the famous cartoonist Tom Webster joked that 'the two teams should meet again as neither will be able to get out of Twickenham for at least a month'. As a reflection of the adage that the more things change, the more they remain the same, one of the complaints of journalists covering the 1999 Rugby World Cup tournament was the utter impossibility of getting back into central London from Twickenham after the RWC semi-finals. Waits at the Twickenham train station of up to three hours, in a crowd slowly pressing forward towards the waiting trains, was the normal order of service.

Back to 1928. England played with the wind at their backs in the first half and made all the running. A dash down the wing, a centring kick and the flanker J.S. Tucker was over for a try, which was converted. 5–0 to England. Could the leg-weary Waratahs respond?

Wallace, an inspirational captain, made several breaks in the centre and then told Cyril Towers to loop outside him when he broke again. The move, which is still played by the Wallabies, was executed brilliantly and with the conversion the scores were tied 5–5. Then it was 10–5 to England and just before half-time England scored again, converted and stretched their lead to a seemingly unreachable 15–5. Another try to England and the score was 18–5 with 25 minutes to play.

The Waratahs showed their great fighting spirit by going into an extra-Waratah mode, attacking from everywhere, with John Ford, the massive number 8, taking the ball up time after time. Towers scored. 18–8. Then the winger Eric Ford raced through the England defence. 18–11. The Waratahs were still attacking the England line, desperate to snatch the victory, when the whistle blew for full-time. The crowd roared its appreciation of a great game of rugby, with the applause continuing long after the players had retired to the changing rooms and the hot tubs.

At the official dinner that night, nine of Rev. Mullineux's touring team of 1899 were present. One of these old-timers, Admiral Percy Royds, described the wonderful Waratahs of 1927–28 as 'the greatest band of sportsmen who have ever visited us'.

A Wallaby in Winter

His eye is as glittering still as that of the Ancient Mariner. His handshake is firm. Despite his great age, his shoulders are square and he retains the ranginess of the lively flanker he once was. Myer Rosenblum was born in Pretoria on 10 January 1907. At the beginning of the twenty-first century he is the oldest living Wallaby. With his mind brimming with memories and opinions, he is the epitome of the Wallaby in winter.

He remembers the Tests he played in New Zealand in 1928, three against the All Blacks and one against the New Zealand Maori, as if he were still back on the mud of Athletic Park more than 70 years ago. 'I scored two tries, you know, in the first Test,' he said. 'Even though I was marked by the great wing forward, Cliff Porter. We later became great friends. The New Zealanders were big and tough but they weren't dirty. Not like the game now, which is full of biff and bang.'

The Australians lost the Test series but New Zealand journalists were full of praise for the tourists. 'A picturesque, fleet-footed, mobile force,' one rugby writer described the Wallabies, 'which tossed the ball with gay abandon and at times exhibited such dazzling speed and combination as to make the New Zealanders look sluggish.'

Some of the Wallabies had taken part in the Waratahs tour of Britain in 1927–28, where dazzling speed and combinations were made irrevocably into the template for the Australian style of playing rugby.

Rosenblum's first Test try came, according to a press report, after 'the ball swung across the breadth of the field and back, passing from hand to hand, before the harassed defence finally yielded'. His second try came after an Australian attack of more than 50 metres before the ball rolled clear of the ruck for Rosenblum to seize it and dive across the line.

'I'll tell you my secret,' he said. 'I kept close to Cyril Towers every time he had the ball. Cyril was a wonderful player with a great change of pace. He could always beat a man. But no great speed. I'd follow Cyril and finish off his breaks.'

Rosenblum was so elated at the way he played in the Test that he decided it was an appropriate time to lose his virginity. 'We were staying at the Waterloo Hotel, down by the Wellington Railway Station,' he said with a wry smile on his face. 'I had a room to myself. So I made a proposition to one of the wait-resses. "You'll be number 13 in line," she told me.

' "I can't wait that long," I told her.'

In Dunedin, after the second Test, he and Towers spoke with Vic Cavanagh senior, the coaching guru who developed the famous Otago rucking game. 'The trouble with you Australians,' Cavanagh told them, 'is that you deprecate kicking too much. Your forwards are much smaller than ours. You should kick more to take the strain off them.'

When the Australian Rugby Union reinstated the limited kick-into-touch law in 1934 – the Australian Dispensation, as it was called around the rugby world, which punished kicking out on the full with a lineout from where the kick was made – Rosenblum wrote a vigorous letter of objection: 'I have played and watched games under both rules, and consider that the old rule makes for better football. Under the proposed new rule, which of course is adopted from the league game, play will become more scrappy and disjointed. When the game starts from a set position of a scrum or a lineout much better rugby is seen, for it is then a case of forwards against forwards and backs against backs.'

He put this theory, which is essentially the British way of

thinking, into practice when he coached Scots College to a GPS championship in 1960. His team had the Boyce twins on the wings to score tries and his son Rupert – along with Paul McLean and Michael Lynagh one of Australian rugby's most adroit kickers – to kick for position and convert the tries and penalties.

The Rosenblums are one of the few father-and-son families to play for the Wallabies. 'The thing about Rupert is that he just didn't kick the ball anywhere, like they do nowadays,' Myer Rosenblum said. 'He could put the ball exactly where he wanted it to land. People forget that his kicking game helped to destroy Scotland in 1970 at the SCG when the Wallabies won 23–3 and ran in six tries.'

I asked Myer why he didn't play for Australia again after that 1928 tour. He said he was too busy getting his law degree and educating himself. 'I was avid for life, you know.'

A profile of him published in 1990 in the *Australian Jewish Times* was headed: 'The Renaissance Man'. An apt description. His life is a classic example of a successful, first-generation Australian who over-achieves to assimilate into the mainstream of law, music and sport, and who over-compensates, perhaps, for his Russian–Jewish background with a multitude of good works in Sydney's Jewish community.

Living, for Myer Rosenblum, meant teaching himself French and German so he could become an expert in comparative literature. He also understands Yiddish and Latin. He won a scholarship to the Sydney Conservatorium of Music in the 1920s, where he became an excellent bassoon player. Alfred Hill, the famous New Zealand composer, was his tutor. 'I got first in the class for composition one year and then finished last the next year,' he said. 'When Hill asked me what happened, I told him, "There was rugby".'

He was an Australian record holder in the hammer throw and competed in the 1938 Empire Games, thus becoming that rare breed of sportsman, a double Australian representative. How did he get on? 'No good. Wasn't up to it.'

It was his practice as a solicitor only to accept articled clerks who played rugby or who competed in athletics. There was one exception. His firm acted for a local garage owner. The owner's wife came to see him about her son who had passed his law exams but couldn't get placed in a legal firm to do his articles. As a favour, she asked, could he take the young man on? And this is how John Howard, later to become the Prime Minister of Australia, became an articled clerk to Myer Rosenblum.

Rosenblum established a company called 'Australian Concerts and Artists' which organised visits by overseas musical celebrities. These celebrities often stayed with Myer and his New Zealand-born wife, Lyla, who entertained them with lieder and piano duets. One of the celebrities, the New Zealand bass Oscar Natzka, drank a bottle of whisky after each performance. 'We lost money on his tour,' Myer conceded.

As well, he was the first secretary of Sydney's Musica Viva, winner of the White City tennis doubles competition, president of the NSW Amateur Athletic Association, treasurer of the Sydney Rugby Union, and a member and later secretary of the Great Synagogue choir. The renaissance man.

The game of the 'muddied oafs' has remained a constant passion, however. Early on a Sunday morning during the 1999 RWC tournament, in his large house with its fine view of Sydney Harbour, Rosenblum rose to watch his beloved Wallabies become the world champions of rugby for the second time. With rugby as with his life, the real thing. No replays for him.

His life has spanned most of the history of the Wallabies. He was two years old when Dr Moran's Australian rugby team (the first side to carry the name of Wallabies) made its pioneering tour of Britain. As the pictures flickered in front of the old man, therefore, and Ben Tune ran away from opponents in the electrifying manner of, say, Daniel Carroll, there was only one degree of separation – an old Wallaby in his winter years – between the golden Wallabies at the end of the twentieth century and those first golden Wallabies, the gold medal winners for rugby at the 1908 London Olympic Games.

Roaring Lions

When the 1908 Wallabies played at Oxford University, the Australian captain, Dr Herbert Moran, spent some time in the rugby pavilion watching the match with a friend from Sydney University, Garnett Vere Portus, a Rhodes Scholar, who played two Tests for England that year. Portus came back to Australia and became a professor of economics. He was a Wallaby selector in the 1920s and for two decades wrote masterly accounts of rugby Tests played in Australia in the 1920s and 1930s.

'Awakening much earlier than usual on Saturday morning last,' he wrote in the 3 September 1930 edition of the *Sydney Mail*, 'I puzzled my drowsy brain for some reason. Then it flashed on me. This was the day of the Test match . . . The sun was making millions of winking diamonds on the water . . . We parked ourselves in one of the front rows of the Ladies Stand at the Sydney Cricket Ground. And none too early, either. By 1.45 p.m. the Sheridan Stand was full, the Grandstand had been full for some time, and there was standing room only in the Ladies Stand . . . "Spread out a bit, please," whispered a perfect stranger on my right. "I'm trying to keep a place for my husband, who can't get away from the office until one." '

Professor Portus and the perfect stranger saw a wonderful Test won by the Wallabies against the British Lions 6–5. Right on time, the Lions streaked towards the corner; a Test-winning try seemed to be inevitable. Professor Portus takes up the story. 'Britain was staging its familiar last-minute win once again. Then from somewhere – the clouds, I think – came Cyril Towers, catching the big forward Jones with every stride. But there was no time for a race. The Green flung himself at Jones' heels, and the pair crashed scarcely a yard from the chalk line.'

This was the first Wallaby victory against a fully-fledged Lions side. The victory confirmed Australia's stature as a leading rugby nation.

In 1899 there had been talk, after all, of a combined Australasian side to play Mullineux's side of English and other home union players. The victory in 1930 against the Lions ended this talk for all time. It also made the Australian Rugby Union determined to host a Lions tour to Australia only, and not be tagged on to a major tour of New Zealand.

This dream of the Lions touring Australia specifically was achieved in 1989, when the Lions won a sternly contested Test series 2–1. The Lions adopted dirty tactics throughout the series, in the British manner, to encourage the Wallabies to trade biff for biff and to forgo the usual clever Wallaby style. The distinguished Australian rugby writer Evan Whitton deplored these tactics by the Lions in a colourful article with a memorable headline: 'The Scum Also Rises.'

In the last Test of the series, won by the Lions 19–18, a wayward pass by David Campese on his tryline allowed the Lions to go into the lead. Towards the end of the match a rabbit appeared behind the Australian tryline. The nervous nibbling of the rabbit symbolised the anxiousness of the 40,000 spectators as they watched the Wallabies trying, unsuccessfully, to win the Test.

'Chattering Charlie' Bledisloe and His Cup

There is no evidence that Lord Bledisloe, the Governor-General of New Zealand between 1929 and 1935 and the alleged donor of the Bledisloe Cup, knew one end of a rugby ball from the other. The remarkable files of the *Sydney Morning Herald*'s library hold a typewritten biography on oilskin paper of Lord Bledisloe, 'The English Statesman', that was sent to newspaper offices throughout the British Empire by a Whitehall press officer in October 1929, to mark his New Zealand

appointment. 'Charles Bathurst, barrister, politician, agricultur-
alist and First Baron BLEDISLOE, was born in Sept. 1867, and
educated at Sherborne, Eton and University College, Oxford.
After leaving Oxford he was called to the bar in 1894 and practised as a Chancery barrister and conveyancer for 16 years. In
1910 he was elected Conservative MP for S. Wilts and made a
member of the Council of the Duchy of Lancaster.'

Lord Bledisloe was a politician–aristocrat with a passion for
agriculture (somewhat in the slightly eccentric manner of P.G.
Wodehouse's Lord Emsworth and his obsession for pigs) and a
talent for the telling PR gesture. He saw his mission as
Governor-General – as Governor Carrington had in Australia
in 1888 – to 'strengthen the Empire bond in New Zealand'. He
presented the Treaty House at Waitangi to the New Zealand
people in 1932. This house is one of New Zealand's sacred sites.
He made it known that every article of clothing he wore was
made from New Zealand materials. And in 1931 he gave his
name to a trophy for rugby competition between New Zealand
and Australia, the Bledisloe Cup.

This is the official picture of Lord Bledisloe.

Bruce Hewitt, a distinguished New Zealand journalist, the
head of the NZ Press Association for many years, and later in his
career a successful journalist in Melbourne, remembers Lord
Bledisloe differently. In an article in the *Sun Herald* published in
1988, Hewitt depicted Lord Bledisloe as a 'man who had little
interest in football, and his outdoor activities were limited to
farming and long-winded speech-making at country shows.'

Lord Bledisloe was once photographed at the Canterbury
Agricultural Show at Christchurch, according to a story that
Hewitt tells. The next day the photograph of a beaming Lord
Bledisloe was run in the *Christchurch Times* – with a caption
describing the show's beribboned champion ram. Lord Bledisloe
ordered the newspaper to sack the journalist responsible for the
joke. This incident, Hewitt asserts, triggered off Lord Bledisloe's

'long-running differences with the New Zealand press . . . To a generation of reporters he became "Chattering Charlie", and there were harsher names when his complaints led inevitably to sackings in those bleak, jobless, and depression days.'

By 1931, therefore, with several years of his official stint remaining, Lord Bledisloe was losing the PR battle for the Empire in New Zealand. If the PR battle was lost, the imperial imperative in New Zealand could be endangered, too. This moment of crisis for Lord Bledisloe coincided with a decline in interest by New Zealanders in watching Australian rugby teams, even though the Wallabies had defeated the All Blacks in 1929 in all three Tests. The Lions (1930) and the Springboks (1921) drew great crowds to all their matches in New Zealand. But not the Wallabies.

With a tour coming up by the Wallabies in 1931, and with finances stretched because of the Depression, the NZRU needed something to provoke public interest. Why not set up a trophy to mark the rugby competition between New Zealand and Australia?

Their model for such a trophy, the Ranfurly Shield, was a trophy held by a New Zealand provincial side until it was lost in a home match. Lord Ranfurly had donated the trophy in the early 1900s and it had become an icon of NZ rugby and a tremendous crowd-puller.

Lord Ranfurly's trophy had arrived from Britain as a shield with a centrepiece depicting soccer goalposts and a soccer ball. It was originally a soccer trophy, like the William Webb Ellis trophy. From a consideration of the circumstantial evidence at hand on the origins of the Bledisloe Cup, I would claim that Lord Bledisloe was as ignorant about rugby as his predecessor, Lord Ranfurly. But like his predecessor he could identify a shrewd PR move when it was presented to him.

It served his purpose, therefore, to give his name to the New Zealand–Australia rugby trophy. And it suited the interests of the NZRU to have an international equivalent, the Bledisloe Cup, to go with the Ranfurly Shield.

Some versions of the origins of the Bledisloe Cup have Lord Bledisloe at the first Test match in which his trophy was at stake. Keith Quinn, for instance, in *The Encyclopedia of World Rugby* writes: 'The Bledisloe Cup was presented in 1931 by Lord Bledisloe, then Governor-General of New Zealand, as a trophy to be played between the Test teams of Australia and New Zealand . . . the first game for the trophy was played at Eden Park in Auckland in 1931, New Zealand winning by 20–13. The game, played in front of Lord Bledisloe, was notable for the small crowd that turned out (only 15,000) and for the scoring of 14 points by the New Zealand fullback, Ron Bush of Otago. It was then the NZ record for the greatest number of points scored in a Test match, let alone a debut, though Bush did not get to play for his country again.'

But did Lord Bledisloe actually watch the Test at Eden Park? Gordon Slater, a noted New Zealand author and rugby historian, is adamant that he was not even in Auckland when the Test was being played. 'Neither Lord Bledisloe nor his cup was at the test match,' Slater writes in his momumental *On the Ball: The Centennial Book of New Zealand Rugby*. 'He was in Wellington to attend the commercial travellers' smoke concert, at which he told them the world was topsy-turvy, particularly in the sphere of industry and commerce.'

None of the accounts of the first Bledisloe Cup Test that I have read make any mention at all of either the Bledisloe Cup or Lord Bledisloe being present at Eden Park. The *Sydney Morning Herald* and the *New Zealand Herald*, both newspapers of record at the time, carried long descriptions of the match, without a mention of 'Bledisloe'. There are no photographs, either, of Lord Bledisloe shaking hands with the players at Eden Park in the time-honoured ritual conducted before Tests.

The Australian sporting magazine the *Referee* covered this

first Bledisloe Cup Test extensively. Again, I can find no reference in its many articles to Lord Bledisloe's presence at Eden Park, or to the presentation of the cup he gave his name to. The *Referee* was concerned, virtually to the exclusion of any other consideration, with the fact that the Wallabies scored three tries to none in the Test, and still lost by a wide margin. 'We have the highest regard,' one article stated, 'for New Zealand referees but we are not sure they are interpreting some of the laws in keeping with British rugby.'

A major point of disagreement for Australians was the way the New Zealanders packed a 2–3–2 scrum which allowed their prop/hooker to rake the ball back before it got to the Wallaby hooker in the centre of Australia's three-man front. The 1930 Lions had made a similar complaint but in the manner of the Rugbyocracy had insisted that the New Zealanders were 'cheating' with their seven-man diamond scrum. This scrum was regarded by New Zealanders as the best scrum formation devised, allowing for a quick release of the ball and its transfer to the backs for one-on-one attacks. To preserve the scrum, the NZRU had proposed to the IRB several times that teams should comprise 14 rather than 15 players. In September 1930, however, the IRB ruled that the ball had to pass three feet in the front row before it could be hooked. This killed the 2–3–2 scrum.

Lord Bledisloe's name, though, was enough as far as the NZRU were concerned to lift the profile of All Black–Wallaby contests. His presence was not needed at Eden Park. The All Blacks retained the Bledisloe Cup on their tour of Australia in 1932. In a two-Test series in 1934, the All Blacks were thrashed by the Wallabies at the Sydney Cricket Ground 25–11 (the heaviest defeat inflicted by Australia against New Zealand) and then held to a draw at Brisbane.

The All Blacks won back the trophy in 1936 with wins against the Wallabies at Athletic Park, Wellington (before 30,000 spectators) and at Carisbrook, Dunedin (25,000). The size of the

SATURDAY, JUNE 24, 1899.

A SANCTIFIED SPORT!

The cover of the *Bulletin* before the first Test match in 1899. The Rev. Mullineux, with irony, is given a halo. The Australians are pictured as villains with spikes, rather than sprigs, on their boots. (*Bulletin*, 1899)

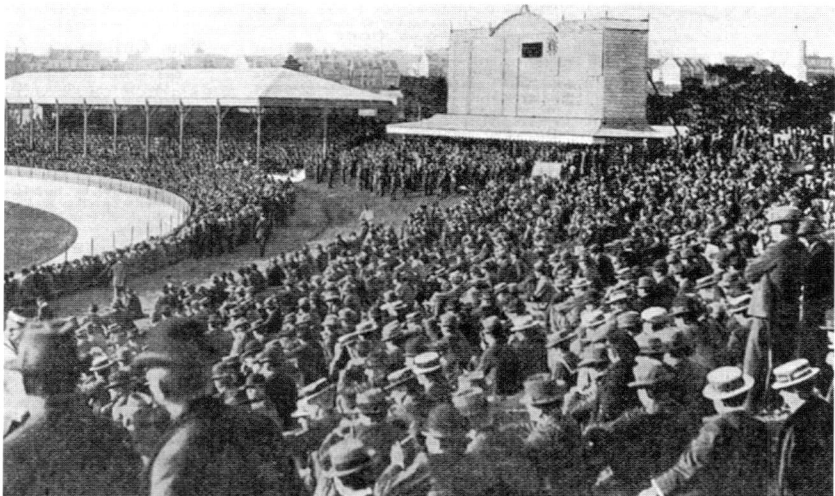

The crowd on the hill at the Sydney Cricket Ground for the first Test played by an Australian rugby team. When the weather is fine, boater hats, and the occasional bowler hat, seem to be the order of the day. (*Sydney Mail*, 1899)

The Rev. Mullineux's side shortly before the first Test at the SCG. The red, white and blue striped jerseys worn on this occasion were revived by England in 1999 for the first rugby Test played at the Olympic Stadium, Homebush, in Sydney. (*Sydney Mail*, 1899)

Another view of the massive crowd on the hill at the SCG for the first Test. The sobriety of the crowd is noticeable. Sydney had a population of almost 400,000 at the time. With over 30,000 at the SCG, the impact of the Test on the male population of the city is obvious. (*Sydney Mail*, 1899)

The very first Australian national rugby team played its first Test match at the SCG in 1899, getting Australian rugby off to a winning start. (*Sydney Mail*, 1899)

The Rev. Mullineux's team on the left and the Australian national rugby team, with their dark-blue pantaloons rather than shorts, eye each other warily before the start of their historic match. A small boy, inevitably, has managed to become part of the tableau. (*Sydney Mail*, 1899)

The Rev. Mullineux's side brought the passing skills developed by Welsh players to Australia. The Australians are stretched to hold out an attack by the opposing three-quarters. This is not a problem faced by the modern Wallabies. (*Sydney Mail*, 1899)

The first try scored by Australia in a rugby Test. In the manner of the day, neither team shows much emotion. (*Sydney Mail*, 1899)

The first Wallabies, on their 1908 tour of the United Kingdom, performing the war-cry that their captain, Dr Herbert Moran, claimed was 'a wretched caricature of a native corroboree'. Moran hid in the back row.
(*Sydney Mail*, 1908)

AUSTRALIA'S OLYMPIC FIFTEEN.

BACK ROW : T. Richards, F. Bede Smith, C. McMurtrie, P. A. McCue, S. A. Middleton, J. T. Barnett.
SECOND ROW : F. Roberts (touch-judge), R. R. Craig, A. J. McCabe, C. H. McKivat, J. Hickey, C. Russell, T. J. Griffen.
FRONT ROW : M. McArthur, D. B. Carroll, and P. Carmichael.

match, and the numerous bunches and rosettes of blue ribbon demonstrated the Colonial element in the crowd.

After bathing, the team returned to London, to find that the Cornish team were also staying at the Imperial. Sunday was essentially a day of rest, though a party of Wallabies risked themselves and their reputations by exploring the Sunday markets of Petticoat Lane.

THE OLYMPIC VICTORY.

Owing to France's withdrawal from the Olympic Rugby contest on the plea of want of training and play, the Cornwall and Australian teams payed on the Monday in the Stadium. Consequently on Monday afternoon, despite the heavy rains and fogs, they "tubed" by underground railway to Wood Lane, the Exhibition Ground's new station. About 3600 spectators lined a few seats of this vast enclosure. A large section singing the Welsh football song, "Sospan Fach," in one isolated corner of the pavilion, sounded like representation from gallant Wales. The back converted. Hickey ran beautifully, and making a splendid chance for Carroll, the St. George greyhound made no mistake about scoring, but no goal resulted. Australia, 21 points.

From a pretty knock-back from the line-out all the backs handled, and Carroll raced over again. The angle was too much for Carmichael. Australia, 24 points. For Cornwall, Davy raced off, and passing out well, Bert Solomons scored. It was only a spasdomic effort, however, and the Blues made every post a winning post. McKivat scored a regular Freddy Roberts try by racing and dodging serenely on his own quite 35 yards. Carmichael's kick made the score 29 to 3. Before the whistle, McCabe scored another try, which was not converted, thus Australia put up 32 points, their biggest score to date. McKivat was a distinct success behind the scrum. Lord Desborough personally congratulated the team after the match. And many others did so, too. The team is to receive medals commemorative of the contest, and the other members of the team will receive competitors' badges. Both are highly ornamental in design. In years to come they prominence of service uniforms very evident. The sun shooting out occasionally through the clouds made the different players in hooped Red and Blue (Service) and Blue (Australia) a very bright contrast. Mr. A. O. Jones, in his International blazer, officiated as referee very efficiently, not, however, clear of errors.

AUSTRALIANS.—P. Carmichael, full back ; C. Russell, J. Hickey, F. B. Smith, and D. B. Carroll, three-quarters ; C. H. McKivat, five-eighth ; F. Woods, half ; T. Richards, Dr. Moran, N. E. Row, S. A. Middleton, P. A. McCue, T. Griffin, C. A. Hammond, and T. J. Barnett, forwards.

LONDON.—H. Lyons (United Service), full back ; D. Lambert (Harlequins), W. N. Lapage (United Service), W. C. Wilson, Richmond, H. T. Lewis (Harlequins), three-quarters ; A. S. Henle, outside half ; H. J. Sibree (Harlequins), half ; E. McEwan (London Hospital), J. McHaffey (London Hospital), A. D. Warrington-Morris (United Service), A. E. Evans, St. Bart.'s Hospital), H. Archer (Guy's Hospital), J. G. Bussell (Harlequins), G. H. Hind (Guy's Hospital), J. M. Weddell (St. Bart's Hospital).

The United Service were big, hefty, men, very fit, lithe, and strong, their athletic appearance suggesting that they had had plenty of gymnasium work. Right from the kick off they made the pace very

A SCRUMMAGE IN THE OLYMPIC MATCH.

C. H. McKivat is picking up the ball. T. Richards is standing to the right alongside the English half-back.
R. R. Craig on the left side of the scrummage is facing McKivat.

The Wallaby Olympic XV looking purposefully into their destiny. The photo of the scrummage is a rare image of the match. The Cornwall side appears to be wearing the red, white and blue stripes of the United Kingdom.
(*The Referee,* 1908)

Trevor Allan, the greatest Australian outside centre, wearing headgear as usual, makes a break against the All Blacks at the SCG in a 1947 Test won by New Zealand 27–14. Allan kicked a conversion and three penalties.
(John Fairfax, 1947)

Phil Hawthorne slips a pass to the champion halfback Ken Catchpole, who races across for a try against England at Twickenham, 1967. Australia 23–England 11. (John Fairfax, 1967)

Tony Shaw and Stan Pilecki find an unsual way to celebrate the Wallabies'
defeat of the All Blacks at the SCG in 1979 – with 'champoo'!
Australia 12–New Zealand 6. (John Fairfax, 1979)

The master Mark Ella slips away a pass despite the attention of two England
defenders. On the first Test of the Wallaby Grand Slam in 1984, Australia
recorded a 19–3 victory, one of the largest margins of points conceded
by England at Twickenham. (AP, 1984)

David Campese about to score after running a remarkable angle across the New Zealand defence, which did not adjust for the subtlety of Campese's break. (AP, 1991)

Captain Nick Farr-Jones receives the Rugby World Cup trophy from Queen Elizabeth II after Australia defeated England 12–6 in the final at Twickenham, 2 November 1991. (Reuters, 1991)

crowds suggests that by this time the magic of the Bledisloe Cup trophy was working with NZ supporters.

The Wallaby captain in 1931 was the mercurial halfback Syd Malcolm, a tiny but brilliant player with a face like Punch and the brain and talent of a rugby god. Malcolm mixed business with pleasure on the tour by taking an order book along with his rugby gear. He was able to make a full quota of sales in New Zealand of the novelty sweet he was selling, Lifesavers.

This product's name can stand as a symbol, too, for the impact of the Bledisloe Cup on Australian and New Zealand rugby. It has become a symbol for excellence. The Sydney-based gossip writer Jane Fraser has referred to 'Bledisloe Cup sex' – the best sex you can possibly have. Bledisloe Cup rugby, similarly, has produced the best Test rugby that can be envisaged.

'Chattering Charlie' Bledisloe, almost unwittingly, delivered a lifesaver for the rugby game in Australia and New Zealand.

PART IV: A Half-century of Wallaby Triumphs

Eye Witness to the State of Rugby

The Final Whistle

Brave on the rugby field and defending the values they held dear, virtually all the grade rugby players in Sydney and Brisbane joined up as volunteers to fight overseas during the First World War. The ARU Archivist, John Mulford, estimates that 'over 2000 players from all levels of the game' joined up. This grand gesture meant that the Sydney and Brisbane grade championships had to be cancelled. The loss of young rugby players was so acute in Queensland that the QRU became extinct. It was finally revived in 1929, but by then rugby league had entrenched itself in what had been a powerhouse of Australian rugby. In addition, many of the young men who went away to war never came back. The 1916 NSWRU Annual Report listed the loss of 115 former players. Seven Wallabies were buried on cemeteries on the Dardanelles Peninsula. Most of those who did return never played rugby again. A generation of players and leaders, of the game and their communities, was lost, therefore.

What they suffered on the battlefields, though, lives on. For this was an era of letter writing. Even young men who were never schooled beyond primary school could write honestly and eloquently about what was happening to them. The *Referee*, a popular sporting magazine, realised this and published a series of moving letters from players relating their war experiences. In these letters there was a haunting nostalgia for the simple pleasures of home life and of chasing a rugby ball around a field with a team of mates. Clarrie Wallach, a noted after-match baritone singer and a Wallaby against the All Blacks in 1913, wrote in this simple but memorable vein: 'We arrived at Hellopolis about three weeks ago. We have been in pretty solid work, but expect the real stuff next week. All the rugby union men are well here, from the Major down to the privates. "Twit" Tasker told me how Harold George died a death of deaths — a hero's — never beaten until the final whistle went.'

William 'Twit' Tasker was the first Wallaby sent off the field. This happened on the tour of the United States in 1912 when Tasker's rough play upset an American referee. He died of wounds on the Western Front in France in 1918. The Major was Major James McManamey, a leading NSW rugby official. He died at Gallipoli a few weeks after Wallach's letter was written. Clarrie Wallach, too, was killed at Gallipoli. He was awarded the Military Cross for his bravery in action.

The fact that all the players mentioned in Wallach's letter perished during the First World War provides an awful indicator about how ruthless that conflict was. In 1919, as a way of restoring some normality to life after the war, a great rugby tournament was played in England between soldiers' teams from Britain, South Africa, New Zealand, Canada and Australia. New Zealand won the tournament but the Australians defeated the eventual winners in one of the round-robin matches in a magnificent exhibition of hard tackling and forthright running.

This Australian Imperial Forces (AIF) team played a series of wonderful matches against local sides on its return to Australia which re-established rugby in NSW. The returned soldiers were incredibly hard and fit, in superb condition for playing exuberant rugby. After their terrible experiences on many battlefields, they regarded rugby as an activity to be played as a game above all, while kicking for touch was a form of trench warfare to be avoided at all costs.

This enthusiasm for vibrant running became the model for the Waratahs that was perfected on the tour of Britain in 1927–28. The Waratahs style – clever, incisive and hard – became the Wallabies style.

Bruce Scates, a senior lecturer in Australian history at the University of New South Wales, has made a special study of the backpacker-Anzac phenomenon. He says that young people seek out the grave of someone their age, or from the same township, or even of the same name. 'The young,' he claims, 'seem especially taken with inscriptions on the headstones which evoke the Australian character or celebrate the Australian climate or landscape.' They give the sense that Australian values are worth fighting for and, possibly, dying for. In war – and in rugby – the Australian ideal was tempered with the concept of fighting hard for what you valued, right to the final whistle.

Thinking about the rugby men who died and those who returned brings to mind Stephen Spender's moving poem 'I Think Continually of Those Who Were Truly Great', in which the men travelled towards the sun and signed the air with their honour.

Ken Catchpole, 'The Genius'

It is common for youngsters to refer to star sportsmen as 'legends'. So any sportsman or woman with attitude – or even a curious haircut, or someone who wears his cap back-to-front – is invested with saintly qualities. The word is generally over-used. But not so in the case of Ken Catchpole, the immortal 'Catchy', captain of the Wallabies at 20 and captain–coach of the Wallabies on a tour to South Africa at the age of 21. Peter Crittle, a good all-round Wallaby forward in the 1960s and a keen historian of rugby, told a rugby dinner I attended in 1994 that 'Ken Catchpole was the greatest player ever to represent Australia at rugby union.'

Extravagant praise? Perhaps not. T.P. McLean, knighted for his services to rugby journalism in New Zealand, covered rugby from the 1920s to the beginning of the twenty-first century. This is what McLean wrote in 1979: 'Ken Catchpole I rate for many reasons which start with courage and end with loyalty to the game. The fine point was his pass. Years ago, I talked with the great Welshman, Hadyn Tanner, who would be a candidate for the greatest scrumhalf of all time . . . We talked passing. "There are," said he, "three elements to the halfback's pass. They are length versus speed versus accuracy. The greatest of these is speed." Enter Ken Catchpole. His was not so much a pass as an instantaneous flip. His partner was given a yard, even two yards, before opponents grouped and rushed. At various times in various sorts of company, with players and alickadoos and pressmen, I have discussed the great players we have seen and our candidate for the greatest in the various positions. At our most conservative estimate, Catchpole has been first choice of 80 per cent of us. The president of the RFU endorsed this view at the dinner for the 1966–67 Wallabies after Australia had defeated England 23–11, with this unequivocal statement: "Ken Catchpole is the greatest halfback rugby has known." '

For those of us who did not see him play, our only glimpse of the genius comes from television footage that is played from time to time. When his five-eighth partner, Phil Hawthorne, died in September 1994 some of the television channels showed archive footage of the immortal pair in action. One clip reveals a darting Catchpole running flat from a scrum before putting a perfect scissors pass into the hands of Hawthorne, who virtually strolls across for a try through a bemused Welsh defence. Randwick Rugby Club, too, has a video of a miracle try scored by Catchpole in a club grand final against Norths. Once again Catchpole is caught by the camera running across the field, along the same tight line that David Campese ran to score his try against the All Blacks in the 1991 RWC semi-final at Dublin. But Catchpole is about 40 metres out, not 15 or so metres like Campese. Suddenly he breaks around the opposition inside centre and bolts on an angle to the corner flag. The fullback comes across and Catchpole jinks and shakes his hips, all at high speed, slips inside the cover defence and scores under the posts.

It was a remarkable try from a remarkably gifted player, physically and intellectually. It was Ken Catchpole 'The Genius' at his usual best.

The Tourist of the Century

The 1984 Grand Slam tour of Britain was the last of the block-buster tours lasting over four months. It was fitting, therefore, that in the team was the tourist of the century, Stanislaus Pilecki, 'Stan The Man', born at Augsdorf, Germany, on 4 February 1947.

He was one of the few Wallabies to make two major tours to Britain, even though he didn't play his first representative game until he was 29. At age 37, and older than coach Alan Jones, Pilecki was selected for the 1984 Wallabies on his second British tour.

From a book on his life, *Stan The Man*, the proceeds of which have been donated to various Asthma Foundations and the Cerebral Palsy Association, a collection of Pileckisms can be put together.

- In Argentina he was asked to warm up to replace Mark Loane. 'Haven't got time to warm up,' he told coach Bob Templeton, 'I'm only halfway through my smoke.'
- After giving him a hard time one match, the tough Welsh prop Ray Prosser asked Pilecki how he thought he'd played. Pilecki answered: 'Under an assumed name.'
- After the Wallabies had watched the ballet in London, the first time Pilecki had seen dancers cavorting around on their points, he asked a team-mate why they didn't just get taller dancers.
- On one of his tours Templeton took Pilecki aside and told him, 'Mate, we're playing you on Saturday because we need your grunt and your commitment to the hard stuff. Can we count on you?'

  'Bob,' Pilecki told him, 'you just want me because there's no one left to play.'
- He was once asked if he was interested in playing rugby league. He replied: 'The Queensland players are my mates, and you don't leave your mates to play league.'
- His favourite food, he said, was seconds.

- He once wondered on the 1984 tour why a youngster kept on coming up to him asking him for his autograph. The youngster finally told him: 'Ten of yours is worth one of Mark Ella's.'

Behind the gruff humour, Stan Pilecki was a master prop. And as a mark of respect for his contribution to Australian rugby, he was selected in the Wallaby side to play the Barbarians at the end of the 1984 tour, even though he wasn't one of the Test props. At the team meeting before the match there was a lively discussion about all the contrived moves the team could put on to entertain the crowd. Pilecki was asked his opinion. 'Kick the bloody thing out,' he told the team meeting.

The Inevitable Question

Nick Farr-Jones, in the diverting book *Nicks and Cuts: Wallaby Tales*, which he co-authored with Steve Cutler, calls it 'that inevitable question'. He can't recall, he writes, any occasion at the numerous rugby dinners and presentation nights over the years 'when that inevitable question hasn't been asked: "Who do you rate as the better coach: Alan Jones or Bob Dwyer?" '

Farr-Jones (although he is a lawyer) relies on telling stories (many of them hilarious) about the two coaches. He then leaves it up to the reader, as an entertained jury, to come to a conclusion about the question.

Just reading between the lines of many of the splendid anecdotes about Alan Jones, however, my feeling is that Cutler, in particular, retains a special regard for the former Wallaby coach. There is a wonderful photograph of Alan Jones in brown face singing in the style of Al Jolson. 'What a performance,' Cutler writes. 'Jonesy had donned the full kit – including brown boot polish – and proceeded to sing and dance his way through a medley of Jolson tunes.'

The next morning, Jones gave his Wallaby team a day off

from training. 'I think Jonesy needed some time to get all the boot polish off his face,' Farr-Jones suggests. There is an entertaining chapter, too, by Farr-Jones on David Brockhoff, a Wallaby in the 1940s and 1950s, an Australian coach, and a passionate coach and supporter of the Sydney University Rugby Club. There's Brock, before an Anzac Day match against the great rivals Randwick, arranging for the door of the dressing room to be taken off its hinges. He makes a passionate pre-match speech culminating in: 'If it was good enough for the boys at Gallipoli, it's good enough for us' pause, then slow and deliberately, 'and today fellas' pause, 'WE . . . DO . . . BATTLE.'

Farr-Jones finishes: 'As Brock motioned his troops out of the trenches he was seen to rip the door off its hinges slamming it down on the cement floor so that the players had to pass across it on their way out. Rumour has it that University players suffered a similar defeat to the one in 1915 (with no disrespect to our soldiers).'

The Great 'Campo'
August 1990

David Campese, the erratic, tackle-shy and confused 'should I run it or not?' rugby player, shouldn't be in the Wallaby Test side. Campo, the goose-stepping, electric and bewildering broken-field runner, the world-record holder of Test tries, should be.

When Campese played his first Test as a 19-year-old back in 1982 he was 'Campo', a fearless and confident runner who threw the All Black backline into a panic whenever he touched the ball. His then coach Bob Dwyer likes to tell of Campo's first touch of a ball in a Test match. Campo had no support near him, so the safe thing to do was kick for touch. Instead, he chose to take on his opposite winger, Stu Wilson, a veteran of 26 Tests and at that time the leading try-scorer in Tests for the All Blacks. With a brilliant change of pace, he left Wilson stranded.

In the second Test, Campo made a startling break, beating three All Blacks including that ferocious tackler Bill Osborne with, according to Evan Whitton, the most 'prodigious side-steps since Prince Obolensky cutting back from the right wing, spread-eagled the All Blacks at Twickenham in 1935'. The overweight Scottish referee, Alan Hosie, who was left metres behind along with 12 All Blacks, ruled that Campo's pass to Andrew Slack was forward, thereby depriving the Wallabies of a famous victory.

In 1988, at the conclusion of the British tour by the Wallabies, Stephen Jones, the rugby writer for the *Sunday Times*, compared Campo with Gerald Davies, the brilliant Welsh winger of the 1970s. 'We can leave Gerald and his era in peace,' Jones wrote. 'But we can also say that David Campese is the greatest rugby player of his generation.'

A potted history of accolades for Campo is necessary because most rugby followers in Australia do not realise what a remarkable player he is. Perhaps it's his flashy style, or his loquaciousness, or the fact that he plays in Italy, but there is something about Campese that upsets people. When he makes mistakes, people never forgive him. Somehow Campo's astonishing record of try-scoring is overlooked.

Nick Farr-Jones says that Campo is such a dangerous player to the opposition because 'brain doesn't always know where his legs are carrying him'. To play well, Campo has to play instinctively. When he is made to think and play like a conventional player, by an overbearing coach or from too much public or team pressure, he becomes David Campese, a conventional player. The electrifying running is short-circuited by fear, and he makes mistakes.

When he made a careless pass in the third Test last year that set up a match-winning try for the Lions, Andrew Slack made this damning comment: 'What of Campese's stupendous genius? How often do we see it when it matters, and does it stack up favourably against the number of times he turns damn fool?'

This season Campese has missed tackles on Serge Blanco and John Kirwan. His running has lacked the unpredictability and explosiveness of other years. Kirwan now has the wood on him the way the young Campo had the wood on Stu Wilson.

Should he be dropped from the Wallaby Test side, then? In my view, such a thought should not be contemplated. Campo has played 52 Tests. He has taken more risks in any one of those Tests than someone like Slack did in all his Tests put together. It is remarkable, though, how few mistakes Campo has actually made. Critics of his play forget that in a rugby match sins of omission are often more telling in the final outcome of a match than sins of commission. The kick for touch may be the safe play but it won't score points.

Even safety-first players make mistakes. Slack once tried to run the ball from under his goal-posts, was tackled and the All Blacks scored a try. There was hardly a mention of this after the match. Last Saturday, Ian Williams and Greg Martin muffed a rolling ball and the All Blacks scored. The outcry would have been overwhelming if Campese had been involved. There has hardly been any criticism, either, of the way Va'aiga Tuigamala pushed Paul Carozza off him like a fly in the Auckland match.

Campo has that rare try-scoring gift. There have been hundreds of players, for instance, who have played as competently as, say, Slack. Few players in the history of rugby can match Campo's try-scoring achievements. Not playing him in a Test is like dropping Don Bradman because he scored the occasional duck.

Sour Notes from a Whistle-blowing Rhapsody
26 August 1991

The referee 33 (penalties), Wallabies/All Blacks 0. That was one of the decisive outcomes, unfortunately, from Saturday's Test at

Eden Park. There were far too many penalties from the Scottish referee Ken McCartney and too few (none, in fact, that come to mind) advantages played.

The problem with the majority of UK referees is that they believe set pieces – the scrums and the lineouts – are an end in themselves. Referees in this part of the world, on the other hand, correctly regard the set pieces as a way of starting play. So when McCartney blew his whistle on Saturday for a collapsed scrum when the ball was already in the halfback's hands, an Australian or New Zealand referee would have let the game flow on. We can now see why UK sides favour huge, virtually immobile front rows, and why penalties, not tries, dominate their scoring.

If the game had been allowed to flow, it is difficult to say with certainty which side would have been advantaged. The All Blacks played superbly in the first half, and with a more flowing game allowed might have scored more points. The Wallabies were the better side in the second half, although not as dominant as the New Zealanders in their half of ascendancy. As the game continued, the harder driving and greater weight of the Wallaby pack, more than 6 kg a man heavier on average, began to assert itself. The statistics bear this out: the Wallabies won the penalties 18–15, with Michael Lynagh having more kicks at goal (seven) than Grant Fox (five); the lineouts went to the Wallabies 15–14; and although there were no tightheads, the Australian pack won its own ball more comfortably than the All Blacks, despite the greasy footing.

Wallaby coach Bob Dwyer is probably right when he says his team should have taken more time towards the end of the match to get a proper platform for the final decisive assault. Against this is the fact that the All Blacks' back row was metres quicker than their opponents, and applied tremendous pressure on Michael Lynagh and Tim Horan. The All Blacks are now Rugby's equivalent of the West Indies cricket team: difficult to beat on their best days, as Saturday's Test indicated, but with the best days becoming increasingly rare, as the Sydney Test revealed.

> **24 August 1991, at Auckland.** Australia **3** (M. Lynagh 1 penalty goal) lost to New Zealand **6** (G. Fox 2 penalty goals)

Keeping the Score on Jones
August 1991

Two weeks ago, the rugby league referee Chris Ward was subjected to a furious tirade from Alan Jones. On Sunday, on radio 2BL, following another loss by his Balmain side, a further broadside was fired, this time at the Fairfax newspapers. Jones's case is that the *Sydney Morning Herald* and other Fairfax papers have treated him without journalistic integrity with their 'persistent attack . . . against me in particular and Balmain in general'.

A look through the *Herald*'s files reveals that this accusation doesn't hold much water.

A key document in the relationship between Jones and the *Herald* was an editorial written just before his appointment as coach of the Wallabies in February 1984. The editorial insisted that the incumbent, Bob Dwyer, was more likely than Jones 'to encourage the exciting, running rugby that has characterised our national team in recent years'. Jones's achievement in guiding Manly to the Sydney premiership was acknowledged, 'but one winter doesn't make an Australian coach'.

After Jones was dropped as the Wallaby coach in 1988, he wrote an article for the *Sun Herald* (one of the newspapers he is now criticising) claiming that when he was appointed in 1984 'the equivalent of all hell broke loose, unleashing then and often since upon me and the team forces of emotion and vilification which were hard to combat'. He instanced the *Sydney Morning Herald* running 'an editorial imploring the ARU not to appoint Mr Jones'. After citing his record as Wallaby coach – the 1984 Grand Slam, the 1986 Bledisloe Cup victory, the 89 victories out of 102 outings – Jones noted that 'only a fool would bother to search for such a *Sydney Morning Herald* editorial in defence of Alan Jones'.

As it happens, if that fool had bothered to look, he would have found such an editorial. On 10 December 1984, the *Herald* published an editorial titled: 'Grand Slam Wallabies'. The editorial said the Wallabies' triumph 'vindicated the appointment of Alan Jones earlier this year as coach, an appointment which in certain quarters received sharp criticism. Indeed, the further the achievements of 1984 recede into history, the greater the credit, probably, Jones will be given for them.'

Throughout Jones's time as Wallaby coach, the *Herald* had two rugby writers, Jim Webster and Greg Growden. The basic reporting during his tenure (and therefore the bulk of the stories about him and his teams) was handled by these two journalists. There has never been a suggestion from Jones that either Growden or Webster were anything less than even-handed in their reporting. After Jones was dumped as Wallaby coach in February 1988, Growden praised Jones for the Grand Slam and Bledisloe Cup victories: 'These two successes were recognised as among the greatest achievements in Australian rugby history ... But everything went amiss last season when the team's standards dropped alarmingly.'

It is fair to say, however, that two of the *Herald*'s commentators on rugby during this same period, Roland Fishman and Evan Whitton, are the writers Jones generally refers to when he complains about a lack of journalistic integrity at that paper.

Roland Fishman, who had been taught by Jones at The King's School, was initially enthusiastic about Jones's promotion to the position of Wallaby coach. He wrote: 'One Manly player said that if Jones wanted his players to run through a brick wall, they would.' Jones, Fishman says, sent him a note about this particular article saying how much he liked it. Fishman wrote a further article, however, about the 'politicisation' of rugby in the lead-up to Jones's appointment. The article quoted various personalities critical of Jones. 'Two days later,' he wrote in 1988, 'I spoke to him on the phone. "An absolute disgrace, Roly," he said. "The performance of the Fairfax organisation has been appalling. And you, of all people, would know better . . . How dare you set yourself up as my critic?" '

Evan Whitton has won a bagful of Walkley awards (journalism's equivalent of the Logies). He is a fearless commentator on politics, crime and rugby. When Jones won the NSWRU's nomination for Australian coach in 1984, Whitton was typically direct: 'To say that this decision is a disgrace will seem, to many supporters of the game, to elaborate the obvious.' One of Whitton's criticisms was that in the 1984 Sydney premiership final, 'Mr Jones employed the Bob Templeton-type of forward game that is quite useless for Australia at international level.'

This theme, that the Wallabies had to play running rugby to be a force at the international level, infused virtually all of Whitton's comment pieces on rugby. The Grand Slam Wallabies, for instance, were successful because Jones 'clearly an intelligent and thoughtful man . . . was sensible enough to see, or allow himself to be persuaded, that the running game was required . . . Whatever the merit of Jones's original appointment as assistant manager, he will always have, as the ultimate organiser of our greatest achievement, a significant place in Australian rugby history.'

Whitton repeatedly called for the reinstatement of Bob Dwyer as Wallaby coach, using the argument that Dwyer understood the running game better than Jones. In August 1987, the *Herald* published a letter from five Wallabies, including the captain, Nick Farr-Jones, saying that Whitton's criticisms of the performance of the Australian team and its coach, Jones, were 'neither valid, nor objective'.

Whitton, who saw Jones's hand behind the letter, wrote a cheerful reply making a point he repeated when Jones was made coach of Balmain, that 'he was appointed [Wallaby coach] mainly to handle the media hype'. Whitton was inclined in his articles to attribute the technical skills of the Wallabies to Jones's assistant coach, Alex Evans. This obviously grated with Jones.

Whitton told me that when the Wallabies played a night match at Swansea, Wales, in 1984, the journalists were offered the privilege of going back to London in the team bus. As Whitton went to board, Jones said: 'Not you.' Whitton says one of the least pleasant moments in his life was standing in the rain in Swansea at about eleven o'clock at night watching a warm bus pull away into the darkness bound for London.

Harold Wilson, a controversial British prime minister, once noted that people in the spotlight had to learn to face the fast bowling. This is what Jones expects of the bureaucrats, the judges, the politicians and the journalists he savages morning after morning on his radio program. It is a test, though, as his tirades against his critics when things go wrong for him demonstrate, which he has not learned to master himself.

Tim Terrific
26 May 1992
On a scale of one to ten, Queensland centre Tim Horan scored an 11 in Sunday's NSW v. Queensland game. Horan's perfect match, one of the most complete and effective displays of rugby skills I've seen in decades of watching the game, was the decisive factor in the Reds' 23–18 victory.

In the opening minutes, when the Waratahs rolled relentlessly forward and a try was inevitable, the ball was shifted to the blind side after a series of savage mauls. Horan read the play, formed the first line of defence to prevent the run, and then dropped back to cover a grubber kick when the Reds' line was exposed. One saved try to Horan.

A little later, when the Waratahs were leading 6–3, and still in control of the match, Willie Ofahengaue was set free with no one in front of him on a 25-metre charge to the line. A searing burst from nowhere by Horan, an adroit ankle-tap, and Ofahengaue tumbled to the ground. Another try saved. Later in the first half, with the Waratahs still in control, the NSW centres fumbled, Queensland recovered, Paul Carozza burst away, put through a long kick and with another searing burst of speed Horan raced past the chasers, toed through skilfully and slammed across for a try. A try gained by Horan.

Then just into the second half, with NSW only a point behind and still with a strong chance of winning the match, Nick Farr-Jones kicked a cross-field bomb from a penalty. Horan caught the ball with several Waratahs challenging him. He glided across the field, drew in the Waratahs' outside backs and passed to Jason Little, giving him a clear 30-metre dash to the tryline. Little's score, but Horan's try. Later in the match, when the Waratahs were pressing hard time and again for the winning try, Horan frequently tackled his opponent on the blind-side and somehow managed to get across to the open-side when the Waratahs shifted play and had the numbers to make a further try-saving tackle. With Horan playing in such a commanding fashion, it was astonishing that the Queensland tactics seemed to be designed to prevent him from getting the ball. My notes of the match suggested he received the ball from the set pieces perhaps twice in the match. Paul Kahl, the five-eighth, obviously under instructions, banged the ball downfield or in the air virtually every time he received it.

With Horan in such majestic form, it was an insult to his talents that Queensland played its traditional slow-motion, kicking, defence-obsessed style.

Australia Prove Themselves a Champion Side
20 July 1992

This is a special Wallabies team. It doesn't know how to lose. The two crucial Australian tries in yesterday's second Test at Ballymore came within minutes of the half-time and the full-time whistle. What this tells us is that the Wallabies play out the entire gut-wrenching 80 minutes of their matches and have a confidence that when they have to score points, they will score them.

It's as if a divine spark ignites the team at moments of truth and its will to win forces the opposition and the fates to succumb to its pressure. That last try scored by Paul Carozza, for instance, was the culmination of a perfect two-hand jump in the lineout by John Eales; a metre-perfect bomb by Michael Lynagh; a fierce chase and disciplined driving maul by the forwards that unsettled the All Blacks and led to the ball being kicked through to the Wallabies; a perfect cut-out pass by Nick Farr-Jones; Lynagh committing the defence before making a perfect pass to Carozza who charged like a little rhino for the line. All this perfect play was accomplished while the All Blacks defended their line with a take-no-prisoners passion and with the knowledge by the Wallabies that this sequence of play had to be the game's final, decisive thrust.

The Wallabies right now are a rugby side with no weaknesses for an opposition to exploit. As in the first Test at Sydney, the All Blacks gave away critical penalties with undisciplined play. And they were never able to get a grip on the match, even when they were in front and playing well. In fact, the All Blacks penetrated the Wallabies' 22 infrequently. The Wallabies, on the other hand, played a large percentage of the match inside or just outside the All Blacks' 22.

Occasionally in sport everything comes together – the right coach, an inspiring captain, players of supreme ability in virtually every position and that indefinable team spirit that makes the whole better than the parts. This is what has happened with the Wallabies. The team is entitled to make the claim that it is now one of the great rugby sides of the modern era.

19 July 1992, at Brisbane. Australia **19** (P. Carozza 2 tries; M. Lynagh 3 penalty goals) defeated New Zealand **17** (J. Timu, J. Kirwan tries; G. Fox 2 conversions, 1 penalty goal)

'Poido', You'll Be Missed
18 March 1993

Certain things seem to be immutable and when they finally end you feel that a part of your life has been diminished. The news of Simon Poidevin's retirement from all rugby has created one of those diminishing events. It's hard to contemplate a winter without Poidevin, Australia's greatest loose forward, snarling at the end of the lineouts, nostrils flaring, eyes narrow and hard, his chest heaving from the effort to suck in more oxygen before taking up the challenge to make the life of his marker and the opposing five-eighth as difficult and as miserable as possible.

The extended golden period of Wallaby rugby, which began with the Bledisloe Cup triumph in 1980 and still continues, has exactly duplicated Poidevin's career. The only series the Wallabies were terrorised in the forwards in this period, in 1989 against the Lions, Poidevin wasn't in the team. Poidevin's contribution to the success of the golden era has been immense for his play was founded on the, undeniably correct, notion that the forwards are the vanguard and that the breakaways are the elite of that vanguard. This is a concept that New Zealand rugby (but not Australian rugby until recently) has known from the days of Davy Gallaher, the loose forward theorist and captain of the famous 1905 side. Most All Black sides, through an adherence to the forward-power concept, are captained by forwards, often breakaways. And ever since Gallaher's time, coaches handling youngsters in New Zealand have always put the most athletic and competitive player in their squad on the side of the scrum.

In Australia, the tendency is to play similar athletic and competitive youngsters in the centres. Consequently, Australia has produced a glittering litany of great centres but few masterful breakaways. The New Zealand experience is the exact opposite.

Poidevin's role, especially when the Wallabies played the All Blacks, was to nullify that traditional New Zealand advantage in the loose play. Against Wayne Shelford's 1988 side, one of the finest All Black sides ever, Poidevin virtually played the New Zealand pack on his own. His struggles with Shelford in the mauls were mesmeric and titanic. Poidevin was sometimes criticised for being deficient in pace and in the ball-running skills of, say, the All Black Michael Jones. But the strength of his game lay in his courage, his toughness of character, his tirelessness and his infectious commitment to winning.

Who can forget the mighty tackle Mike Teague made on him in the 1991 World Cup final against England and the way Poidevin bounced back immediately to his feet in a gesture that told the English players the Wallabies believed they were invincible that day?

His first-class rugby career in Australia ended quietly. After playing a leading role in Sydney's demolition of the All Blacks last year at Penrith, Poidevin left the field with 20 minutes remaining in the match to give Tony Dempsey the thrill of playing in a side that was thrashing the old enemy.

The Wallabies Ambushed
20 July 1993
SATURDAY, DUNEDIN, 4.45 P.M.

Phil Kearns, the Wallaby captain, patiently points out to the New Zealand rugby writers in the cramped media room in the main stand at Carisbrook that the Wallabies needed a match or two more before they get the rust out of their game. 'It went from a two-Test series to one Test and instead of being played after our series with South Africa, it went before. Also, instead of being played in Australia, it was played in New Zealand.'

The suggestion here is that the Wallabies were ambushed. But in all probability the Wallabies were ambushed by Australian rugby officials who somehow agreed to a one-off Test for the Bledisloe Cup to be played in that graveyard of Wallaby Test hopes, Carisbrook Park, Dunedin. Why did the ARU acquiesce in an arrangement that clearly was against the interests of the

Wallabies and, therefore, of Australian rugby? As someone said to me at Sydney Airport on the way to Dunedin: 'We're the world champions. Why aren't they playing us in Sydney?'

SATURDAY, DUNEDIN, 2.53 P.M.

Pat Howard's drop kick to begin the game after Grant Fox has kicked a penalty for the All Blacks doesn't go the required 10 metres and the Wallaby forwards trudge back for a scrum on the halfway mark. Forget Howard's dropped pass and the badly considered attempt to beat Frank Bunce — these were predictable mistakes from a young, inexperienced player in his first Test. The really weak area of his play, and that of Tim Kelaher and David Campese, was in the kickoffs.

This was where Michael Lynagh's absence was most greatly felt by the Wallabies. For over a decade we've been used to Lynagh putting the ball up high enough and far enough for the forwards to win back or crash the opponent catching the ball to the ground. But hardly one Australian kickoff gave an advantage to the Wallabies.

THURSDAY, SYDNEY AIRPORT, 11.30 A.M.

The flight carrying the Wallabies to Dunedin is supposed to have left. The fog lifts to allow the plane to take off at 12.15. It's nearly five o'clock New Zealand time when they arrive at Christchurch and there is another flight of about 40 minutes before they, finally, arrive in Dunedin. The whole of Thursday, basically, is wasted for the Wallabies. While they're trapped in the boredom and discomfort (for players with sore backs and legs) of a long-distance air flight, the All Blacks have a long, detailed training session and a boat excursion around Dunedin harbour.

WEDNESDAY, SYDNEY, 6.00 P.M.

'The team could be heading for the abattoir.' Three days before the Test, this is the anguished assessment of David Brockhoff, a former Wallaby and Wallaby coach.

SATURDAY, DUNEDIN, 4.00 P.M.

In the end, however, the Wallabies did surprisingly well despite all the problems they had to counter. The tight five, particularly, won their battle in the lineouts and scrums, except for those crucial few minutes after half-time. The problem was that the rolling-maul method, which seemed to be the main offensive tactic, was successfully (but illegally according to Bob Dwyer) resisted by the All Blacks.

As a consequence, even though the Wallabies were on attack inside the New Zealand 22 for long periods of play, they never quite looked like cracking the defence. A critical question must now be posed: 'Was this failure due to a rustiness of skills or a rustiness of method?'

The real lesson to emerge from the loss of the Bledisloe Cup, it seems to me, is that even when the rust is removed from the skills, the Wallabies will still be playing the wrong style. The rolling-maul game will have to be replaced by a quick-release game, which rewards flair and dash (or flashes of it, as it did for the All Blacks on Saturday), if the Wallabies want to remain the best team in the world.

---

17 July 1993, at Dunedin. Australia **10** (T. Horan 1 try; T. Kelaher 1 conversion and 1 penalty goal) lost to New Zealand **25** (F. Bunce, S. Fitzpatrick tries; G. Fox 5 penalty goals)

Marvellous Theatre, Pity About the Script
3 August 1993

Under a black velvet sky, Marty Roebuck kicked off for the Wallabies . . .

Despite the fact that the Wallabies were comprehensively defeated by the Springboks (the talk about 'refereeing errors' from the Wallaby camp is self-deluding), this was a significant rugby occasion and marvellous theatre. Journalists will have to get used to writing intros along the lines of the above.

My guess is that within five years or so, most Tests will be played at night. This will have its effect on the outcome of Tests. Both Scott Bowen and Nick Farr-Jones, for example, when they were discussing the Test on Channel 10's 'Rugby World' program, made the point that the ball was slippery because of the night dew. Knowing that this would be the case, David Campese, in hindsight, might have fallen on that rolling ball and then tried to stand in a maul rather than attempting (unsuccessfully) the sliding pick-up that led to the first Springbok try.

Another intriguing point Bowen made was that the crisp night air seemed to invigorate the South Africans. Against the NSW Waratahs, he said, the Springboks tired noticeably in the second half. On Saturday night, though, they were full of running for the entire 80 minutes. At the end of the Test, defending their line, there were Springboks everywhere.

There is probably something in this. The slower pace the Wallaby pack played at, though, compared with the Waratahs forwards, must have had an effect. Also, the probability of a victory from half-time onwards would have concentrated the determination of the Springboks.

By playing Tests at night, rugby administrators can solve a number of their scheduling problems. The club and schoolboys matches can be played during the day and everyone involved still has plenty of time to get to the Test. The imperatives of television, anyway, will force the hand of the administrators. The big television audiences are at night. The sponsors want big audiences and are prepared to put a great deal of money into rugby, if the television audiences are delivered. Under lights, too, rugby takes on a magical aspect. This was certainly the case on Saturday night. The lights, like the original theatre limelights, gave a focus to the playing field and the players on it. Under the vast, black Sydney sky this became a gleaming arena. The sense of being at a theatre where great deeds would be accomplished was overpowering.

Pity about the Wallabies muffing their lines.

---

31 July 1993, at Sydney. Australia **12** (M. Roebuck 4 penalty goals) lost to South Africa **19** (J. Small 2, P. Muller tries; J. van Rensburg 2 conversions)

Wallabies Prove That Glitter Can Be Golden
16 August 1993

This was a vibrant, inventive performance by the Wallabies in a great Test, because the Springboks played about as well as any team can when it cannot win ball. The atmosphere of the occasion was heightened by a passionate, focused crowd, which sang 'Waltzing Matilda' throughout the match and then roared when the Wallabies threw assault after assault at the Springboks' line before Australia recorded their convincing 28–20 win.

At half-time, the scoreline was 10–10, even though the Springboks had hardly entered the Australian side of the field. Five-eighth Joel Stransky's penalty was taken from 56 metres out and sailed over the crossbar as inevitably as any of those massive kicks from rugby's longest goal-kicker, Don Clarke. Then again, it was Stransky who read a complicated Wallaby backline movement, which involved centre Jason Little passing blind (to Stransky, as it happened), and the South African raced away for a long-distance try. At the press conference after the match, captain Phil Kearns said Little had gasped out, 'Oh no!' as soon as he passed the ball. But a released pass, like a jump from a bridge, cannot be brought back.

To their credit, the Wallabies continued to run the fabled and complicated backline manoeuvres of which we have heard so much before matches but never actually seen. Let it be recorded now that the glittering moves do exist, and when they are carried out with the panache the Wallabies brought to their play on Saturday, they are thrilling and effective.

Little's second try was an example of how well the Wallabies can play when they attempt ball-in-hand rugby. Instead of a bomb from a tap penalty, the forwards did some passing as they thundered into and through the South African defensive line. By the time Little made his charge down the middle of the field, South Africa's Maginot Line had crumbled and the strong-running centre was able to shrug off defenders who were out of position and off-balance. During the week, the Wallaby camp made statements about why the media had been, perhaps, too critical. The players, it was said, had stopped reading the papers. They were aware of what was being written, though, from reports from relatives and friends. The Wallaby coach Bob Dwyer also talked about the axe which would be used on those 'dud' players who did not lift their performance. This threat (and the media comment) concentrated the players' minds.

It also concentrated the mind of the coach who, for the first time this year, was able to get a quick-release, running-the-ball game plan implemented. We reptiles of the press predicted when we pushed hard for the Wallabies to play this expansive style that it would be effective. No great credit should go to those who point out the obvious, although it has taken the Wallaby management four Tests to see it staring them in the face.

It should be an easy thing to see the obvious. It is another and much harder thing to make the obvious work. The Wallabies did this with a memorable performance.

---

14 August 1993, at Brisbane. Australia **28** (J. Little 2, T. Horan tries; M. Roebuck 2 conversions and 3 penalty goals) defeated South Africa **20** (J. Stransky, J. Olivier tries; J. Stransky 2 conversions and 2 penalty goals)

Farr-Jones Makes His Mark
17 August 1993

The day the music stopped for Elvis Presley, Nick Farr-Jones carved on a tree these words: 'Elvis Presley died today, 17 August 1977'.

This is one of many fascinating details and incidents in Peter FitzSimons's engrossing biography, *Nick Farr-Jones: The Authorised Biography*, an essential book that explores the life, mind and pysche of one of Australia's most complex and successful athletes.

Because Farr-Jones's career embraces the glory years of Australian rugby, from the 1984 Grand Slam tour of the UK through to the 1991 World Cup triumph and the 1992 Bledisloe Cup-winning series against the All Blacks, the biography provides an insider's view (FitzSimons was a Wallaby, too, during this period) of how a remarkably successful team was put together, then disintegrated and was reconstructed with Farr-Jones as captain.

This rise–decline–rise process also involves the story of Alan Jones, the wordy, relentless, antagonistic, brilliant, ambitious Wallaby coach whose career in rugby, like a hero of a Greek tragedy, finally ended in hubris.

Chapter 7, '1987 – The Decline and Fall of Alan Jones', is compulsory reading for anyone interested in the pressures of big-time sport and how coaches and players respond to these pressures. Perhaps the most disturbing revelation from the chapter is that Alan Jones was prepared to carry on with the tour of Argentina without Farr-Jones. Jones, for example, is quoted as telling the Wallaby physiotherapist, Greg Craig, after Farr-Jones had gone through a tough fitness test on his damaged knee, that the halfback would be 'taking no further part in the tour'.

At Ballymore on Saturday, as the Wallabies lined up in front of the McLean Stand for the national anthem, this humiliating episode in Farr-Jones's rugby career resonated in my mind. We expect the players to play faultless rugby under the most intense pressure but we often don't know the pressures off the field that the players are enduring. Some players can absorb this pressure, on and off the field, better than others. Farr-Jones is clearly one of those. This is why he is one of rugby's greatest players.

On that tour of Argentina, for example, he played a blinder on his return in spite of the coach's apparent misgivings about his fitness and his worth to the team. It was the same again on Saturday. The most vocal protests about his return to the Wallabies came from Queensland officials. But from the first pass, he was on his game. It was his unobtrusive efficiency in clearing up bad ball and choosing the right side of the field to attack from that made possible the expansive game the Wallabies played.

And then, especially when the score was 10–10, he began to 'captain' the side. FitzSimons quotes Farr-Jones's reaction when he was made captain of the Wallabies by Bob Dwyer: 'Like quick tap kicks, for example, I liked not having to ask, "Can I do this?" I'm captain. I gave myself permission.' He was at it again on Saturday, charging from the mark from one of the taps and, later, setting up the forward drive that culminated in Jason Little's second try from another.

Like all natural leaders, Farr-Jones has a sense of his own destiny, that he is a winner. The way I deconstruct the Elvis Presley carving, for instance, is that the young Farr-Jones somehow identified with 'The King', and wanted to mark this identification in a permanent way.

It's hard to accept that Nick Farr-Jones will be playing for the Wallabies for the last time. Can the great side survive his departure? When will Australian rugby see his like again?

Mozart Magic Makes Wallabies Sing
28 August 1993
The Wallabies' 19–12 defeat of the Springboks at the Sydney Football Stadium was a triumph for the true believers. For the

victory was achieved by the traditional 'Australian method' of running the ball through the backs, except for a curious reluctance to use Tim Horan, Jason Little and David Campese (our greatest centre/wing combination?) inside the South African 22. The result of this strange strategy was that penalties rather than tries were forced by the Wallabies; all four penalty kicks were landed by Marty Roebuck.

The Australian try, however, was a classic, worth about a dozen normal tries. The Wallabies secured the ball from the kick-off, mauled forward, halfback Nick Farr-Jones (brilliant all day) worked the blind-side for Campese, the forwards, led by hooker Phil Kearns, put on a series of charges before the ball was put across the backline for Campese, again, to break the Springbok defence and float a pass for Horan to turbojet on to and score.

What more can be said about Campese? The Mozart of rugby kicked huge punts, guarded his wing securely and popped up all over the field to torment the South Africans with dazzling runs always at the heart of the defence where a missed tackle could be made to count. Just as Mozart extended the limits and range of classical music while always being on song, Campese is redefining the role and effectiveness of the winger to encompass being the second fullback, second five-eighth and the third centre on attack, making the winger the focus of the assault on the opposition's tryline.

After the match, Kearns was surprised when the crowd dissented from his comment that the series was the cleanest in which he'd played. Surprised at the reaction, he repeated it and shook his head when the crowd dissented even more loudly. The crowd was right, though. The South African foul play throughout the series ranged from continual grand dirt by Uli Schmidt to continual petty dirt from many of the other Springboks, and the crowd was in no mood to forgive them.

When Horan scored his try, for instance, James Small, the Springbok winger, was stranded near the sidelines but he still tried to trip replacement winger Matt Burke in the vain hope that he, in turn, might tumble into Horan. There was rough justice, therefore, in Small giving away a penalty at the end of the game for (unnecessarily) holding back Campese when Springbok fullback Andre Joubert was streaming away to touch down under the posts and level the scores. At the final whistle, Farr-Jones cleverly snaffled the game ball from a Springbok forward. And that incident summed up the Test: the Wallabies were too fast and too clever all day at winning the ball from the Springboks.

> **21 August 1993, at Sydney.** Australia **19** (T. Horan 1 try; M. Roebuck 1 conversion and 4 penalty goals) defeated South Africa **12** (J. Small, J. Pienaar tries; J. Stransky 1 conversion)

Rising Star George Gregan
March 1994

The Hong Kong Sevens must rate as one of the most exciting one-off sports tournaments in the world, in any code. It is a sports lover's Sevens Heaven. The most devoted lover of confrontational sports can thrill at the bone-jarring tackles of the Wallaby, Ilie Tabua, and all the Western Samoan players.

The best way to get a fix on Sevens Rugby, though, is to perceive it more in terms of basketball than rugby. As in basketball, the idea is to create a hard pressure on defence, without over-committing too many players to any one individual in the opposition. On attack, the opposite principle applies. Players try to move the ball behind the normal 15-man rugby advantage line, drawing out the opposition, until a player is put into the position to break for the goal-line. The advantage line in Sevens Rugby is really based on where the ball is rather than where the set-piece play started from.

Before the tournament, George Gregan was praised as a new star in Australian rugby, a year out from the 1995 Rugby World Cup tournament. Bob Dwyer talked about his Mark

Ella-like skills and 'his courage to have a go'. The first we saw of him on television against Japan, he backflicked a pass about 15 metres and then doubled around Tim Horan wide out to take a pass and race away for a try. Against New Zealand in the final, he showed extraordinary speed and determination to race through tight gaps in the manner of a young David Campese.

It is tempting to argue that he might be the answer to Australian rugby's halfback problem in the 15-man game. In Sevens Rugby, as in boxing, you can run but you can't hide. Gregan didn't hide but he did achieve some superb running.

Knox's Match
8 August 1994

The astonishing record annihilation of Western Samoa by Australia at the Sydney Football Stadium on Saturday night raises this question: is David Knox now the incumbent Wallaby five-eighth? Put simply, Knox played the finest five-eighth's game by any Australian since Mark Ella. It was based on the same elements as the Randwick flatline, ball-in-hand game that Ella made so effective. Knox kicked rarely, and only when the pack was on the back foot or if he couldn't run on to the ball. Otherwise he ran at the Samoan defensive line, and revealed a conjurer's collection of slick passes, behind the back, inside to a storming Willie Ofahengaue and outside in long cutouts to Pat Howard and Jason Little. The Wallaby outside backs received so much good running ball that David Campese went down with a cramp from the sheer exhaustion of being forced to run a dozen or more times at the Western Samoa backs.

There was one significant moment that summed up the difference Knox, with his running instincts, brought to the back play. After some fractured play, with both sides scrambling, winning and losing the ball in a succession of drives and runs, the Wallabies in retreat finally secured the ball with the centres and

Campese in place and only two Samoans out in defence. Above the roar of the crowd, the cry of 'wide, wide, wide' could be heard from Campese. And wide the ball went from Knox to set up another attack.

Around the ground after the match, there were references to the Wallaby halfback, George Gregan, the man of the match, as 'another Catchpole'. This is the highest praise any halfback can be offered. Gregan's passing lacks a little in the wristiness of the master but the deft, soft passes to runners in broken play and the aggressive corner-flag tackling had the hallmark of authenticity. It was a cover tackle by Gregan that snuffed out any hope the Samoans had of being competitive after a storming start by the Wallabies. Western Samoa attacked down the left and Toa Samania was launching himself for a try when Gregan came across to knock him off balance. A converted try at this point would have had the Samoans only ten points adrift and possibly back in the game.

But this was to be their only chance as the Wallabies played a match of breathtaking brilliance. If there is any consolation for the Samoans to be taken from the hiding, it is, perhaps, this: no team in the world could have got within 20 points of the Wallabies in the mood they were in on Saturday night.

---

6 August 1994, at Sydney. Australia **73** (J. Little 2, D. Smith 2, T. Gavin, V. Ofahengaue, G. Gregan, M. Pini, D. Campese, P. Howard, D. Junee tries; D. Knox 6 conversions and 2 penalty goals) defeated Western Samoa **3** (D. Kellett 1 penalty goal)

A Victory to Savour
18 August 1994

What a Test, one of the most pulsating in the long history of rugby matches between Australia and New Zealand which began at the Sydney Cricket Ground in 1903.

It took a tackle by George Gregan coming from nowhere to knock the ball out of the hands of the All Blacks' winger Jeff

Wilson just as he was going to score the try which would have won the Test for the All Blacks. Wilson, who is called 'Goldie' by his team-mates for his prodigious sporting talents, beat four or five players in a run to the line and, in what seemed to be a storybook ending to his controversial selection, launched himself into a triumphant dive. And then came Gregan . . .

The Wallabies kept the All Blacks waiting for some minutes before coming on to the field. David Campese and David Knox nonchalantly kicked the ball to each other while the All Blacks were doing an impassioned haka. The point of all this, it seemed, was to give the New Zealanders the impression that the Wallabies were supremely confident.

The opening seconds of the match confirmed this approach. Knox kicked high, the Wallaby forwards recovered the ball, Knox then kicked a monstrously high ball to the All Blacks goal line and Jason Little soared up like an Australian Rules footballer, caught the ball and fell across the line. For an All Blacks side which was under intense pressure and criticism, this was the worst possible start.

As the first half proceeded, the All Blacks knocked the ball on, missed passes, gave away penalties and generally played like a side which did not expect to win. When the Wallabies produced a well-rehearsed and unstoppable move from the back of the scrum to score their second try, it looked as if the All Blacks were being prepared for the sort of massacre that was inflicted on Manu Samoa recently. Knox's kicking from re-starts and general play had the ball hanging agonisingly in the air for the All Blacks, and with John Eales charging through to put pressure on the catcher, the All Blacks spent the half in push and shove towards their goal line.

At half-time I came across an All Black from the 1970s, Joe Karam. I asked him what he thought about what was happening out on the field. 'They're playing with no confidence,' Karam said. 'Too many players have been dropped, too many players have been played out of position. Senior players like John Kirwan should be in the side.'

But in the second half the All Blacks reached back to that New Zealand genius for rugby and played a magnificent 40 minutes. The bounce of the ball, which had gone against them in the first half, started to turn their way. They began to win a sequence of lineouts. I wrote in my notes: 'The All Blacks are getting on top but do they have enough time to win the game?' A certain try was lost when Zinzan Brooke passed forward to an unmarked Michael Jones who crossed for a try – disallowed.

The errant pass had followed a sustained series of attacks by the All Blacks from one side of the field to the other, time after time until there were no Wallabies left to defend. Series after series of similar attacks were launched but the Wallabies' tackling was as secure and thorough and often pile-driving in its effect.

Shane Howarth scored the try that had to come and the All Blacks were finally within a score of winning the game. Howarth missed a penalty. Knox kicked a penalty and then Jeff Wilson made the wonderful run into the same corner where John Kirwan had fumbled a ball two years ago and lost a try that would have probably won the Test for the All Blacks. The corner has become Hell's Corner for the New Zealanders.

In a finish that a master of melodrama might have concocted, the All Blacks ran the ball from behind their goal line with holes opening up in the Wallaby defence all over the field. People beside me were standing on their seats and screaming out, 'Tackle Wallabies, tackle, tackle.'

The desperation off the field was matched with a similar desperation on the field.

---

17 August 1994, at Sydney. Australia **20** (J. Little, P. Kearns tries; D. Knox 2 conversions and 2 penalty goals) defeated New Zealand **16** (S. Howarth 1 try, 1 conversion and 3 penalty goals)

The Tackle of the Century
August 1994

The front page of the *Sydney Morning Herald* on Thursday 18 August 1994 carried one of the most dramatic photographs of a rugby match ever taken. The match was the 1994 Bledisloe Cup battle, the ninety-eighth rugby Test between the two countries. It was won by the Wallabies 20–16, in a contest that provided a memorable finish that no writer of schoolboy yarns could ever dare to present to readers and hope to retain credibility. This was the match that will be remembered a hundred years on as 'The Test That Was Won By Gregan's Tackle'.

The headline above the *Herald's* photograph, which was taken with only four minutes of the Test to go, was a triumphant, nationalistic shout of pleasure: 'Gotcha! The All Black That Didn't Get Away'. The photograph shows a focused, calm-faced, All Black winger, Jeff Wilson, his brain not yet registering the disaster that has happened to him, diving for the tryline with both feet off the ground, the force of dive making his blond hair stand literally on end – and the ball is spilling centimetres away from his left hand. His right hand is stretching and tensing in what is an instinctive, unavailing grab to bring in the ball floating away from him like a fabulous, gleaming, elusive spheroid. The ball, in this frozen fraction of time, is still tantalisingly close. Still reachable perhaps. Over his right shoulder, about 20 metres back in the distance, can be seen the blurred features of Sean Fitzpatrick, the All Blacks' hooker and captain, running up in support as ever, his arms held high to pump air into his aching lungs, his face with the hint of a smile beginning to form. Have some phrases of a victory speech come into his mind? For the match-winning try is surely about to be scored, he believes.

Over the other shoulder of the diving Wilson is to be seen the face, inscrutable as a Japanese mask, of the All Blacks' halfback, Graeme Bachop, who is running beside his captain.

And standing less than a metre away from Wilson unmarked, is the All Blacks' fullback, Shane Howarth. If the ball somehow spills back across to him, if it just spills back anywhere nearby, it is the simplest of exercises for Howarth to pick it up and score.

Howarth's feet are forced into the turf of the Sydney Football Stadium like the hooves of a quarterhorse trying to stop and then turn. He is leaning back, bracing himself for the dash, in any direction – if the ball is spilled from the grasp of Wilson. The message of despair has not yet passed right through the nerves and sinews of his body. But his fists are clenched. His mouth has the bared-teeth tightness of the grin of death. For his eyes are looking directly at the ball which is floating away from his diving team-mate – floating away, and with it the glory of an improbable New Zealand victory.

No Wallabies are fully visible in the photograph. For at this point in the play the Wallabies are beaten in every aspect of the Test except on the scoreboard. Over Howarth's tensed right thigh can be seen the blobs of the boots of David Wilson, the Wallaby flanker, lying prone and defeated on the ground, one of the four Wallabies whom Jeff Wilson has beaten with swerves and sidesteps on his dash to the tryline.

The right arm and left leg, only, of George Gregan are visible. His tackle on Jeff Wilson has been made from behind, rather than from the side. And because of this miracle of timing and positioning he has hit the diving winger on the back, with great force. A tackle from the side might not have come up on Wilson so unexpectedly. It might, too, have jolted Wilson's left arm more securely around the ball rather than propelling it from his grasp.

The power of Gregan's tackle has come from the impetus generated by a strongly planted left leg. Gregan's arms encircle the waist of the All Blacks' winger. And the ball is floating away . . . floating away, along with the tackle of the century, into the collective memory of thousands of people who watched the Test live and the millions of people around the world who watched it on television. For every person involved, players and spectators, this moment, frozen in the hundreds of dots of a newspaper photograph, will always be the infinity of 'Gregan's Tackle'.

Time, though, in reality never actually stops. Many things were happening in those seconds just before and just after the photograph was taken. Jeff Wilson says he was aware of George Gregan bearing down on him. He believed he was short of the tryline, so instead of tucking the ball under his arm to protect it from the impact of the tackle, he decided to stretch out and thump it across the tryline. But as he was extending his arms, at the precise moment when his control over the ball was at its most precarious, he was whacked from behind by Gregan.

The tackle was a carefully calculated one, too, In the Test against Manu Samoa, ten days earlier, Gregan had made a similar tackle, going in hard for the ribs, using the theory that the shock to the body from such a jarring, painful tackle could cause the player to involuntarily spill the ball. So, as he was coming across the field towards the corner and trying to line up Wilson as he wove in and away from defenders like a skier on a brilliant run through the gates, the memory of the tackle he'd made against Manu Samoa came into his mind. Corner-flagging, but too far away from the ball to make a play, Phil Kearns, the Wallaby hooker and captain and one of the match's most vibrant players, was praying to himself: 'Make the tackle, George. Make the tackle.'

Just as Wilson was reaching out for his moment of glory, the tackle was made. It was hard and it was accurate. Wilson's back was smashed by Gregan's shoulders. Gregan's arms clamped on to Wilson's ribcage. And, just as Gregan's reasoning suggested, the ball flew out in front of the two falling players.

Women's Test Rugby – It's Just the Start
6 September 1994

Women playing Test rugby? I'd like to see that.

I went to North Sydney Oval last Friday night to see the first women's rugby Test between Australia and New Zealand. The New Zealanders were favourites, with officials talking in some awe of their two 80-plus points victories in lead-up matches and their determination to exact revenge on Australian rugby. 'The men have lost the Bledisloe Cup. The New Zealand women want to balance up the scoreboard,' was the favoured line.

The predictions were almost correct, with the New Zealanders scoring seven tries in a 37–0 victory.

After the match, Mark Ella, the incomparable Wallaby five-eighth and intrepid advocate of running rugby, told journalists that the New Zealanders had played 'technically perfect rugby'. This excellence was demonstrated from the beginning of the match. Australia (the Wallaroos) kicked off, as their male counterparts did in the first men's Test between the two countries back in 1903. The New Zealand centre, Vivienne Rees, ran the ball almost to the halfway mark. She turned in the tackle and the forwards came in as a pack, drove in low and hard, to set up a maul. The ball was then released for the winger, Tasha Williams, to make a dash down the sidelines.

For the next half-hour or so, the New Zealanders won all the lineouts, rucks, mauls and scrums. With the halfback, Anna Richards (the best player on the field), attacking the advantage line to link up with the loose forwards or spiralling out long passes to a lively set of backs, the Wallaroos were confronted with wave after wave of runners.

Before the match, I mentioned to some friends that I was going to watch a women's rugby Test. The response, generally, was: 'Not for me. I like women to be feminine.' This raises an interesting cultural point. Is playing rugby an unfeminine activity? Those people who insist it is reflect the unfortunate

Victorian mentality that women 'glow' rather than 'perspire'.

This construct, that women are somehow ethereal creatures, purports to put women on a pedestal. In fact it demeans the flesh and blood reality of women. For if it is deemed unfeminine to perspire, the freedom of women to engage in activities that makes them raise a sweat is undermined. The pedestal construct, the 'God's angels' syndrome, has been used over the generations by reactionaries of both sexes to keep women out of participating in all the activities that have been dominated by men. Sport is only one manifestation of this.

The rugby the women played was assertive rather than aggressive. The Wallaroos' five-eighth and captain, Helen Taylor, was quick on the break and resolute in her tackling. But, like all the other players, she had to rely more on her brain and skills than on any brawn to make the telling plays. There were several head-high tackles, mainly through faulty technique, one injury and one brief scuffle. For the purist, there was the revelation as the backline movements unfurled, mainly elegantly constructed movements by the New Zealanders, of what a beautiful game rugby is when the power element is taken out of it.

Sinners Are Grinners
13 April 1995
Professionalism was rugby union's secret sin. The unequivocal and measured statement made yesterday by the NSWRU finally exposes and purges that sin.

At the beginning of the Laws of the Game of Rugby Football is this Declaration of Amateurism: 'The Game is an amateur game. No-one is allowed to seek or to receive payment or other material reward for taking part in the Game.'

The heading to the NSWRU's media release states: 'RUGBY IS NO LONGER AMATEUR'. The statement goes on to make the obvious point that the 'rugby world has been remunerating players and coaches in various ways for a very long time . . . Amateurism as a concept is outmoded and should be dispensed with in the modern game.' This blatant and timely rejection of the official stance has the great merit of putting to an end the hypocritical insistence by administrators, mainly in the United Kingdom, that there is some inherent virtue in denying the players who generate vast amounts of money in Test matches a level of remuneration the administrators are prepared to pay themselves.

The obsession with professionalism dates back to 1895 when a group of rugby clubs in the North of England requested a change in the Laws to reimburse injured players for the time lost off work. The request was denied and the clubs broke away from the Rugby Union to form their own Northern League. According to an emotional article written by E. Ensor in 1898, the point behind keeping rugby union an amateur game was to destroy a rapidly growing system of 'petty trickery, mean cheating, and espionage which almost passes belief'. He cited tales 'of ingenious devices, of money dropped into men's boots or slipped into the hand in lavatories by seeming virtuous officials, of tons of coal arriving from nowhere and stopping outside football players' houses'.

The Northern League, which developed the game of rugby league, eliminated this problem of bribery and corruption by instituting an officially sanctioned system of expenses and payments. This system was adopted in Australia when rugby league was started in Sydney in 1908. The Rugby Union opted for a middle-class vision of a lilywhite game, with players to be untainted by any recompense for their investment of time, energy and skill – and broken bones – in the cause of the game.

From the beginning, the opposition to the breakaway rugby league code was confused with an opposition to professionalism. In 1895, the Rugby Union declared that it was an 'act of professionalism to play on any ground where gate money is taken in any match or contest where it is previously agreed that less than 15 players on each side shall take part'. This was an attempt to stymie league's contraction of the rugby team from 15 to 13. Later, when Sevens Rugby was invented, though, the organisers found that they were inviting players to become professionals.

For a hundred years these types of incongruities bedevilled rugby administrators as they tried to square what became a vicious circle – how to keep rugby union amateur while the game was drawing huge crowds to Tests and while rugby league clubs were picking off the code's great players. At one point, the section on amateurism was one of the longest sections in the Laws of Rugby Football. The Laws forbade a player who had 'turned' to rugby league from returning to rugby union, in any capacity. Former players were driven out of coaching and administration, too, for earning money from books about their careers. Trust funds for their children were devised to get around this problem. In Wales and France, particularly, players found money deposited in their boots, a reversion to the corruption of the 1890s. Overseas players in the Italian club championship somehow returned home with well-padded wallets as officials turned a blind eye.

The effect of the NSWRU's historic statement will be to put an end to this sort of hypocrisy. That it was inspired by Rupert Murdoch's raid on rugby league to set up a rival super league is a final irony a century after the Northern League broke away from the mainstream rugby game.

Trevor Allan's Ordeal
13 April 1995

The case of the magnificent centre of the late 1940s, Trevor Allan, epitomises the stupidity of rugby union's obsession with amateurism. In 1949, Allan established the record of captaining Australia in ten successive Tests. His team won the Bledisloe Cup in New Zealand for the first time. Allan, with his trademark head-gear, his devastating, hard, straight running and his punishing tackling, was Australian rugby's best and most charismatic player. The New Zealand Rugby *Almanac* named him one of its 'Five Best Players' in 1949. The BBC described him, at age 21, as 'one of the three greatest players of the century' after his triumphant tour of Europe with the 1947–48 Wallabies which he captained.

To save money to afford the 1947–48 tour to Europe, Allan gave up a lowly paid clerical job and worked on an ice run. With Allan as captain, the Third Wallabies played 35 matches in Europe, won 29 and three of their five Tests. This record was unmatched until the Grand Slam tour of 1984. The manager of the Third Wallabies was Arthur Tancred, a star player for the 1927/28 Waratahs. And so the rugby knowledge and the spirit of the Australian game was handed down from one generation of Australians to another.

The wonderful Third Wallabies, like their counterparts the original Waratahs, had players who had endured the traumas of war. It was a team of characters and a team of character. They played rugby with the zest of men who had faced death and had prevailed. Denzil Batchelor, a noted British writer, in a memorable article on the England–Australia Test on this tour insisted that 'the whole trend of Australian football is to do away with as many forwards as possible to give the ball plenty of air in passing movements, and to discourage ground too easily gained by the punt to touch, which slows the game up with that undignified shenanigan, the lineout.'

The Test, wrote Batchelor, was a pitched battle between 'Australia's cohesiveness and strategic conception' and England's hope that 'one of these days 15 uncoordinated geniuses will be graced by the miracle of enveloping good fortune'. Fifty years ago, then, England had no idea about the way rugby should be played while Australian rugby had already developed a system that suited the Australian type. What is more, Batchelor was so despondent about the low level of thinking from the Rugbyocracy that the odds of England getting its act together were on a par, he reckoned, 'with a chimpanzee sooner or later typing out Hamlet'.

Twenty minutes into the Test, however, England somehow managed a breakout. D.W. Swarbrick was over the Australian tryline. All he had to do was fall on to the ground for the points. 'A dead man must have scored us three points,' Batchelor writes. But as Swarbrick was falling down, he was hit by a rocket-like tackle from Trevor Allan. 'Have you ever seen this sight,' asks Batchelor, 'the whirling into touch, by a side-on tackle, of the wing who had crossed the goal-line? You have never seen rugby at its most thrilling unless you have.'

Allan's Gregan-like tackle ensured an 11–0 Wallaby victory and the achievement of a unique record by a touring side – of not conceding a try in their Tests in Britain.

After he married, Trevor Allan finally relented to the unceasing pressure inflicted on him over five years to join a rugby league club. When the story broke that he was 'turning to league', Allan was still in the middle of the 1949 rugby season. He denied that he had signed a contract with Leeds. Subsequently he joined Leigh for £6000.

The denial, then the acceptance of a contract to play rugby league, provoked newspaper editorials pillorying his 'turncoat' behaviour. The decision split his family, deeply wounding his father, the famous 'Slab' Allan, coach of Gordon and a staunch advocate of the amateur ideals. The Allan family, though, should never have been subjected to this ordeal, and would never have been if rugby had adopted the sensible practice of paying players for time off injured and away from work on tours.

Like most of the rugby league 'defectors' Allan came back to rugby as soon as his professional playing career was over. He played rugby league for two years with the North Sydney club after his stint in Lancashire and then became a respected rugby union broadcaster for the ABC for many years.

Since 1989, the Australian Rugby Union and the New Zealand Rugby Union have lobbied the International Rugby Board to bring in a regime that rewards players financially. Earlier this year, yet another attempt to break the cruel and stupid grip of the amateur ethic for the top players was thwarted. The NSWRU's statement yesterday that 'rugby is no longer an amateur game' must be the circuit-breaker that ends this hostility to players making money out of the game by exposing the hypocrisy behind the amateur law.

They Fell to Their Knees
27 June 1995

In the end, 15 All Blacks and a couple of reserves couldn't defeat 15 Springboks and a couple of reserves, who had a nation of 43 million people willing them on to victory, and one charismatic president. The part played by President Nelson Mandela in South Africa's victory in the 1995 RWC final can't be overestimated. It was a touch of PR genius for the national treasure, the greatest South African, to perform his official duties at Ellis Park in a number 6 Springboks jersey, the number of the inspirational captain, Francois Pienaar. Imagine Jim Bolger wearing an All Black jersey on a similar occasion? Or Paul Keating giving up his Italian suits to wear a Wallaby jersey to inspire Australia to a famous victory? It wouldn't work.

With President Mandela, though, the gesture seemed right and inevitable. It was the great man's way of telling the South African players, and a nation so divided in the past, that the national rugby team (formerly the team of the Whites Only) could be, and should be, a symbol of national unity and regeneration.

On the field, the South Africans embarked on the bold strategy of playing to their restrictions. There was an element of a belief in predestination in this. God was going to give them victory. When He did, after extra time was played, the Springboks fell to their knees in thanks at the final whistle.

Great Expectations, Even Greater Fears
1 August 1995

These are the best of times and the worst of times for rugby lovers, as the code enters an exciting and treacherous era of an officially professional sport. The rule for the next few months, with all the rumours and disinformation rising to the surface like scum, is: believe everything and believe nothing.

A vibrant Bledisloe Cup match was played on Saturday, the one-hundredth Test between Australia and New Zealand. To celebrate the occasion there were lunches on Friday and a dinner on Saturday night with the present players and 50 greats from the past. In pubs and at the various press conferences too, most of the talk was about the contracts being offered to the players and the possibility of a rebel rugby organisation. I was at several of these functions and here are some notes from hell.

John Hart, the man who created the Auckland side of the 1980s, the brains behind the International Rugby Hall of Fame and a member of the controlling board of the Auckland Rugby Union – an establishment figure in other words – addressing a lunch on the Friday was extremely critical of the way administrators had treated, and were treating, players. That a feeling of disenchantment with the administration is particularly strong among the present All Blacks was clear from what they told former players at the Saturday night dinner. One former All Black told me he chatted with one of the best young All Blacks about the contracts and was amazed at how blinkered he was to the implications of playing rebel rugby.

One of the reasons for the blinkered approach may be that the New Zealand Rugby Union initially offered players $150,000 a year. This was then raised a few days later to $200,000 and then again to $300,000. No wonder the players

are stringing out the negotiations. The NZRU made a fundamental mistake by not putting its best offer forward straight
away. I can't understand, either, why the people in the Murdoch
organisation, who are skilled at negotiating contracts, weren't
asked to help the rugby officials, who are amateurs in this shark-
infested sea.

Throughout the weekend, officials were asking journalists
what they knew. Greg Growden and I saw David Moffet, the
chief executive of South African, New Zealand and Australian
Rugby (SANZAR), at the Saturday night dinner. 'What's happening?' we asked him.

'I was going to ask you the same question,' he replied.

No one, apart from the players, really knows what is going
on. Do the players even know? In hindsight, officials in Australia
and New Zealand were too sensitive to the outmoded conditions of the amateur regulations when the Murdoch deal was
put together. The players should have been signed then. Instead,
the formula was accepted from the players that 'we want to
concentrate on rugby and get the Bledisloe Cup Tests out of the
way before talking about money'. While nothing was being
done, the vultures moved in with absurd offers ($300,000
signing-on fee and an additional $300,000 for the season).

The players are being tempted with the contract equivalent
of a seven veils dance by the rebel organisers. They are being
asked to sign a letter of intent now – which stops them from
signing with the ARU – and on November 22 (two days after
the All Blacks' tour of France ends) a real contract will supposedly be offered, if the rebel organisers raise the $US100 million
($136 million) required to run the circus.

Will the seventh veil finally fall, however? Gordon Bray, who
is close to the heart of Australian rugby, told a New Zealand
radio audience on Saturday morning he was confident that in
the end the Wallabies would sign with the ARU. He also questioned the figure of $US100 million reputedly needed to create

the rebel rugby circus. In the early '80s, he said, that was the amount David Lord required for a similar venture but couldn't raise it. Bray's guess was that the amount needed now would be around $US500 million for the first year. That is about two-thirds of what Rupert Murdoch is offering for 10 years.

In New Zealand, at the player level and among some administrators, there is a great deal of hostility to the Murdoch deal. The feeling is that Ken Cowley, Murdoch's chief executive in Australia, is too enamoured of rugby league to have the interests of rugby union at heart. Cowley's contention that rugby league only has to be presented to the world for the world to accept it as 'the greatest game' was specifically mentioned to me by one of the officials closest to the All Blacks at the Saturday night dinner. This hostility to aspects of the Murdoch deal is tied in with the feeling that the Murdoch camp was too eager to sign up All Blacks to play in Super League earlier this year.

'Why is New Zealand rugby going to bed with the rapist?' was the brutal comment made to me by a NZ rugby identity.

---

29 July 1995, at Sydney. Australia **23** (D. Smith, V. Ofahengaue tries; M. Burke 2 conversions and 3 penalty goals) lost to New Zealand **34** (F. Bunce 2, J. Lomu, A. Mehrtens, J. Wilson tries; A. Mehrtens 3 conversions and 1 penalty goal)

The WRC Won, Wink/Wink
17 August 1995

At 2.36 p.m. yesterday in the corridor outside room 5, level 5, of the Wentworth Sheraton Hotel, there was the sound of jocular voices and the calls of television cameramen that Phil Kearns was arriving for the fateful media conference that would announce the future of Australian rugby. The laughter, with its implication that all was well, that a resolution had been achieved, confirmed for those journalists gathered at the conference that after weeks of arm-twisting, rumour and disinformation, World Rugby Corporation had failed in its attempt to take over the game in Australia.

A minute or so earlier, Geoff Levy, an elfin-looking lawyer and the brains behind the WRC, had slipped into the room and taken a seat at the head table. Inside the conference room, the chairman of the NSWRU, Ian Ferrier, handed Kearns a three-page press release with the logo of the Australian Rugby Union at the top.

The Wallaby captain carefully read through the release, which announced that the ARU and the WRC and a group representing most of the leading players had 'reached an agreement on a blueprint for the future of the game that would ensure the players remaining with the unions'. About the only news of substance in the release (other than this confirmation that the ARU had defeated the WRC takeover bid) was 'the historic move' to admit two players on to the executive board of the ARU and two players to the boards of the NSW, Queensland and ACT unions.

The press release ended with a comment attributed to Kearns: 'Everyone involved is happy that the focus will now go back to the playing field where it belongs.' When he finished reading the press release, Kearns murmured to Ferrier: 'That's good.'

The conference itself involved the journalists, in the main, trying unsuccessfully to find out from Levy just what the WRC had lost and won now that the war was over. Levy and Ferrier (who was punctilious about maintaining the fiction that the WRC had not been routed) came back consistently to the assertion that a 'win/win compromise' had been achieved and that the WRC had been a 'constructive catalyst'.

How much, Levy was asked, had it cost WRC to be the catalyst? It was an amount not worked out yet, he replied, but no one was going to be hurt financially.

Did Kerry Packer withdraw funding? Levy was then asked. More clichés were trotted out about the Packer-owned sports marketing company PBL being 'a catalyst in the outcome'. The question, and the answer which did not even attempt to reply to the substance of what was asked, gave the game away.

The WRC could not win any long-term financial backing from Packer and because of this the great rugby war had ended (thankfully) with a whimper rather than a bang.

Reforming the Rugby World Cup Tournament
August 1995

While Japan was being thrashed by New Zealand and the Ivory Coast was being taken apart by Scotland, France and Tonga during the 1995 RWC tournament, Fiji played a vibrant game against England A at Suva, outrunning a side that had defeated an Australian XV only a few days earlier.

One of the few weaknesses of the 1995 World Cup tournament was that the Ivory Coast side shouldn't really have been in the competition, while Fiji weren't in South Africa but should have been there.

In 1999 the RWC tournament will be expanded to 20 teams, so the problem of excluding teams that deserve to be competing will be lessened. My own preference, though, is for a 24-team tournament, with the four-pool system retained. Each side, also, should be allowed to have a squad of 30 players rather than the 26 allowed at present.

This 24-team, 30-squad tournament would take a week longer to play, with each team playing a minimum of five matches. The teams competing in the final would have to play eight matches, rather than the present six. But with a squad of 30, teams would be able to rest all their players for several matches.

Why a 24-team tournament? The main reason is that virtually all the national sides that play a reasonable standard of rugby or have a history of playing quite well from time to time would get a chance to compete. The expanded tournament, in other words, would be a true showcase of the international spread of the code. There is an obvious commercial factor involved, too. Why are the Olympics, with their coterie of obscure sports clustered around athletics and swimming, so commercially successful? Because virtually every country on the globe has an athlete competing. This gives an incentive to a TV broadcaster to pay for and carry pictures of the events in the hope of picking up the national champion.

The International Rugby Board is aware of this obvious marketing ploy, which is why the World Cup tournament has been extended to 20 teams in 1999. With the present 16-team format there was always the possibility that Japan might not qualify. Without Japan in the tournament, the lucrative Japanese sponsorship market (and the international market for Japanese products) was in danger of being closed off. The other major market that has been closed to organisers so far is the United States. The irony here is that rugby has been played in the US for more than a hundred years. The Wallabies played their eighteenth Test against the America All-Stars in 1912 at Berkeley, California, winning 12–8.

In fact, the Wallabies played a Test against the USA before they played a Test against the South Africans. An expanded World Cup tournament would allow the entry of an American team, and an interest in – and, therefore, a television market for – the RWC in the USA.

Rugby is beginning to make some progress in China, too, where the code has been designated one of the official sports of the Red Army. This exposes rugby to a potential playing pool of three million male adults. The Hong Kong Sevens, too, has given rugby an Asian presence and the marketing potential of having a Chinese/Hong Kong side in the RWC could be substantial.

There will be a number of matches in the 24-team World Cup tournament that will be walkovers, of course. But there were several such matches (most of them involving the Ivory Coast and Japan) in this year's 16-team tournament. Even though they are being defeated, my guess is that lesser teams will relish the chance of having a month together practising and playing rugby and having their code getting publicity and coverage back home. The Canadian side I saw being overwhelmed a few weeks before the RWC tournament by New Zealand 73–7 bore no resemblance to the side that Australia strained to defeat 27–11 some weeks later. The Canadians showed how just being at the World Cup can lift players to a level of performance that was previously beyond them.

Flat Backline Theories
August 1995

The flat backline, like monetarism, is an ideology rather than a system. Just as there are many ways or systems of applying the principles of monetarism, there are many flat backline systems. During the 1995 WRC tournament the Wallabies were like strict monetarists and played an extremely flat backline. There is nothing intrinsically wrong with this. The problem was that the halfback, George Gregan, lost confidence and was standing up to pass. The time lost put additional pressure on Michael Lynagh at five-eighths. As Lynagh drifted across the field, the pass-receiver had to drift out to keep his distance. The result was that the Wallaby backline ran across field and were sitting targets for the sideswipe tackle, the easiest tackle to make in rugby.

The consequence of all this was that the Wallaby centres were getting the ball with one opponent hitting them from the side and several others from the front. When the England winger Tony Underwood scored that vital try against the Wallabies in the RWC quarter-final, for instance, Lynagh passed behind the inside-centre to bring the fullback into the line. But it was Rob Andrew, the England five-eighth, sliding with the Lynagh drift, who was able to pick up the dropped ball and release it to set up the try.

While doing research, I came across a diagram drawn up by

Syd Malcolm, the outstanding Australian halfback and captain, on the way the Wallaby and All Black backs lined out during the 1932 Bledisloe Cup series. The Wallabies, from a scrum on the halfway mark, had their open-side winger just inside the 22 using a stepladder formation. The All Blacks' backline from the five-eighth to the outside-centre was lined out in Indian file, in Malcolm's words 'almost in a vertical line behind the other'. One of the Australian centres in that series was the brilliant Cyril Towers. He became the guru of the flat backline, rugby's Milton Friedman. Possibly as a reaction against the extreme depth played by backlines in his era, Towers argued for an extremely flat backline.

His theory was that the flatter the attacking line played, the greater the pressure on the opposition. The reaction time for the defence to adjust to an attack was reduced to fractions of a second. And when the attacking side made the break, there was little chance of a defence in depth cutting off the raid. Towers espoused his ideology of the flat backline in the Randwick clubrooms for decades. The consequence is that Randwick are devoted to the flat backline and are the most successful club team in Australia. The club is the Reserve Bank of the 'flat backline' ideology. One of these 'bankers' contacted me recently to offer his thoughts on backline play. Geoff Mould, coach of the famous 1977 Australian Schoolboys side (perhaps the greatest team Australian rugby has produced) and a Randwick identity who taught Dwyer the principles of running rugby, told me the problem in South Africa was not the ideology or the system used but the inability of the halfback and five-eighth to master the quick hands required to make the flat backline work.

Mould gave a telling analogy to describe how the five-eighth had to take the ball with his arms extended and pass across his body to the centres in one motion. 'He's got to be like an elephant,' he said, 'with the legs going forward in a straight line and the arms swinging across the body like the elephant's trunk.'

The Rise and Fall of a Stylish Man
30 September 1995

In rugby, as in politics, you have to have the numbers to be a winner. Bob Dwyer ran out of numbers, on and off the field. His inevitable dumping from the position of coach of the Australian team, now that the NSWRU has decided to support Greg Smith, is as simple and as brutal as the dumping of Bill Hayden as the ALP leader back in 1983 by the pragmatic numbers men who wanted Bob Hawke to get up.

Dwyer, a man of style, in appearance and behaviour, even though he has known for some time that his number was up, decided to tough out the contest and force the ARU officials to face up to the uncomfortable decision of dropping Australia's most successful coach.

There will be some quiet pleasure over the NSWRU's decision from a number of Queensland rugby officials. They have never forgiven Dwyer for, in his first Test as the Wallaby coach, dropping the Queensland star fullback, Roger Gould, for Glen Ella and retaining Mark Ella in place of the local hero Paul McLean, at Ballymore of all places. The parochial crowd booed Glen Ella. The Wallabies lost to Scotland 12–7. However, Australia won the second Test in Sydney 33–9, the first demonstration of Dwyer's remarkable ability to inspire the Wallabies to win crucial matches.

The turning point for him, and for Australian rugby, came in the third Test against New Zealand in Wellington in 1990. With the first two Tests lost, another defeat would have meant the necessity of a clean-out of Wallaby personnel, players, coach and selectors, in preparation for the 1991 World Rugby Cup. It is history now that the Wallabies won that Test at Wellington, with Phil Kearns scoring the decisive try and swinging his arm up in a triumphant and defiant uppercut. That victory saved Dwyer, Nick Farr-Jones, Michael Lynagh and a number of other senior players. These survivors, the players and the coach, became the hard core that organised, plotted and achieved the greatest feat in Australia's rugby history, the winning of the 1991 World Cup.

This victory and the results in the following three years revealed Dwyer as the master coach, the best in the world, according to many European commentators. Dwyer once compared coaching a rugby team to writing a great piece of music. The backs and the forwards had to work together in a sweeping symphony of movement. In the early 1990s the Wallabies were often on song. For three years, they were the best team in the world and the most admired team, two compliments that do not necessarily go together.

Last season, as well as winning that memorable Sydney Test against New Zealand 20–16, the Wallabies won five other Tests, including a thrashing of Western Samoa, in which Australia gave a perfect display of the running and winning rugby that Dwyer has espoused over the years. The six Test victories and no losses represented the best single season achieved by a Wallaby side.

However, coaches, like politicians, are only as secure as their last victory. This season, the Wallabies played a lacklustre 1995 RWC tournament and finished with two losing Tests against the All Blacks. Despite the way in which his second term is ending, Dwyer will rank as one of the greatest of the Wallaby coaches. He has been articulate, tough, stylish and often innovative. And if his training as an engineer made him perhaps over-fond of rehearsed moves, especially those involving the back row, his teams often played exhilarating and winning rugby.

The dropping of Bob Dwyer leaves open this haunting question, though: Will his successor prove to be the Bob Hawke of Australian rugby?

Open Rugby
2 February 1996

Since rugby union became an 'open' code last year, a great deal of effort has gone into making the game as seamless as possible in an administrative and structural sense. Rugby is assuming a similar shape to cricket and golf, with a thousand or so top players being paid handsomely and the hundreds of thousands of players at the grassroots playing the game because of the pleasure of being, in Kipling's phrase, 'muddied oafs'.

The next challenge for the administrators is to transfer this seamless quality from off the field to play on it. The latest four changes to the laws of rugby help this process in a significant manner. The most important change – or 'variation', according to the International Rugby Board – relates to Law 20 concerning the scrum. A scrum will now consist of eight players. Presumably this definition will outlaw the South African tactic of the halfback and five-eighth packing in for pushover tries. The eight members of the scrum will have to stay bound until the ball is released.

The integrity of the scrum will be restored by this change. The best way to prevent the side feeding the scrum from launching backrow moves to an unprotected blind-side, and to clear the ball quickly to force one-on-one plays in the backline, is for the defending scrum to exert its own pressure, so crumbling the opposing pack.

It is a pity the IRB stopped at this point. The Australian and New Zealand delegates at the IRB meeting wanted the backs to stand back 10 metres from the middle line of the scrum. This suggestion, unfortunately, was not accepted. Antipodean delegates were defeated, too, on the suggestions that a scrum at the halfway should follow a kick going dead; that a 22 drop-out should be lawful even if some of the players are offside but in the process of retiring behind the line; that there should be no loitering in the in-goal area; and outlawing pretending to pass by halfbacks from rucks and mauls.

The IRB did, however, adopt proposals to allow a catcher to mark the ball with both feet off the ground, to allow a jumper to be supported in the lineout after he has made his jump, and to allow the use of either hand to deflect the ball if a two-handed attempt is made to catch the ball. The tackled player, as well as the tackler, must now get to his feet or roll clear.

Academic Nonsense
20 February 1996

Academics know more and more about less and less, or so they tell us. But if the analysis of the matches at the 1995 Rugby World Cup tournament by Gareth Potter and Alun Carter of the Centre for Notational Analysis at the Cardiff Institute of Higher Education is any guide, the definition should be changed to understanding less and less about more and more.

Potter and Carter analysed the 45 hours of RWC rugby and found that the most action in the tournament was in the Australia versus Canada match, when the ball was in play for 32 minutes. The least action was in Tonga versus Ivory Coast, with 23 minutes of play achieved. A second finding was that, with the exception of the French, teams that passed the ball 'generally' lost. When England beat Australia they passed the ball 64 times to 94. Against New Zealand, in a Test in which they were mass-acred, England passed 120 times to 72.

The implications the academics drew from their finding are that kicking rather than passing wins rugby matches and that time getting the ball into play is 'lost' time. Both implications are nonsense. Danie Craven, who knew everything about rugby and had two PhDs, always made the point that there are limits to what the body can endure. Rugby had to remain a game that could be played at many levels, Craven maintained. With rugby union opting to become a game with a small professional top and a huge grassroots spread of amateur players, the 'playability' of the game at all levels must always be kept in mind.

Paul Ackford, the rugby writer for the UK *Daily Telegraph*, would like to see a rugby match set at 40 minutes of actual playing time, 20 minutes each spell. My preference would be to keep the 80-minute framework but for timekeepers to allow, say, only 15 seconds for each restart of play. If play has not restarted after 15 seconds, the clock is stopped until the ball finally goes into play.

The point needs to be made, though, that something is going on when the ball is out of play. The players and the crowd are given time to contemplate what will happen next. All good playwrights understand the drama of the pause. The roar that follows the winning of a crucial lineout, for instance, is an indication of how the pause helps to involve spectators in the drama of the game.

There is a great deal of difference, too, between activity and action. Rugby league is a game full of activity but little actually happens within this activity. The ball is in play when the one-off hit-ups are made, admittedly, but the outcome of these hit-ups is predictable more than 90 per cent of the time. If the actual time play is on in a rugby league match is measured it is about 18 minutes. Rugby union, on the other hand, involves more action than activity. Possession is always being contested, which makes for a more engrossing spectacle.

It needs to be remembered, too, that in terms of the ratio between the time played and ball in play, rugby union has a high rating. A Wimbledon tennis final of five sets, a match lasting several hours, will have fewer than 30 minutes of actual play. A six-hour day of Test cricket has about 30 minutes of actual play.

This gets us to the matter of the team passing the ball most generally losing. The correct implication to draw from this is that there is passing and passing. The 1995 All Blacks, the most exciting team for years, virtually gave away the hit-ups from rucks and mauls and concentrated on putting the ball wide to the wingers. The All Blacks passed less often but scored more tries than any other team, more than 30 in the World Cup. It is not correct, therefore, to conclude from this that because they passed less it was their kicking that gave them their victories. It was the style of their wide passing that was crucial.

One of the ironies of all this is that the All Blacks played a style the Wallabies should have been playing, for they virtually duplicated the game Randwick played when they won their succession of grand finals as the 'Galloping Greens'. When told during this era that Gordon, beaten heavily by a Randwick team he was coaching, actually 'won' the rucks and mauls by a wide margin, Bob Dwyer made the valid point: 'It's what you do with the ball that matters.'

Fragile Talent on Display, and Gone
5 March 1996

There is a row of seats outside the press box at the Sydney Football Stadium for the overspill of reporters. I like to sit there. You get the game, and the crowd's reaction to it, direct, without the muffling of the press-box glass.

As a creature of habit, I moved my customary five seats down the row on Friday night before the NSW v. Transvaal match, the first-ever Super 12 at the SFS, sat down and also claimed the seat beside me. Over the past couple of years, Wanda Jamrozik, a sports writer on the *Australian* and formerly a colleague on the *Herald*, would bustle in, take the seat I'd saved for her, roll a cigarette and ask: 'How's things, mate?'

At the *Herald*, Wanda attracted international fame from an article about the appalling dress sense of the Duchess of York on a trip to Australia. The London *Sun* ran a photo of Wanda in her grunge clothing – tramping boots, short socks, long skirt and nondescript jersey – captioned: 'This Woman Says Fergie Is Badly Dressed!'

During the 1991 World Cup Wanda discovered rugby, and David Campese, and became besotted. Every morning at work she'd ask me to explain the more arcane aspects of the game. Although not typical in terms of lifestyle, talents or temperament, Wanda was like tens of thousands of Australians who became rugby followers as the Wallabies established themselves as the best team in the world in the early 1990s. Wanda entrenched her interest in rugby by writing a colourful and confessional profile of Campese for the *Independent Monthly*.

At last year's Bledisloe Cup match, she remarked with a satisfied grin: 'Two wogs covering the rugby. That's something, isn't it?'

With her Polish background, I knew what she meant. On radio a few weeks ago I was asked: 'What's a good old Greek chap like you doing writing about rugby?'

'This good old Greek chap,' I replied, 'was born in New Zealand.'

For Wanda, the attraction of rugby was based on a passion for David Campese, the success of the Wallabies in the 1990s and a growing understanding of the beautiful and intricate hardness (for mind and body) of the rugby game. And the attraction for Campese related to his ethnic background and the great winger's style, the brilliant running, the inventiveness, the class and the sense that his rugby was always played on the edge.

She identified personally, I am sure, with Campese's risk-taking approach, for it was the way she lived her own life too. At a rugby dinner last year she approached Campese and spoke to him. Her eyes became lustrous and her manner animated whenever she talked about the meeting.

Last year and the beginning of this year, though, have not been good times for Campese. He was dropped by Australia and on the Waratahs' recent UK tour there were reports that he had lost his form totally. Waratah coach Chris Hawkins was quoted as saying he had never seen Campese play so poorly.

All these thoughts crowded my mind as I waited for the

Super 12 match to begin on Friday night. There was a final realisation, too, that there'd be no Wanda to claim her seat. Never ever. Earlier this year, she was found dead in her flat at Bondi from a drug overdose.

As the NSW Waratahs streamed on to the field, with Campo out last as usual, this affirmation came spontaneously to me: 'Play a great one for Wanda, Campo.' On Friday night, though, Campese had trouble finding touch with his kicks. When he tried to run, he was cut down before he could spreadeagle the opposition. The instinct to do the fabulous was still there, as it will be for as long as he plays. But the genius that worked off that instinct is fading.

Walking out of the SFS after NSW's comprehensive victory, a Latin phrase came to my mind, '*lacrimae rerum*' (the tears of things), Virgil's gentle warning about the fragility of life and wondrous talents.

The Wallabies Changing Colour
1 June 1996

The new Wallabies lineup announced tomorrow night will not be that different from those of the past. But that is all about to change over the next few years as Australia's indigenous population and Pacific Islanders begin to stake their claim on rugby. The Wallaby team to play Wales at Ballymore next Saturday, therefore, will be regarded in perhaps ten years time as an historic anomaly, the white Wallabies.

A sociological process, a growing inclusiveness in Australian rugby, has been gathering such force in recent years that it is likely more than half the Wallaby team in the early twenty-first century will comprise Aborigines, Torres Strait Islanders and Pacific Islanders.

This browning of the Wallabies has already begun. Last year's Wallaby back row against the All Blacks had two Islanders in it, Daniel Manu and Willie Ofahengaue. Fijian Ilie Tabua was a

Wallaby loose forward at the 1995 RWC tournament. The Wallabies sometimes had three Aborigines in the backline during the Ella brothers' reign of the 1980s.

The number of Aborigines and Pacific Islanders playing for or having been considered for the three Australian teams in this year's Super 12 tournament indicates the inevitability of the browning process. In the Super 12 media guide, NSW gave pen portraits of Graeme Bond (from Terrigal), Sam Domoni (former Fijian international), Fili Finau, Manu and Ofahengaue. The ACT portraits included Ipolito Fenukitau (Tongan international who turned out to be one of the best loose forwards in the tournament), George Gregan (whose mother was born in Zambia) and Timote Tavalea (Tongan international). Queensland named Tabua.

During the tournament, though, a breakaway with a Tongan background, Toutai Kefu, was brought into the Queensland squad. Kefu played so well that David Brockhoff, the former Wallaby player and coach, said that he'd be a Wallaby sooner rather than later.

'Willie O', Vilaime Ofahengaue, came to Australia in 1989 with a New Zealand Schoolboys side and played a robust match at number 8 against the Australian Schoolboys at Waratah Oval. Returning home, he was refused entry into New Zealand at Auckland airport because he lacked the appropriate visa. Quick-thinking and compassionate Australian rugby officials organised a visa for him to live in Australia with an uncle. I have often wondered what happened to the NZRU official who let Ofahengaue slip away from NZ rugby.

In the past ten years, immigration from Fiji to Australia has risen, and the number of Fijians living here has risen from 13,000 to 37,500. From other parts of the Pacific, including Tonga and Western Samoa, the numbers have also risen, from 35,500 to 52,000. Closer to home, professional rugby means that for the first time Aboriginal players will be able to afford to play rugby. This theory was put to Mark Ella recently. 'If there's a quid in it, Aborigines will be in it,' he said. In the past, sport has been the main way out of poverty for Aborigines. A sport such as rugby, though, which was basically amateur, did not meet the needs of young Aborigines who had to convert their speed and ball skills into a living. Talented Aborigines did not consider rugby an option, therefore. They turned to the professional sports – Australian football, rugby league, boxing and, as with Charles Perkins, professional soccer.

Professor Colin Tatz's book, *Black Diamonds* (Allen & Unwin), with its compelling photographs of the Aboriginal and Torres Straits Islander Hall of Fame athletes, provides a sad commentary on the talent lost to rugby over the decades. There is a photograph of a handsome Glen Alfred (Paddy) Crouch in his Queensland Rugby League jersey, arms folded, chin up and steadfast eyes. Tatz's text reveals Crouch was 'the first Aboriginal footballer in any code to tour abroad. Born in Dunwich, Stradbroke Island, Queensland, in 1904, he began his career as a union player, switching to rugby league in 1922 . . .'

And Frank Ivory, with his John Newcombe moustache and wearing a Queensland cap, 'the first Aborigine to play representative football (in any code)'. Born in 1872, of a Scottish father and an Aboriginal mother, Ivory attended Maryborough Grammar School and in 1893 played rugby union for Queensland as a fullback in a side that defeated NSW. Tatz notes, 'there is a strongish suggestion that the crowds gave him a rough time because he was black'.

And Lloyd McDermott, whose 'parents were anxious that he have a good education to get out of the ruck of all the usual discrimination'. McDermott went to a private school on a scholarship and then studied law at Queensland University. While studying, McDermott played two Tests on the wing for the Wallabies against New Zealand in 1962. Two years later, 'to finance a house, he played rugby league for Wynnum–Manly'.

Now a prominent barrister in Sydney, McDermott is the guiding spirit behind the Lloyd McDermott Development Team, a group of Aboriginal youngsters brought to Sydney every year to play rugby and to be introduced into the rugby culture.

And the marvellous Ellas, Mark ('the only Australian inducted into the International Rugby Hall of Fame'), Glen and Gary, and their cousin Lloyd Walker. The happiest coincidence in Australian rugby, surely, is that Matraville High School happened to play rugby when the Ellas attended it and that a master at the school was Geoff Mould, a knowledgeable coach with a passion for running rugby and a gift for identifying and encouraging talented players.

Tatz makes the point that the success of Aborigines in professional 'gladiatorial' sports has been 'quite phenomenal for a group less than 2 per cent of the population'. He estimates that in recent times, Aborigines have formed about 10 per cent of the playing line-up in Australian Rules and rugby league. This success, he argues, is founded on a hunger to win and risk-taking, and not genetic factors.

Speaking at the launch of *Black Diamonds*, Mark Ella supported this contention: 'People watched us play and put down our tricks and skills to natural ability and talent. But hours and hours and hours of practice and scheming went into making our play look as natural and as spontaneous as possible.'

With the professionalism of rugby now in force, Aboriginal players who start off in the rugby union code (such as Eastern Suburbs rugby league star Andrew Walker) may now finish their careers in rugby union. These Aboriginal players will be joined by Pacific Islanders. Ian Paterson, a New Zealander who manages the West Harbour Rugby Union club, has noticed an increasing number of Fijian and Tongan players turning up to practice these days. He is impressed with their dedication to hard training and their determination to succeed. 'Immigrants have everything to lose, in a sense, if they don't prosper in their new country,' he said. 'These players have an impressive drive and commitment.'

Why the Rugby Codes Will Never Merge
17 June 1996

Two into one won't go.

There will never be a merger between rugby union and rugby league to create a unified world rugby game. The people promoting the fanciful notion about a merger are in despair about the future of rugby league, with good reason. Moreover, these league adherents know nothing about the history, culture and practice of the two codes.

It is a significant fact about the debate that the leading proponents of a merger are rugby league officials. Leading the charge, for instance, is Maurice Lindsay, the shrewd chief executive of the British Rugby League. Lindsay's motivation is obvious. British rugby league is essentially bankrupt. Only money from Rupert Murdoch is keeping it afloat. Rugby union, on the other hand, is flush with money, or potentially flush with money. Already some of this money has been used to buy back former rugby union stars like Scott Quinnell and Jonathan Davies. The next step for the rugby union clubs in England is to begin buying rugby league stars, and then a major rugby league club like Wigan.

Rugby league prides itself on being the working man's game. You can trace the history of rugby league in the few countries in which it is played by following the coal seams. Union tends to appeal to a middle-class and professional audience. As one insider in the Murdoch organisation said: 'Why would we want to turn two games that have their own distinct audiences into one game that might not have any audience?' The economics of a merger, therefore, do not add up.

But even if a merger was wanted by officials from both codes and even if it had the backing of the big television companies, it still couldn't happen. To understand why, we must go back to between 1850 and 1900 when there was a fascinating battle between a number of English schools and clubs to establish the dominant football code. A decisive year was 1863, when representatives of a number of English clubs meeting at a tavern in Great Queen Street, London, formed the Football Association ('soccer' is a play on the word 'association'). The association, using a framework of 10 rules for 'The Simplest Game' written by J.C. Thring, of Uppingham School, set out the rules for a football game in which there was no 'hacking' (the savage rucking favoured by players of the Rugby School rules) and where handling, except for the goalkeeper, was abolished.

This 1863 meeting created the first great divide in football, with the non-handling code, soccer, becoming the world football game. Throughout the 1860s and 1870s, the hackers developed a set of laws (rugby union has upper-class laws) that refined the hacking practices but did not outlaw them, allowed handling, set the numbers of players in a team at 15, created an offside line behind the ball, formulated the role of the referees and codified the lineouts and scrums.

In 1895, the inclusive, upper-class domination of rugby was challenged by a group of clubs from the mining towns of Yorkshire and Lancashire. When their players were not granted a small financial consideration for injuries and time off work, these clubs broke away from the rugby union and established their own league, the Northern League. The Northern League several years later developed the laws of rugby league.

The fundamental difference between the two rugby codes is the simple fact that possession of the ball is generally not contested at restarts in rugby league. Even the play-the-ball follows this principle. The rugby league authorities in recent years have diminished the contest for possession even more by restricting striking out in play-the-balls, stopping reefing the ball in tackles and endorsing second-row scrum feeds.

The result is that rugby league has a great deal of activity but often little real action. There is a numbing sameness about the play. It has been calculated that if play is timed only when players have their hands on the ball (and the uncontested set pieces at the tackle and the scrum are not counted), there can be less than 20 minutes of (predictable) play in a rugby league match.

Rugby union, however, retained a principle from soccer of possession being continually challenged. Play, as a consequence, is never predictable. The continual challenge for possession gives rugby union at its worst a scrambling, incoherent, muddling game. But at its best, and especially with the changes to the laws introduced this year to encourage handling, rugby union has a sweep and flow that make it one of the most exciting and thrilling of all sporting spectacles.

Winning the ball from restarts requires rugby union players to have many skills and has created an ethic of clever thinking about the game. The game, too, is physically democratic (far more so than rugby league) in that the variety of ball-winning contests requires players in some instances who are squat and solid (the scrums), tall and athletic (the lineouts), indefatigable and strong (the rucks and mauls).

A merged code, therefore, would have to decide between a contest for possession of the ball at restarts or no contest. If the contest principle is accepted, the merged game will quickly evolve into rugby union. If the no-contest principle is accepted, it will evolve into rugby league.

Two into one will never go.

A Desperate Victory
15 July 1996

Australia 21, South Africa 16, at the Sydney Football Stadium on 13 July 1996 . . . a beautiful set of figures. Occasionally a sports event transcends the actual contest and becomes a symbol for something much greater. The credibility of Australian rugby was

at stake on Saturday night. Since 1991, rugby supporters around
the world had automatically placed the Wallabies in the same
league as the Springboks and the All Blacks. This hard-won
right of primacy would have been lost if the Springboks had
inflicted a heavy defeat on them. Once the aura of authority and
competency goes, it doesn't take very long for results to slide
precariously.

It's hard to remember, for instance, that as late as the 1970s
Wales was regarded, along with the inevitable South Africa and
New Zealand, as one of the top three rugby nations in the
world. Now Wales is the sick man of world rugby. It is not being
melodramatic to have foreseen a similar fall from grace for the
Wallabies following a hiding from the Springboks. And in the
early stages of the match, this outcome seemed to be a distinct
possibility. The Springboks absorbed the early fire of the
Wallabies, then kicked the first penalty in one of their rare visits
into Australian territory.

Then, instead of opening up play and putting the ball wide to
stretch the impassioned Wallaby defenders, the South African
backs kicked and kicked. In modern rugby, it is hard to score
points when the other side has the ball. The effect of the kicking
was to give the Wallabies more ball than they anticipated. Some
strong running from Daniel Manu finished off with a slick
behind-the-back pass led to Joe Roff smashing his way over for
a try. A scuffle was started by the South Africans as the referee
awarded the try. This provided the first indication that they were
beginning to panic.

The Springboks had gone into the match with the traditional South African game plan, remarkably successful for nearly
a hundred years, of subdue the opposition pack, kick for field
position, force penalties and achieve the occasional try by the
three-quarters from sharp dashes from close in. This style was
perfectly suited to the old laws of rugby, which favoured the
kicking game. It is now obsolete. The proof of this is that South

Africa won nine consecutive penalties in the half and still could not claw their way into the lead.

It was the penalty count and nothing else that kept the South Africans in the Test at the end. But their restricted game plan and the instinct of virtually all the backs to kick meant that the task of keeping them out, while difficult, was not impossible. Despite the inadequacies of the Springboks, though, it was a famous – and important – victory for the Wallabies.

> **13 July 1996, at Sydney.** Australia **21** (J. Roff, T. Horan tries; M. Burke 1 conversion and 3 penalty goals) defeated South Africa **16** (P. Hendriks 1 try; H. Honiball 1 conversion and 2 penalty goals, A. Joubert 1 penalty goal)

The Great Escape
29 July 1996

In the record books, the 32–25 victory to New Zealand against Australia at Suncorp Stadium will look reasonably comfortable. But it was the Great Escape that should never have happened for the All Blacks. At the press conference after the Test, the New Zealand captain, Sean Fitzpatrick, was asked: 'Sean, how did you feel when there were only 20 minutes left to play and you were behind 22–9?'

'I felt like Kieren Perkins on Friday,' the All Blacks captain replied. Then a Cheshire cat grin spread across his face as he paused to deliver the punchline. 'And when the referee blew the whistle for full time, I felt like Kieren Perkins today.'

For an hour, the Wallabies played dedicated and effective Test rugby. Michael Brial hit everything that moved on the New Zealand side of the field, figuratively and, unfortunately, literally as well. Matthew Burke was magnificent with his goal kicking, his taking of the bombs, his defence and his inspiring 90-metre run for a try when the Wallabies messed up a backline movement and looked like conceding one instead.

Burke, now a great Wallaby fullback in the tradition of

Dr Alex Ross and Roger Gould, beat all three of the NZ back row from broken play, proof once again that the All Blacks are the Spartans of rugby: anything predictable they counter ruthlessly but the unpredictable often confuses them.

John Eales won three New Zealand lineouts early in the second half. The Wallabies were awarded six of their seven penalties in this period and the lead was stretched, through successful penalties, to 22–9. In 1984 at Ballymore, the All Blacks came back from a 12-point deficit to win the Test, the largest deficit the New Zealanders had ever turned into a victory in a Test. The 13-point lead, therefore, should now have been decisive. But the Wallabies fell into the error of either not closing down the All Blacks' game by kicking for the corners or not putting the ball wide for Joe Roff, Ben Tune and Burke to run around the lumbering Jonah Lomu. The best way, after all, to convert a 13-point lead into an unbeatable lead is to make it a 20-point lead.

The Wallabies, as they did in 1984, started playing the ball down the middle of the field, particularly with their kicking. Christian Cullen ran one of Pat Howard's hopefully booted kicks back, linked up with Lomu, the All Blacks hit the ruck low and at pace and Justin Marshall was given a clear run to the try-line on the blind-side. Then from the last scrum of the Test Andrew Mehrtens decided against the dropped-goal option. Instead, he looped with Frank Bunce and put Cullen into the gap. When tackled, Cullen calmly placed the ball for Bunce to bulldoze his way across for the winning try.

The match clock showed 1.42 seconds when the try was scored. But the All Blacks allowed the time to ooze away as they jumped all over Mehrtens in congratulation and embraced each other with relief. As the successful conversion was on its way, the fateful bell signifying the end of the match sounded. The Wallabies were left behind their tryline trying to work out how a Test that should have been recorded as a well-deserved and historic victory somehow turned so violently and cruelly against them.

But, as the old baseball coach once said: 'The game's not over until it's over.'

---

27 July 1996, at Brisbane. Australia **25** (G. Gregan, M. Burke tries; M. Burke 5 penalty goals) lost to New Zealand **32** (J. Marshall, F. Bunce tries; A. Mehrtens 2 conversions and 6 penalty goals)

Musings at Dusk
27 July 1996

The players were drifting off the field after the finish of a tight First XV match between The King's School and St Joseph's. Parents were checking on the weekend plans of their sons. A soft dusk was setting in. It was that time when for nearly a hundred years the enthusiastic and committed play of the teams has warmed the emotions of all those watching, when you catch up with old friends you see once a year and chat about rugby and life.

A GPS stalwart, a teacher and a selector, suggested to me that King's perhaps should have run the ball at the St Joseph's defence in the last 20 minutes instead of trying to drop goals. We chatted about one of my sons whom the stalwart had managed on a cricket tour to England some years before. And then he mused about new laws. 'I don't know about the lifting in the lineout,' he said. 'They're grabbing them before they jump now and the referees are letting them get away with it. Someone will get hurt, too, being taken out at the top of their jump.'

Rugby is a clever game. People who support it like the stalwart are forever thinking about the implications of its laws and how the game can be improved. My argument to the stalwart was that when you put the ball into the scrum, you almost certainly win it. Why shouldn't the same principle apply with the lineout?

This season saw the initial exploitation of the new laws result in an explosion of tries. Phil Gould, the rugby league coach, from a position of supreme ignorance, talked about the 'Mickey

Mouse' tackling in rugby union. This is the coach whose team, Sydney City, is benefiting directly from the attacking skills of his rugby union-trained backs, Andrew Walker, Darren Junee and Peter Jorgensen (who watched the King's and St Joseph's match and stayed on to talk to his old coaches).

The point about the Gould criticism is that it did not take into account the ebb and flow of thinking about rugby. Or the inventiveness of those involved in the game. When the new laws came in, the first reaction of coaches was to work out ways of exploiting them for attacking purposes. The tendency in rugby union, but not generally in rugby league – which tends to be a defence-oriented game – is to work out ways of making breaks and scoring tries. Now, however, the deep thinkers of rugby have started to work out ways of nullifying the impact of the new laws.

The King's School were within one break of defeating St Joseph's, the side all the other GPS teams set themselves to defeat. The winning of matches and working out ways of winning matches never ends. In a real sense, the game begins after the final whistle.

As Good as Gold
10 September 1996

It looks as though the rugby community will have to adjust to a dramatic change in the jersey worn by the Wallabies. Reebok apparently has conducted some market research and, surprise, surprise, the research has revealed that there is support for a change in the jersey from the present gold to a more dramatic one involving slashes of green, gold and white.

There is nothing immutable about the colours a team plays in. Moreover, the Wallabies have played in many different jerseys over the decades. A glance through Jack Pollard's magisterial *Australian Rugby: The Game and the Players* reveals a photograph of Dally Messenger in his 1907 Australian jersey of thick and thin maroon hoops (representing Queensland) inter-spersed with thick light blue hoops (representing the colour of NSW).

But in 1905 on a tour of New Zealand, the Australian jersey was thin blue and maroon hoops. Dr Moran's 1907–08 Wallabies wore the light blue. And the 1914 Australian team that played New Zealand wore the Queensland maroon with a huge A on the left side of the jersey. After the First World War, the changes in the jersey continued. The 1934 Wallabies (with 'Weary' Dunlop in the second row) played in dark green jerseys. In 1937 against the Springboks, the jersey went back to something like the design used in 1907, NSW blue with one thick Queensland maroon hoop and a maroon collar.

After the Second World War, the Wallabies wore a dark green jersey that was changed in the early 1960s to the now familiar gold jersey. But even this jersey has had design modifications with dark green stripes being added to and then taken away from the sleeves.

Despite the history of the jersey being a movable visual feast, the argument can be made that any desire to change it now will be driven essentially by the desire to sell more Wallaby rugby products, particularly to young people. Many people would insist the present jersey epitomises the spirit of the Wallabies, it is identified with the team all over the world, and should be retained. The gold colour is a sign of the gloss and the glow of a fine Wallaby side playing at its best.

Nothing dates as much as extreme fashion. It is always easy to argue against change. With this in mind, perhaps a compromise is possible. The Wallabies for their tour matches and in tourna-ments like the Hong Kong Sevens might wear whatever modish jersey Reebok devises for them. But for Tests, they should play in the classic jersey.

For in the Tests, we want the Wallabies to look, and be, as good as gold.

The Coach Most Likely
24 May 1997

As a young man, Rod Macqueen was an enforcer. 'He played it very close to the edge when he was a player,' says the doyen of NSW club rugby writers, Phil Wilkins. 'He was a very hard breakaway. Bruising. Rough. But not dirty.' Unfortunately, the same cannot be said of Australian rugby union politics, which is bruising, rough and dirty. In this impatient, pressured and factionalised world, the same power group which ousted Macqueen as coach of NSW several years ago has now installed him as a human guillotine. He is the blade poised over the neck of the Australian coach, Greg Smith. In the coming months, if Australia fails, again, to beat the feared All Blacks, and fails, again, to play open, inventive rugby (the two failures usually go together), then Smith will be out and Macqueen will be in as coach of the Wallabies. 'When he played, everybody on the field knew he was there,' says Wilkins. 'He was quiet, but you sensed his presence. It's the same today.'

Macqueen's presence is now sensed right through Australian rugby. His ACT Brumbies, a team that did not exist until two years ago, has become the most exciting, innovative team Australia has produced in years. While NSW and Queensland have endured high-priced mediocrity and decline in the past two years, the quicksilver Brumbies have reached the semi-finals of the Super 12, the toughest rugby competition in the world, and done it in style. Macqueen built this team with spare parts, with players left over after NSW and Queensland had had their pick, which adds to his aura as a winning coach.

It was not so long ago – 1992 – that Macqueen was forced out as NSW Waratahs coach by an administration that did not see a great deal of merit in his record of 19 matches, 14 wins and a draw, with victories over Wales, England, Scotland, Fiji and Queensland.

'Some real problems have arisen in rugby that will have to be addressed, problems that go to the very nature of the game and what it means,' Macqueen told Paul Sheehan and myself when we interviewed the coach most likely to revive Australian rugby. 'We are very fortunate that we've got intelligent players here, players who have gone to university, who have careers outside football. We have to be very, very careful not to lose this. We are now entering an era of full-time rugby players and that's a concern. We need to address, urgently, how to keep the education and careers of players going. We have to take a step back and look at how we can keep these values alive. Everything is so new, and it's taking a while for rugby's evolution to catch up with the changes. So much changed two years ago when professionalism came.'

Macqueen himself has stepped back and done some hard thinking. 'I've got to say coaching has never been my life. Rugby has never been my life. I make no pretence about that.' He stopped coaching his beloved club team, Warringah, back in 1989 (after taking them to two successive grand finals) when a pituitary tumour was discovered behind his left eye. The operation to remove the tumour was successful, but left him with a permanent loss of peripheral vision in the left eye. A media myth has since grown up that he is blind in one eye. 'The operation certainly did give me a different insight on life. I remember looking out the hospital bed at a golf course I had run on for years and thinking I'd never really stopped to have a look at the view, how beautiful the ocean was.'

Rod Macqueen has values other than rugby: 'I'm proud of my family. I'm very fortunate to have Liz. We have been married 25 years. She's plays an active role in my business. She's very good with a laptop. She even beat me at golf the other day. It was very annoying.' He is also the quintessential Peninsula man. He was born and bred on the Manly–Warringah–Pittwater peninsula, attended Manly Boys' High School, finished secondary education at St Andrew's Cathedral School, married a Peninsula girl, raised two Peninsula children, Jacqui, now 23, and Scott, 21, played over 200 games for the Warringah Rats and became a life member of the Collaroy Surf Life Saving Club, where he was a member of champion crews and club captain.

'I was still rowing surfboats myself four years ago,' says Macqueen, who is 47. With business partner Frank Mannici, he runs a company, Advantage Line, which has a staff of 28. 'I'm basically a commercial artist by trade.' The company is specialised. 'It's a full merchandising service – design, product placement, strategy, securing space in retail environments, installing displays throughout Australia – that we do for a number of very large clients.'

Away from coaching between 1992 and 1996, his company, his family, his love of surfboats, kept him engaged. So he is a man of many parts. But what about his coaching arts? The systems, the brainpower and the creativity that have gone into making Advantage Line a successful company have shaped his coaching style. Macqueen does not rant at his players, nor often fraternise with them socially. He consults, he delegates, he prepares sophisticated match plans. Macqueen is a cerebral coach, a thinker.

Tolstoy categorised thinkers into foxes and hedgehogs: 'The fox knows many things but the hedgehog knows one thing.' Macqueen's strength as a rugby coach lies in the fact that he is a fox and a hedgehog. Most coaches give their teams set moves to put into play at appropriate times in a match. Usually, though, the moves are easy to read by the opposition. The 'one thing' Macqueen understands is that while a set move should be predictable for his players, it should be difficult for the opposition to predict. The set move should be intricate in its formation and possibilities, therefore, but simple to put into practice. Having grasped this elusive knowledge, Macqueen becomes a fox in devising, sometimes on the long flights between Super 12 matches, the fox's many things, the elaborate set moves, from splitting the lineout into two sections to choreographed backline plays with dummy runners going in several directions, players looping and others coming into the line, that confront a defence with difficult formations to read and resist.

The growing number of Macqueen supporters within the rugby power structure see him as possessing, uniquely, all the requirements of the modern rugby coach: he is tactician, motivator, shrewd judge of character and talent, counsellor, rugby historian, innovator and friend to his players. Before every match this season, Macqueen has told his players: 'This is your most important match of the year.'

Before the match against the NSW Waratahs, he was going into his 'this is your most important match' spiel when Owen Finegan, the abrasive loose forward, interrupted him: 'You said that last match.' But for the forward-thinking Macqueen, it is always the next match that is the most important to win.

Farewell to the Illusionist
14 June 1997

A glory is going out of rugby tonight when David Campese, the 'Great Campo', plays (perhaps?) his last representative game for the NSW Waratahs against the Queensland Reds at the Sydney Football Stadium.

To promote the occasion, the NSWRU is handing out 20,000 Campese masks. They should hand out 20,000 tissues, too, for there will never be a player as mesmeric, for spectators and opponents, and such a prolific tryscorer. With 64 tries in 101 Tests, Campese has been more than the rugby equivalent of an illusionist. He is a match-winner.

The hard, unsentimental men of rugby, the All Blacks, were drilled before Tests against the Wallabies in defensive alignments to contain Campese's devastating running. Despite the constant and occasionally brutal attention, he still scored a record eight tries in 26 Tests against the All Blacks. And in the semi-final in Dublin of the 1991 Rugby World Cup tournament, Campese scored a breathtaking (even for him) try against the wary New Zealanders by running an angle almost parallel to the tryline. Later, he put Tim Horan in for the decisive try by gathering a kick, drawing three New Zealanders, and nonchalantly popping the ball over his shoulder as he was thrown to the ground.

Campese burst like a shooting star into the consciousness of the rugby world when he ran down the middle of the field with the ball tucked high on his chest and his body angled away from bewildered opponents as if he was on a motorbike against the NZ Colts in 1982. He created a legendary moment in Australian sport. The several thousand spectators who actually saw this have swollen over the years to tens of thousands who insist that they were there when 'Campo first played at the SCG'.

Tony O'Reilly, the former Lions winger and now businessman, was once asked if he feared death. He replied: 'No, I've already had a taste of mortality. I was a sportsman, you see.' Campese admits he has been dreading his inevitable fate of having to give up big-time rugby. He has retired as many times as Dame Nellie Melba, only to be drawn back to the security of the team and the heady limelight of the big matches.

The NSWRU equates Campese with Sir Donald Bradman, Phar Lap and Dawn Fraser. But a more relevant comparison is with Dally Messenger, 'The Master'. A journalist wrote a tribute to Messenger that fits Campese's career: 'He possessed remarkable stamina, flashing speed, uncanny judgment, amazing intuition, and perfect technique, all the attributes of the champion . . . he always tested the other chap's nerve and carried the fight everlastingly into the enemy territory.'

Messenger damaged rugby union, though, by being the first star convert to league in 1907. Campese deserves all the honours, including face masks and tribute matches, rugby can bestow. He has kept the faith, with his code and with the running game.

Conquering Melbourne Is Against the Rules
27 July 1997

On the morning of the first rugby Test to be played in Melbourne I walked through the Fitzroy Gardens where a statue of Sir Edward 'Weary' Dunlop stands. Drops of dew sparkled like diamonds on the statue, which is, appropriately, a larger-than-life representation of a man who was one of Australia's greatest citizens. He was the hero of Changi prisoner-of-war camp, where he attained heroic status for his dedication, in face of beatings and humiliations, for the captured soldiers. He was also one of Victoria's rare Wallabies.

'Weary', a lanky and aggressive second-rower, played for the successful 1934 Wallabies, a team that retained the Bledisloe Cup at the SCG by 25–11. 'Weary' had his nose smashed in by a thuggish All Black forward. At half-time he broke a toothbrush handle into two pieces and shoved them up his bleeding nostrils, then went back to flatten the perpetrator of the violence to his face.

Playing for a Victorian rugby side rather than AFL was an early sign of the rigorous and sometimes tetchy moralism that 'Weary' brought to his heroic work at Changi. Victorians were (and are) so obsessed with their football invention, Australian Rules, and so fearful of any threat to its hegemony as the state's sport, that shopkeepers in the 1930s wouldn't serve rugby players. Rugby players, too, could be sacked from their jobs for apostasy of the one, true sport of Australian Rules Football.

'Weary' remained true to the rugby faith all his life. He was wearing his Wallaby jersey when he had his fatal collapse out walking. He insisted in his will that he be buried with his Wallaby jersey.

Continuing on with my walk past Melbourne Grammar School on a stroll through the city to pick up the Bledisloe Cup vibes, I saw an Australian Rules match being played by boys of about 13. With the power taken out of the play, I could see how

the game flowed with a ceaseless current and the way the players, as they do in rugby, have to run on and off the ball.

While for the mass of Melburnians hostility to rugby is
becoming a heresy as outmoded as Jansenism, the diehards,
especially those in the media with a career interest in Australian
Rules, remain intransigent. I heard this conversation, for
instance, between two technicians at Channel 9's Melbourne
studios. 'Going to the Bledisloe?' one of them asked.

'No, mate, reckon I'd be asleep by the first quarter.'

'They don't have quarters, mate.'

During the Test, while the Wallabies were having their best
passage of play early on, I heard a Melbourne radio journalist
ring in a report to his station. 'About 80,000 only, even though
30,000 New Zealanders have come over for it,' he was saying.
'Nothing much happening. How's Richmond getting on, mate?'

The MCG members, too, stayed away in their thousands as if
they had a perverse desire to ensure that the Australian Rules
grand final crowd record wasn't broken.

The teams came out into the inky darkness of the night,
under the great lights, to chants of 'Black, black, BLACK!' and
the waving golden flags in the Great Southern Stand seemed
like a huge field of daffodils rustled by the breeze. There was a
full-throated singing of 'Advance Australia Fair', the All Blacks
did a ferocious haka, the Wallabies lined up steely-eyed to accept
the challenge.

And then the match was on . . .

After, outside the MCG, I came across Bryce Courtenay, a
passionate supporter of the Wallabies. 'The All Blacks are one of
the great teams right now,' he said with resignation.

Despite the loss by the Wallabies, though, 'Weary' would have
loved every moment of Melbourne's first sighting of real rugby.

> **26 July 1997, at Melbourne.** Australia **18** (G. Gregan, J. Little tries; M. Burke 1 conversion
> and 2 penalty goals) lost to New Zealand **33** (F. Bunce, J. Wilson, C. Cullen tries; C. Spencer
> 3 conversions and 4 penalty goals)

Football Drama
13 August 1997

A teacher posed this problem to a class I was once in: 'Over 90 per cent of people die in bed. If you don't want to die, you should avoid going to bed.'

This chopped logic is typical of Dr Barry Spurr's argument that the culture of violence in schoolboy sports is not only breeding a nation of sporting yobs, it is driving many young men to suicide. Dr Spurr cites the 'well-documented' increase in violent behaviour in schoolboy sports, 'particularly the football codes'. He insists that 'violent crime, rape, murder, property crimes . . . have all surged in the past 20 years'. He then asserts that this violence is 'committed largely by men who have been encouraged to believe that to be violent is to be masculine'.

This argument, however, is as nonsensical as the example provided by my former teacher. Dr Spurr's correlation between a supposed increase in violence in the body-contact football codes with violence and suicides among young men is as valid (or, invalid) as relating the increased violence and the suicides to, say, the marked increase in the attendance by young people at art galleries and museums.

To begin with, the football codes are much less violent now than at any time in their history. At the turn of the century, for instance, rugby was popularly known as 'the undertaker's friend'. In fact, it was the prevalence of injuries and the refusal of rugby officials to pay for their treatment that led to the Great Split of 1907 and the introduction in Sydney of rugby league.

The behaviour of crowds at football matches over the past hundred years is one of the marvels of law and order in Australia. Football, in all the codes, does not have a history of crowd violence, as soccer does throughout the rest of the world. There are the occasional violent incidents, of course, but they are newsworthy because they are rare. The worst examples of crowd violence at football matches in recent years have had their origins in ethnic tensions and not in the nature of the game.

Cricket, though, had a history of riots in Australia – more at the turn of the century than in recent decades. By 1932, not even the bodyline tactics of the England side could provoke a crowd disturbance.

The only link between suicides and a specific sport involves, curiously enough, a game that does not have a body contact element in it and which is generally regarded as being non-violent. That game is cricket. Admittedly the case against cricket is based on anecdotal evidence but there does appear to be an unusually large number of former first-class cricket players who have suicided. Cricket has a vocabulary with death in it. When the ball hits the stumps, for instance, the batsman hears 'the death rattle'. Players carry their gear in their 'coffins'. Moreover, anyone who has played cricket knows that a dismissal is like a little death to a batsman, as he 'departs the scene' to the gloom of the dressing room.

The vocabulary of football codes does not have this association with death. It does, though, have a bias towards battle metaphors. 'Bombs' are kicked. 'Attacks' are launched down the 'flanks'. Mighty efforts are required for 'victory'.

There is no history of footballers having an above-average rate of suicides. The nature of football, probably, with its tribalism and its regulated violence on the field, allows players and spectators to release their emotions which, if pent-up, might be transformed into violent behaviour. Aristotle justified the horrific violence of the Greek dramas by Sophocles and others – with their eye-gouging and murders a far more violent spectacle than any modern football match – because they had a healthy catharsis on those watching them.

The dramas allowed a public purging and, therefore, an exhaustion of the intense emotions which might lead people to indulge in violent behaviour, Aristotle argued. If he were alive now, he would claim that the football codes are the modern equivalent of the Greek dramas.

More Blood from the Massacre
25 August 1997

South Africa 61, Australia 22 . . . it reads more like a basketball score than the result of a rugby Test. And the Australian rugby tribe will now insist, correctly, on its revenge.

When a great, almost inexplicable disaster strikes, and the 61–22 scoreline represents the most crushing defeat an Australian side has endured in a Test since 1899, tribes seek a sacrifice to appease the game's gods. Wallaby coach Greg Smith must prepare himself, therefore, for the ordeal of being offered up as that sacrifice. The 43 points the Springboks scored in the second half at Pretoria on Saturday were the most conceded by a Wallaby side in 40 minutes of rugby. More importantly, though, the good work established this season to bring the Wallabies into contention as rugby's number 2 team in the world has been destroyed.

The difficulty in understanding what happened in those 40 minutes of humiliation is that at half-time the Wallabies looked as though they might win comfortably. The Springboks started explosively and put points on the board. The Wallabies came back to lead, scoring one of the best ensemble tries an Australian side has put together.

Then David Knox kicked a huge punt to the Springboks' 22. It was the correct thing to do, but along came Andre Joubert, brilliant every time he touched the ball, who carved through and linked with Jannie de Beer, who produced a wonder pass behind his back as he was being pummelled into touch for hooker James Dalton to score.

The second half began without any hints of the impending disaster. What followed was like a thunderstorm coming out of a clear sky. The rangy Springbok winger Pieter Rossouw intercepted a careless Wallaby pass and raced in a runaway try. This try, against the run of play, turned an even, if fluctuating, contest into a rout. Joost van der Westhuizen, so lacklustre throughout the season, started to run with verve and strength. Inventive and telling passes were offered and gathered in. The Springbok backs and forwards played like the rampaging South African teams of old. The tries flooded in.

What happened to the Wallabies? The effectiveness of the front five fell away. The scrum was shoved around. Ominous signs of this had existed in the first half when the Wallabies tried, unsuccessfully, for pushover tries when the ball should have gone out to the backs. The rucks and mauls became a Springbok feast. The loose forwards weren't able to support any of the runners. The tackling of the backs disintegrated as the green jerseys poured through the gaps.

Travel fatigue, accentuated by the physical torture of playing a ferocious and fast game at throat-gripping altitude, clearly gutted the Wallabies of strength and energy. A long season, with some moments of glory, was 40 minutes too long, for the team and, probably, its coach.

---

23 August 1997, at Pretoria. Australia 22 (J. Roff, D. Knox, J. Little tries; D. Knox 2 conversions, 1 penalty goal) lost to South Africa 61 (P. Montgomery 2, J. Erasmus, J. Dalton, M. Andrews, P. Rossouw, W. Brosnihan, J. de Beer tries; J. de Beer 6 conversions and 3 penalty goals)

A Careful Coach
16 September 1997

Rod Macqueen was careful to say nothing controversial at the press conference which announced his appointment as the coach of the Wallabies. He refused to talk about changes in personnel. He refused to comment on the way the Wallabies played. He refused to make comparisons with the deposed Greg Smith.

'Would the Wallabies win the Rugby World Cup in 1999?'

the hacks asked. The reply was an anodyne recital of how the team had to play to the best of its abilities.

A New Zealand official who was at the Australian Rugby Union's headquarters for the completion of the joint Australia–New Zealand application to run the 2003 World Cup, told me at the end of the press conference: 'If the Wallaby five-eighths is as evasive as Rod Macqueen was today, the Wallabies should do well.'

But there was method in the evasiveness. There is a time for straight talking and, occasionally, for the pronouncement of clichés. And the media will, rightly, insist on informed and detailed briefings later this year. But this was not the time. The Wallaby coach had the grace not to dance on the grave of the former coach. And that was the point and justification of the vagueness of the responses.

Smith fell into the trap too early in his tenure as coach of contrasting what he intended to do with the implied failures of the former regime. Players were not going to be played out of position, injured players weren't going to be played, the Wallabies had fallen to about fifth place in the world and so on. These statements came back to haunt him when players were played out of position and when the Wallabies, after establishing themselves as the number 2 team in the world, endured the record hammering in the Test at Pretoria against the Springboks.

The public image of Smith, one that he promoted himself with his taciturn, stiff, pessimistic presentation, was of a man lacking in emotional awareness. Yet in the ABC-TV program 'Australian Story' last Saturday night, in his last days as Wallaby coach, Smith revealed qualities of courage, tenderness and emotional strength. He showed himself as being a lover of literature, a caring father and, in his younger days, a larrikin in the best Australian traditions. It was clear from the program, too, that Smith is still struggling to come to terms with the loss of his close friend Ross Miller, a former player, a teacher at Sydney Boys High School and a man with whom Smith had formed a profound friendship going back to childhood days when they played intense games of cricket in the park using their dogs as fielders.

This loss undoubtedly affected the way Smith reacted to the problems the Wallabies endured during his regime.

Macqueen presented himself, by contrast, as a confident and optimistic person. This optimism may be what the Wallabies need to go to the next plateau. But Macqueen had one criticism of the former coaching regime, telling reporters he wanted to develop a 'Wallaby style'. This comment implied that this year the Wallabies did not have a style, or that the style was the wrong one. But when the reporters pressed Macqueen ('Is it the way the ACT Brumbies play?'), Macqueen said the style would be specifically Wallabies and not Brumbies and then went on to talk about how players had to be 'multi-skilled and thoughtful' and how they had to 'enjoy' playing in the national side.

And so the coaching game and talk goes on.

Let 1000 Coaches Bloom
28 October 1997

China's People's Liberation Army has rugby union as one of its ten major sports. On November 1, the PLA team plays its first Test against Singapore. So much for the Super League football of Asia. Rugby union is entrenching itself as Asia's second football code, soccer being the first.

Aside from learning the rugby culture, the Chinese players must learn the jargon of rugby which, because it reflects the slang of public schoolboys of nineteenth-century England, can be confusing. How do you translate 'in touch', for example, into Chinese? The phrase is a contradiction when carefully considered. A ball that is 'in touch' is actually 'out of touch' as far as the players are concerned.

There are cultural concerns, too. The Chinese, apparently, do not like to play with balls that have gone 'dead', as in 'dead ball'. And shouldn't a shot at goal be a shot at the goal posts? In fact, no.

When rugby first started to get laws in the 1860s, a 'try' (surely a 'success'?) merely allowed the successful side to have a kick at goal. If the kick went over the crossbar, points were scored. Pedants maintain this old terminology to this day by referring to converted tries as 'goals'.

None of this arcane language of rugby seems to have put the Chinese Army off the game. Its officials recently wrote a letter to the New Zealand Rugby Union asking for some coaches. A polite reply in the affirmative asked the Chinese how many coaches were required.

'A thousand, to begin with,' was the reply.

First Step on a Long March
24 November 1997

The last 40 minutes of a long, hard and often disappointing season provided some hope of better things for next year, and the year after, as Australia overwhelmed Scotland with 29 unanswered points to register a record score in 70 years of Tests between the two, 37–8.

From the time of the first Test between the two teams, at Murrayfield in 1927, Scotland have always been a difficult opponent for the Wallabies. The home side won that match 10–6. Up to the weekend, Scotland had won six of the ten Tests played at Murrayfield.

So, from the perspective of history – which usually provides a fair overview – this was a significant victory for Australia. In terms of the future, however, a greater significance may lie in the way the Wallabies played their last 40 minutes: this contained touches of the hard-driving, hard-running, intense, intelligent and sometimes expansive style that marked the great Wallaby side of the early 1990s.

Just as that wonderful Australian team was energised by David Campese, the Wallabies at Murrayfield on Saturday were inspired by the gangly, shy and astonishingly talented Stephen Larkham at fullback. Larkham, as he did against the All Blacks at Dunedin when the Wallabies scored four unanswered tries in the second half, produced a series of runs that were breath-taking. The first at Murrayfield saw him time his clean-up of an attacking wipers kick by beating the chasing winger to the ball, racing down the sideline centimetres from touch, chipping through with his left foot when challenged, kicking on, out-running the cover defence and then picking up the rolling ball centimetres from the ground to dive across the line for a mem-orable try.

The second run started with a difficult take of a high ball under great pressure from the Scottish chasers, which was turned into an astonishing try as he swerved past four defenders, none of whom managed to even put a hand on him before he scored again. The great Campese himself could not have been more magical, or more effective.

The best aspect of Larkham's genius for broken-field running is that it is effective. Tries flow from his incisive thrusts.

The Wallaby scrum, an object of justified derision for most of this season, shoved the Scots around like the proverbial sack of spuds. Whether this means that the problems of technique that were exposed earlier in the season have been overcome (an out-come to be welcomed), or whether the Scots scrum is not up to international standards, won't be seen until next season. But at least the Wallabies have crushed the pack of one of the major rugby-playing nations.

What was obvious, too, was that the Wallabies finally had the confidence to put the ball wide, to give away the safety of the middle of the field and risk exposing Scotland, and themselves, at the more dangerous extremities. The wider the play moved, the better and more like the dashing teams of the past the present Wallabies looked. The point may be made that this expansiveness and flair involved only 40 minutes of play against a poor Scotland side. Some solace exists, though, for Wallaby supporters and their hopes for Australia at the 1999 Rugby World Cup tournament in the Chinese proverb: 'The journey of a thousand miles begins with one step.'

The first steps on a long march finally have been taken.

> **22 November 1997, at Edinburgh.** Australia **37** (S. Larkham 2, G. Gregan, J. Roff, V. Ofahengaue tries; J. Eales 3 conversions and 2 penalty goals) defeated Scotland **8** (S. Murray 1 try; D. Hodge 1 penalty goal)

The Mark of the Ellas
17 February 1998

Gordon Ella died last week, his funeral being held on Friday at St Andrew's Catholic Church at Malabar. The church is one of those in-the-round designs that brings the congregation, in this case hundreds of people including the leading members of the Randwick Club tribe (Simon Poidevin, David Campese, Jeff Sayle, Bruce Malouf, John Maxwell), into something of a community.

John Donne, in a famous sermon, proclaimed that 'no man is an island . . . every man is part of the main . . . therefore never send to know for whom the bell tolls; it tolls for thee.' We were at St Andrew's, I felt, to celebrate a well-lived life and to reflect on that life and on all our lives. Across the road from the church is Matraville High School, an institution that will always be remembered in rugby lore because Gordon Ella's kids performed marvels for its First XV, showing experts who had a vast experience of playing and coaching a rugby game they never conceived could exist.

Mark Ella used to say that if he touched the ball three times in a movement, a try would be scored. His tries in each of the Grand Slam Tests of the 1984 tour of Britain and Ireland will probably never be equalled by another Australian five-eighths. The Ellas showed an ensemble rugby style that was entertaining to watch but which won games. The essence of the style was pragmatism with flair.

The only time I have ever felt ill-at-ease at a rugby match was on those occasions when visiting supporters coming to Coogee Oval to see their team get thrashed by Randwick yelled out racial abuse to the Ellas. So there was a certain compensation in the story told by Mark Ella during a moving eulogy to his father. One day at Coogee Oval someone called to Gordon Ella, 'Have you signed your New Zealand contract yet?'

'What contract?' Gordon Ella replied. 'I don't know about any New Zealand contract.'

'I hear Gordon,' the wit in the crowd responded, 'that they have a contract prepared to put you out to stud in New Zealand.'

These thoughts were with me when I watched the Southern Cross tournament matches, NSW Waratahs against Canterbury, Queensland against Auckland, on television at the weekend. The closest to an Ella among all the players was the ebullient and ruthless Auckland five-eighth, Carlos Spencer. Yet with the Waratahs, and even more so with Queensland, there was a grimness about their play that suggested a 'day at the office' mentality.

Australian rugby will always need an injection of the Ella spirit.

Golden Rugby
7 June 1998

The Wallabies' sensational victory over England by 76 points is a time for Australian rugby to celebrate one of the game's most complete, dynamic, polished and satisfying Test victories.

There were several penalties given away by the Wallabies for killing the ball, Phil Kearns managed to hit an English forward with a couple of his lineout throws, and some kickable shots at goal were missed. A Japanese master potter, however, always puts a slight mistake in his best vases because perfection is boring. The occasional mistakes over 80 minutes of fast and clever play by the Wallabies fall into this category of highlighting the perfection of the finished product.

The Wallabies, moreover, managed one of Test rugby's more difficult assignments by topping their 33 points in the first half with 43 unanswered points in the second, after the England coaching staff had the opportunity to talk to their players about strategies to slow the play.

Out of 10, this victory rates an 11.

In the spotlight of the massive scoreline for the Wallabies, too, it is possible to forget that such a flogging for England (their worst defeat since their first Test, on 26 January 1871, a 20-a-side match against Scotland) was not predicted by many good judges of rugby. 'England Pose Serious Threat', for instance, was the headline given to a piece written by an informed Australian rugby writer. The article made the points also articulated by Roger Uttley, one of the England management team, that with a strong playing base (about 200,000 players) and a strong club system, England had the strongest playing depth of any rugby nation.

The case was made, as well, that on form few of the apparently injured players would have made an England Test side right now, anyway. This line of reasoning set up what was for practical purposes an unwinnable Test for the Wallabies. A convincing victory along the lines, say, of the polished display in Sydney in 1991 against England, which was the harbinger of the subsequent Rugby World Cup triumph, would have been dismissed as unsatisfactory because of the lack of quality of the opposition. A scrambling victory like last year's against England, again in Sydney, would have been classed a loss, or even a 'moral win' for England, by English commentators, because a depleted England were not put to the sword.

The necessity, therefore, not only of having to win but to win in such a manner that the nature of the opposition is taken out of the equation, posed a significant psychological challenge for the Wallabies. The challenge was met with virtually a point a minute spree before the Wallabies declared at the end of the Test. The backs introduced more new angles to their running than Euclid ever dreamt of.

This was a golden match for Australian rugby.

---

6 June 1998, at Brisbane. Australia **76** (S. Larkham 3, B. Tune 3, T. Horan 2, T. Kefu, M. Burke, G. Gregan tries; M. Burke 4 conversions and 3 penalty goals, S. Larkham 2 conversions) defeated England **0**.

The North Turns on the South
July 1998

A nasty and secret war for the control of rugby, on and off the field, is being waged by the northern hemisphere unions, led by the Celtic unions, against southern hemisphere rugby. The fear of the northern unions is that the dominance of southern hemisphere teams on the field will lead in time to dominance in the administration of the game.

The 'field marshal' of the northern campaign is Vernon Pugh, QC. Pugh was both chairman of the Welsh Rugby Union and chairman of the International Rugby Board until he was persuaded by southern officials to accept that a conflict of interest was involved in holding the two positions at once. He opted to remain chairman of the IRB. In my opinion, he has set about trying to become the Juan Antonio Samaranch of world rugby.

The thrust of the war against the south involves a series of attacks aimed at the open, athletic, winning and crowd-pleasing southern hemisphere playing style that has come to be known as Super 12 rugby. A key date in this line of attack is 1890, when a young schoolteacher in Christchurch, J.P. Frith, invented the advantage law. Frith's invention was soon ratified by the newly formed IRB. Yet the northern unions, in the hundred years since, have never accepted the logic of the advantage law. They continue to see rugby as a static game of kicking and set pieces.

The game, for them, begins and ends with set pieces. The advantage law, therefore, which is based on the notion that the game should flow, has been seen as an abomination. The southern hemisphere rugby community, especially in Australia and New Zealand, sees set pieces merely as a device to get the game going. The game is what happens between the set pieces. Hence, an intelligent application of the advantage law is an essential element in maintaining the flowing game.

Northern referees officiate. Southern ones manage games. The IRB, though, is determined to enforce the north's officious, traffic-cop refereeing style throughout the world. It was forced to accept a merit-based list of Test referees. Australian and New Zealand referees featured strongly in this list, with the Australians, Wayne Erickson and Peter Marshall, being regarded – in the south at least – as possibly the world's best. But the panels of assessors have been told by the IRB to base their critiques of the referees on how they applied the black letter of the rugby laws. That is, how effectively they applied the northern hemisphere philosophy of the game and its interpretations.

The soul of rugby is at issue here. Some examples:

- Southern hemisphere referees will point across to a defending backline when the lineout is finished. The backline can then move forward. The IRB forbids this. Why? Presumably because the defending side can be 'caught' offside more frequently.
- The IRB has instructed Test referees to penalise players coming into the tackled-ball situation if they fall over the players on the ground, even accidentally. The point is to produce a static situation, much like rugby league, at the tackled ball. The southern style is to allow the maul to continue, provided

the non-tackler stays on his feet. The ball is then quickly re-cycled and the game continues.

- When the Springboks and the All Blacks played an epic Test in South Africa last year, the Australian referee Peter Marshall received a scathing assessment for alleged mistakes, mainly relating to letting the game flow.
- Some northern hemisphere journalists have become foot-soldiers in the north's campaign against running rugby. Stephen Jones, a Welshman, the rugby writer for the *Sunday Times*, has been scathing and venomous, for instance, in a number of articles about the so-called froth and bubble of Super 12 rugby, writing how the tackling is non-existent and how this rugby is an entertainment rather than a sport.

The veteran English journalist Barry Newcombe seems to have identified the concerns behind these attacks in an article published recently in the NZ *Rugby News*. The IRB, he suggested, had to assess where the game was going after the one-sided contests between southern and northern hemisphere sides. Then came this ominous insight from Newcombe into the northern hemisphere battle plan: 'Some are already suggest-ing that the laws need revising to stop the southern hemisphere running away with the Rugby World Cup next year . . . At least under the old laws a side had a chance of digging in and stopping the rot. But not any more under the free-flow system operating in the Super 12.'

Paying the Price
20 July 1998

No wonder the Springboks jumped around at the final whistle on Saturday night as if they had just been branded with hot irons. Their 14–13 victory over the Wallabies at Subiaco Oval, Perth, represented a great escape from what must have seemed to them only minutes earlier certain defeat.

It would have been a defeat, too, made all the more bitter

because the Springboks deserved to win the Test. But they had failed to make the Wallabies pay for their many errors forced by a combination of a slippery ball and pitch and some thunderous tackling. They had mounted their own offensive on the Wallaby tryline with about 10 minutes of play left, and leading by a single point. They smashed their way to within metres of the Wallaby line with scrum after scrum. Tremendous defence held out the clever back-row and halfback moves the Springboks have perfected from this position. Finally, realising there were no gaps near the scrum, the Springboks moved the ball out wide. But the Wallaby backs were as committed on the tackle as the forwards. The Springboks were forced into a ruck and the Wallabies drove forward to claim the scrum feed. There was a clearing kick. Percy Montgomery tried an up-and-under which went out on the full near halfway. Suddenly the siege was lifted.

More importantly, the Wallabies had a chance to mount a last siege of their own. For only the second time (why?) in the Test – the first occasion was the opening scrum when Stephen Larkham ran the blind-side brilliantly and put Ben Tune in for a try – the Wallabies ran the ball. To one extremity of the field play raced. And then to the other. Matt Cockbain almost touched down for a try between a group of desperately lunging Springboks. Some more charges at the Springbok line and then a scrum and a Wallaby feed within the shadow of the posts. As the Springboks braced themselves for this scrum they must have realised the fate of the Test hung on the next play. All the Wallabies had to do was take the obvious option of dropping a simple goal. But instead of setting two backs on either side of the scrum to act as posts for the Springboks to run around, then setting the designated kicker deep behind the scrum, the Wallabies lined up in an old ACT Brumbies formation of the backs standing one behind each other.

In hindsight, of course, it's always easy to be critical. But as the unusual Wallaby backline formation was setting itself, the rugby journalists sitting with me agreed that a wrong call had been made. As it happened, Willie Ofahengaue drove from the back of the scrum. He was overwhelmed by the defence. The Springboks forced a knock-on and were able to clear to the safety of the touchline. Wallaby coach Rod Macqueen has indicated that Tim Horan wanted to drop a goal but the ball couldn't be worked to him. This suggests to me that Horan's decision came after the initial move broke down. And the main reason why the move failed is that by lining the backs in single file, the Wallabies gave the Springbok loose forwards a single target to home in on when the ball came out of the scrum.

The dropped goal sitter would would have given the Wallabies a two-point lead with about 13 minutes' play left. Since 1992, the Springboks have averaged 15 points a Test against the Wallabies in Australia. So they performed slightly below their average in Perth. The Wallabies have averaged 13.5 points in these Tests. They, too, were slightly off their average. If this trend of playing close to the averages is continued in South Africa for the return Test (with the nit-picking Scotsman, Jim Fleming, as the referee), the Wallabies could struggle. Against the Wallabies in South Africa since 1992, the Springboks have averaged 18.3 points a Test. The Wallabies have averaged only 10.4. A successful dropped goal, though, would have booted these statistics into irrelevance.

---

18 July 1998, at Perth. Australia **13** (B. Tune, G. Gregan tries; M. Burke 1 penalty goal) lost to South Africa **14** (J. van der Westhuizen 1 try; P. Montgomery 3 penalty goals)

The All Blacks Thrashed
2 August 1998

The 27–23 victory for the Wallabies against the All Blacks in Christchurch is merely the result. The fact is that the All Blacks were thrashed more comprehensively than at any time in living memory.

With the Australian and New Zealand players signing contracts with the rebel World Rugby Corporation, there was a possibility that this might harm the last Bledisloe Cup match. Wallaby captain Phil Kearns is showing the strain of the moment after the 1995 Test at the Sydney Football Stadium, won by New Zealand 34–23. (Craig Golding/*Sydney Morning Herald*, 1995)

Colour and pageantry mark the opening of the 1999 Rugby World Cup finals. (Tim Clayton/*Sydney Morning Herald*, 1999)

Tim Horan, the outstanding player of the 1999 Rugby World Cup, sets up his onside backs for another raid on the Welsh try-line.
(Tim Clayton/*Sydney Morning Herald*, 1999)

Damaging Welsh centre Scott Gibbs is tackled by four Wallabies at a crucial moment of the 1999 World Cup quarter-final. The urgency of the Wallabies' tackling was the key to their success in the tournament.
(Tim Clayton/*Sydney Morning Herald*, 1999)

For the first time in the 1999 Rugby World Cup tournament, the Wallabies start to use John Eales in the lineouts, and, as he has done throughout his magnificent career, he rises to the occasion.

(Tim Clayton/*Sydney Morning Herald*, 1999)

Three French defenders can't stop Ben Tune's powerful surge to the try-line in the Rugby World Cup final. (Tim Clayton/*Sydney Morning Herald*, 1999)

George Gregan's leap of triumph after Owen Finegan's try shows that the Wallabies have realised that they have won the Rugby World Cup final. (Tim Clayton/*Sydney Morning Herald*, 1999)

Andrew Blades and David Wilson after the final whistle. The players seem to have taken coach Rod Macqueen's words about going into battle for Australia in a literal sense. (Tim Clayton/*Sydney Morning Herald*, 1999)

Richard Harry celebrates with patriotic fervour before accepting the winner's medal at the end of the Rugby World Cup final.
(Tim Clayton/*Sydney Morning Herald*, 1999)

The towering John Eales and the glum Queen are metaphors for Australian and British rugby at the turn of the century. (Tim Clayton/*Sydney Morning Herald*, 1999)

Dan Crowley holds the William Webb Ellis trophy aloft from the balcony of Sydney Town Hall. (Tim Clayton/*Sydney Morning Herald*, 1999)

John Eales is right to claim that the victory ranks with that in 1991 at Twickenham against England when the Wallabies won the Rugby World Cup. But in terms of a mastery over rugby's historically greatest side, this win stands out as the most definitive and convincing. The All Blacks were outplayed, on and off the field.

The great merit of the Wallabies' achievement is that the dominance started from the kick-off when the All Blacks dithered under the ball and Tom Bowman burst through, grabbed the bounce and ran strongly into the New Zealand 22. This dominance was maintained until victory was inevitable. From this moment on, the Wallabies played like a side that knew they were going to win. And more importantly, knew how they were going to win.

When the All Blacks had the ball inside the Australian 22, the Wallabies worked their number pattern defence to perfection. There was always a player to knock over an All Black, with George Gregan personifying the last-ditch mentality by smashing the ball out of Walter Little's grasp (a re-working of 'Gregan's Tackle' four years ago) when the inside centre looked certain to score beside the posts.

This toughness in defence was crucial because it frustrated an All Black side that had lost confidence in its ability to score tries. The harder it became to score, the more desperate and less calculating and confident the All Blacks became. And the less calculating they became, the harder it became to score. The dogged defence, therefore, created a virtuous circle for the Wallabies. The longer they kept the All Blacks out, the easier it became in a way to continue to keep them out when it mattered.

But as they showed in the last ten minutes, once the knack of try-scoring was regained, New Zealand looked far more dangerous and likely to score. By this time, however, it didn't matter. The game was well won by 70 minutes with the score-line 27–9.

The measure of the Wallabies' superiority can be judged by the fact that about five or six Australians had a claim for the man-of-the-match award. No All Black could challenge any of these players. Dan Crowley in the front row anchored a scrum that did not fold under pressure, his clever play around the field also giving Australia another loose forward. It was clear the destruction of the Wallaby scrum was an important part of the New Zealand match plan. Even with the wind in the first spell, the All Blacks tried to hold the ball in the scrums and drive on. Yet the substitution of Craig Dowd by Carl Hoeft at half-time indicated the tactic hadn't worked. Eales and Bowman were outstanding in the tight and loose, with Bowman's great, charging try, the first of the Test, setting up the Wallabies for victory with an inside swerve. It was noticeable, too, that with the swirling wind making lineout throwing and catching difficult, the Wallabies went to Eales for the harder, must-win lineouts. The captain snatched them all, demonstrating once again that he is one of the greatest second-rowers in the history of rugby.

Stephen Larkham came across on defence after an All Black breakout by Christian Cullen, slid in front of the New Zealander and took the ball virtually off his boot to stop a try and a possible All Black resurgence. Ball in hand, Larkham was the sorcerer's apprentice with an inside pass to Matt Burke to set up a try just before half-time, the whole being brilliantly executed with no fewer than 19 phases of play.

So, what a difference a year makes. In the last Tri Nations match of 1997, the Springboks massacred the Wallabies as the two teams played to see which side would come last in the tournament. In three weeks' time, they'll be playing for the championship, with the rampant Wallabies already possessing the Bledisloe Cup.

---

1 August 1998, at Christchurch. Australia **27** (T. Bowman, M. Burke, J. Little, S. Larkham tries; J. Eales 2 conversions; M. Burke 1 penalty goal) defeated New Zealand **23** (C. Cullen, J. Lomu tries; A. Mehrten 2 conversions and 3 penalty goals)

O'Neill's Remedy Just the Tonic
November 1998

Most of us know the situation where you have a row with your wife or girlfriend, and then you go and kick the cat. Dick McGruther, the former chairman of the Australian Rugby Union, was the cat in the struggle between the ARU and the NSW and Queensland rugby unions.

Before the ARU board voted to replace McGruther with David Clarke from the NSWRU, I spoke to several participants in the power struggle. What emerged from all the talk was that the NSWRU and the QRU had little argument with the performance of McGruther. How could they? It had been exemplary, as the support from players has indicated.

McGruther's high crimes and misdemeanours that led to his virtual impeachment were that 'he doesn't control O'Neill, and Clarke will'. The 'O'Neill' in this context is the smart, efficient and effective chief executive of the ARU, John O'Neill, the first high-profile and highly professional administrator Australian rugby has had. When O'Neill took over the ARU after the 1995 Rugby World Cup, he inherited an organisation in turmoil and in deep financial trouble. Under the amateur system of rugby administration, the ARU had developed an intricate and inefficient system of rule by committees. O'Neill reduced some 25 committees to a handful; this did not endear him to the unpaid old-timers who no longer had a role.

O'Neill also embarked on a tough program to get the finances of the ARU off their deathbed. He was helped in this task by McGruther, a Brisbane accountant. Tough and controversial decisions were taken. A deal was signed with Reebok that brought in many millions of dollars, for instance, and resulted in the change of the gold Wallaby jersey. This decision by itself provoked fury from rugby identities like Peter FitzSimons, who used his sports column in the *Sydney Morning Herald* to wage a campaign against the 'dog vomit' jersey. But the fact of the matter was that the gold jersey wasn't selling and the new jersey did sell.

Nevertheless, the jersey decision alienated many grassroots supporters. But the NSWRU and QRU officials never referred to this when they discussed with me their objections to O'Neill. They were never able to spell out just what they objected to, other than references to speaking too much to the media and centralising power within the ARU.

Most of the objections focused on O'Neill's hostility to the proposed signing by the NSWRU of the disgraced rugby league winger, Adam MacDougall. O'Neill was extremely critical of the move and said so publicly. Of course, he was right. The signal to players and supporters (including parents) would have been disastrous if the NSW Waratahs had signed up a rugby league player facing illegal drug allegations.

The McGruther/O'Neill team has given the ARU its best period of administration in living memory. Initiatives like taking Test matches to Perth, the MCG, Parramatta and Canberra have been successful. The Wallabies have also been successful with their new coach Rod Macqueen, and the age teams have all been defeating their New Zealand counterparts.

The plotters of the NSWRU and the QRU have to understand that there is a connection between good administration and the success of the rugby code in Australia. The history of what has happened to Welsh rugby should provide a lesson about what happens to a rugby union when administrators become obsessed with their power struggles.

England's Number Is Up
28 June 1999

The Australia–England Test at the magnificent Olympic Stadium, won by the Wallabies 22–15, saw a brave and ultimately losing attempt by the visitors to play the modern game of southern hemisphere rugby.

For most of their Tests since 1871 England have played like a side that has the courage of its restrictions, presenting a huge and often intimidating pack and a kick-obsessed five-eighth. So there was a sense of history in the making when England, playing in the dark blue with red and white stripes of Rev. Mullineux's 1899 side, kept the ball in hand for the first 30 minutes of the Test.

This was the period of play when England looked as though they might complete an upset. But in the face of ferocious and technically sound tackling from the Wallabies, England finally reverted to the mean. The ball-in-hand plays, except for the first try which involved a blatant blocking run by one of the forwards and two cut-out passes, took on the aspects of rugby by numbers. Jonny Wilkinson began to kick when the numbers ran out and with some possession, at last, the Wallabies scored two fine tries out wide, exposing the lack of pace of England's pack.

A massive 81,006 spectators turned out, the biggest rugby crowd in Sydney in a century of Tests, and I had the misfortune to sit two seats from a young woman who screamed like a banshee throughout the match: 'Come on England! Play for pride!'

This somewhat defeatist attitude (surely England should have been playing to win?) was reflected by the players after the initial excellent half-hour of dominance. So we saw Richard Cockerill gratuitously knock the ball out of Tim Horan's hands just before a 22 drop-out. Later Cockerill climbed into a maul with a William Webb Ellis-like fine disregard for the laws of the game. When Cockerill was replaced by Phil Greening, who immediately saved a try with a fine covering tackle on a rampant Nathan Grey, other England forwards in the pack maintained the Cockerill rage and the illegalities.

The average score in the 24 Tests played between the Wallabies and England is 20–12 in Australia's favour. Saturday night's 22–15 scoreline represented, therefore, a slightly above average performance on attack and slightly below average performance on defence by the two teams. And this is a reasonable perspective of the Test.

The Wallabies, although they did not play at their best, maintained the official record of not losing to England in Australia since going down 3–1 to the Rev. Mullineux's side in the 1899 series – a remarkable sequence of victories, given England have about four times the number of rugby players as Australia.

But rugby is not about numbers playing but numbers recorded on the scoreboard, a truth England have yet to really comprehend.

> **26 June 1999, at Sydney.** Australia **22** (B. Tune 2, J. Roff, D. Wilson tries; J. Roff 1 conversion) defeated England **15** (M. Perry 2 tries; J. Wilkinson 1 conversion and 1 penalty goal)

Massacre in Brisbane
19 July 1999

How the mighty have fallen!

On Saturday night in Brisbane, the Wallabies recorded their biggest victory in 43 Tests against the Springboks, with a massive scoreline of 32–6. The inept Springboks gave up four tries and never really looked like scoring themselves. In more than 200 Tests, only a handful of sides have crossed the Springboks' try-line four times or more. Remarkably, only a few months ago the Springboks were the world champions in title and performance, being the undefeated winners of the 1998 Tri Nations and looking for a record-breaking 17 successive Test victories.

With only inconsequential victories against Italy in between, the Springboks have lost to England (for the first time since 1994), Wales (for the first time ever), to the All Blacks (by the biggest losing margin ever) and now, comprehensively, to the Wallabies.

What makes Saturday night's massacre even more ignominious for the Springboks is that the Wallabies never really unleashed themselves. The Wallabies played conservatively. They kept the ball in the middle of the ground and rarely used their big wingers to attack from the extremities of the field. This conservative game plan was necessitated in part by the relatively slow hands of manufactured five-eighth Tim Horan. Playing in that position, Horan is an enigma, a great rugby player (unquestionably man of the match on Saturday) but not a great five-eighth. He finds it difficult to catch-and-pass. But being gifted he made a virtue of this defect by continually running hard at the Springboks, especially close to the tryline.

It is a measure of how much the Springboks have fallen in their methods and skills that the loose forwards and inside backs were never able to adjust to a five-eighth running at them, rather than unloading. As a consequence, Horan was able to get in behind the Springboks' defensive line time after time.

The Springboks exhibited a big, powerful scrum, but little else. This was rugby from the dinosaur era. The backline was incompetent, even by northern hemisphere standards. The first play of the Test foretold its outcome with the Springboks moving the ball methodically, almost by rote, from phase to phase without ever looking like making a break before five-eighth Braam van Straaten, with men outside him, kicked the ball upfield with no apparent purpose in mind.

During the same period as the Springboks have fallen from grace, the Wallabies have defeated England and Ireland and recorded ten successive Test victories, the best run of wins since the greatest era of Wallaby rugby in 1991 and 1992.

---

17 July 1999, at Brisbane. Australia **32** (J. Roff 2, T. Horan, M. Burke tries; M. Burke 3 conversions and 2 penalty goals) defeated South Africa **6** (B. van Straaten 2 penalty goals)

Dying League Pigeons
24 August 1999

The chief executive of the Australian Rugby Union, John O'Neill, was the cat among the pigeons last week with his comment that in 20 years' time rugby league might be an endangered game and union the major rugby code in Australia. O'Neill suggested it would be in the best interests of the International Rugby Board to pour most of its profits from the 1999 Rugby World Cup tournament, about $100 million, into the development of rugby in Australia.

He did not advocate a hybrid code, part union and part league. The reason is that it can't be done. Either you have a continuous and often scrappy contest for possession (rugby union), or you have certainty of possession and an often one-dimensional man–on–man contest (rugby league). These subtleties escaped the pigeons, the rugby league writers and broadcasters, who fluttered into print and over the airways condemning O'Neill without bothering to read or understand what he was saying. The pigeons pointed to the upsurge in crowds, the best since the Super League war began, and the tremendous television ratings that State of Origin matches achieve.

These flustered cooings of the pigeons evoke no sympathy from union supporters, who have had 92 years of league officials and journalists in Australia trying to destroy their code. Union players who were enticed to league to pay their mortgages were called 'converts', as if they had come across to the one true faith. Rugby union players were disparaged, too, as not being as tough, skilful or professional as their league counterparts. But when league players like Willie Carne came across to union they couldn't make the grade.

Then in 1995 league tried to destroy union with the announcement that any league club that bought a union player could fund the transfer without affecting its salary cap. This was an invitation to the league clubs to take all the talent out of rugby union. This decision coincided with, and was part of, the expansion of the NSW Rugby League into a 20-team competition. The league pigeons wrote and broadcast stories predicting the demise of union in New Zealand and the Pacific Islands because the Auckland Warriors would replace the All Blacks as national icons.

Five years later, this trumpeting has become a case of once were Warriors. Rugby union was saved by the Rugby World Cup in South Africa in 1995. During the tournament came the announcement of the $700 million News Limited deal that gave rugby the money and the television coverage through Foxtel to become a successful and expanding professional game.

League's comparative advantage over union until 1995 was that it was a professional game. Players could make a living out of it. The public also invested a greater worth in a professional, rather than an amateur, product. That advantage has gone. Now union has the comparative advantage because it is a global game. The Rugby World Cup tournament in Britain in October will be the biggest international sporting event in the world for 1999. The television audience in Australia for the Wallabies playing the All Blacks at the Olympic Stadium on Saturday night will not match those for the State of Origin matches, in Australia. But out of Australia there is a potential audience of 300 million viewers.

In the long run, possibly within 20 years, a sport that attracts 300 million viewers around the world for its big matches against, say, three million in Australia, should emerge in the era of globalisation as the dominant product.

This is O'Neill's point.

Waltzing Wallabies
30 August 1999
With rain falling, giving the illusion to the world-record crowd of 107,042 at the Olympic Stadium that they were watching through a screen of glistening pearls, Matt Burke calmly kicked

a penalty minutes from full-time to give the Wallabies a 28–7 lead and the biggest winning margin achieved by any side in a Test against the All Blacks.

For 71 years the 17–0 defeat by the Springboks at Durban in 1928 had stood as the blackest day in New Zealand rugby. Until Saturday night's showing, the Wallabies' best result against the All Blacks was a 26–10 win in Sydney in 1980.

Before the Test began and at the beginning of the second half, John Williamson stirred the massive crowd into full-throated renditions of 'Waltzing Matilda'. Australian rugby has been looking for most of this century for a patriotic response to the haka. The response may have been found. It is tempting to say the Wallabies waltzed to victory. But, in fact, the victory and the retention of the Bledisloe Cup were gained the hard way. They were based on ferocious defence.

The winning margin for the Wallabies seemed to come almost accidentally. They were favoured by a 5–2 penalty count after 10 minutes, with Matt Burke kicking two penalties. Then Andrew Mehrtens scored with a 60-metre run after the All Blacks' loose forwards confused George Gregan at a scrum. The All Black five-eighth scooted down the blind-side, beat Gregan's attempted covering tackle, dummied Matt Burke and forced down near the posts.

The All Blacks seemed to have the game under control. They surged back after the kick-off with Christian Cullen, Tana Umaga, Justin Marshall and later Jeff Wilson almost crossing for tries. The defence held. Mehrtens missed an easy penalty. And as suddenly as the All Black dominance had been asserted, it disappeared. A try to Mark Connors for the Wallabies from a thunderous rolling maul right on half-time provided the killer thrust.

Then as the second half began, the rain came. The All Blacks started to drop passes under the pressure of having to handle a slippery ball and a defence that was picking them up and dumping them on the ground. The Wallaby pack, so slow and passionless against the Springboks two weeks earlier, held its scrum and smashed the All Blacks in the rucks and mauls. Rod Kafer played superbly in his first Test. With his first touch he threw a cut-out pass to outside-centre Daniel Herbert. He sent soaring up-and-unders into the glare of the stadium lights. He flick-passed. He skidded long kicks into the corners when it came time to close down the game.

Toutai Kefu resurrected his running game. Two of his charges early in the Test found holes in the opposing defensive line and created doubts about the mastery of the All Blacks that were intensified as Burke calmly kicked seven penalties.

Can the Wallabies now transfer the spirit of 'Waltzing Matilda' to the stadiums of Britain for the 1999 Rugby World Cup?

> **28 August 1999, at Sydney.** Australia **28** (M. Connors 1 try; M. Burke 1 conversion and 7 penalty goals) defeated New Zealand **7** (A. Mehrtens 1 try and 1 conversion)

Sitting on Defence
8 December 1999

Is rugby's great divide, the southern and northern hemisphere split, finally at an end?

The five-day International Rugby Board 'Conference on the Game' ended in Sydney on Monday with journalists offered rare, informal access to a clutch of distinguished coaches (including Rod Macqueen, Ian McGeechan, Nick Mallett and Graham Henry), a blast of referees (Peter Marshall, Andre Watson, Colin Hawke) and leading officials and former players (Sean Fitzpatrick, Jeremy Guscott).

There were 60 delegates, and one was tempted to paraphrase a line from President John F. Kennedy, that this was the greatest collection of rugby brains since Danie Craven walked the grounds of Stellenbosch University by himself. The task of the conference was to produce recommendations about changes to rugby laws that should be approved by the IRB. And the general impression was that while the 1999 Rugby World Cup produced memorable matches, notably the France–New Zealand, Australia–South Africa semi-finals, defence was too dominant in deciding the outcome of most games.

A meeting of South African, New Zealand and Australian Rugby (SANZAR) officials earlier this month produced a list of recommendations designed to create more space for teams with the ball. Its key recommendation was the requirement for players at the tackle to come into the ruck or maul from behind the ball. The IRB conference took up the SANZAR recommendations and added several others.

At the end of it, IRB game-development manager Lee Smith explained to a small gathering of journalists what had been decided. He was in shorts and sports shirt and his friendly, open manner could not have been further removed from the 'old farts' accusation levelled by Will Carling at officials in 1995. The main changes recommended were for the 'use-it-or-lose-it' law to be applied to scrums, which would encourage number 8s to pick and run when a scrum began to screw. Another recommendation was that mauls could be pulled down, and lineout alterations were proposed to allow for steadier jumping and more options for the side winning the ball.

The conference had endorsed SANZAR's tackled ball recommendation because with the present law, which allowed players to jump in front of the ball before the ruck formed, referees can never be wrong, no matter which side they penalised. Ireland and Scotland, notable for their resistance to change, supported SANZAR on this recommendation. Russell Trotter, the ARU referee manager, told me a trial on Sunday, using NSW under-19 representatives, showed the tackled ball recommendation greatly improved flow and continuity of play.

I wandered into the dining room and came across Tim

Gresson, the IRB's referee committee chairman. He had an important message. The 'myth' of the great rugby divide between north and south had been killed off, if it ever existed, he said. The conference delegates discarded personal agendas and concentrated on the best outcomes for rugby. Gresson called over Syd Millar, IRB technical committee chairman, and Allan Hosie, IRB laws committee chairman, to confirm this. Both agreed the northern and southern hemisphere division was over.

'When will we see the conference's recommendations in place?' I asked. In time for the Super 12 and Six Nations tournament in 2000?

'Well, there is the problem of process,' I was told. There are 80 nations affiliated with the IRB and they have to be given a chance to respond. There was no guarantee, therefore, about a quick adoption by the IRB of the conference recommendations.

Rod Macqueen is right, therefore, to link the credibility of the IRB with an approval of the recommendations in time for the Super 12 trials in February 2000. 'The ball really is in the IRB's court,' he said.

Towards 2003 and All That
January 2000

Jeremy Guscott finished his Test career for England by scoring an 80-metre runaway try against Tonga in the 1999 Rugby World Cup tournament. Then he predicted that a British team would win the next Rugby World Cup in Australia and New Zealand in 2003. There is as much chance of this happening as Guscott himself coming out of retirement and scoring an 80-metre try against the Wallabies in 2003.

The 1999 RWC tournament was the first held since rugby went professional. What is revealed is that going into the twenty-first century the three major southern hemisphere countries have embraced professionalism in the right way. The players are fit, mentally and physically. The coaching staffs have developed clever technological devices to plot the way their opponents are playing and to devise counterattacks. And the rugby community in these three countries, the thousands of players not playing at the elite level, the hundreds of coaches, the millions of supporters, the referees and, it has to be said, the rugby writers, all understand the best practice in rugby as it has evolved over the decades.

The British rugby community (with the exception of the French and perhaps the Welsh), and especially the British Rugbyocracy, still see rugby in terms of the nineteenth century, rugby as football with hacking and a bit of handling, but not too much handling. They see rugby as being fundamentally a kicking/handling game when the southern hemisphere countries see rugby as a handling/running/kicking game. The results achieved by the southern hemisphere countries throughout the twentieth century suggest that they are right and the Rugbyocracy is wrong. And the six or so major reforms to the laws of the game since the 1860s have been characterised by a meandering resolution (despite the continued opposition of the Rugbyocracy) towards rugby being a handling/running/kicking game.

Going into the twenty-first century it is safe to say that Scotland and Ireland will not win the William Webb Ellis trophy within our lifetimes. Yet these two countries – plus England, as the first of the Test-playing countries – have an inordinate representation within the IRB. Wales, like Scotland and Ireland, is relying heavily on imports, Welsh only by the accident of the birth of one of the players' grandparents. And in the case of the four teenage South Africans they are recruiting, without even blood ties. Like Scotland and Ireland, the Welsh seem to have no idea about the realities of modern rugby. Their officials have rejected the calls from the New Zealander, Graham Henry ('The Great Redeemer') for British referees to officiate in the southern hemisphere manner. Foul play remains the norm in the British game, with administrators trying to stop the imposition of a sin-bin. The Welsh management proclaimed that its side in the 1999 RWC was the fittest Wales had ever fielded. But David Campese was right when he accused the Welsh players of being too fat.

The only British side that has a hope of winning a future RWC tournament is England, rugby's great under-achiever. But this won't happen in 2003 at Sydney's Olympic Stadium. England rugby has the soccer disease of not playing well away from home. England had its chance in 1999 when it could have had a semi-final at Twickenham. The next time England will be a RWC contender will be when the RWC tournament is played in Europe, probably in France in 2007.

Even then England will be a long shot because the team rarely rises to the greatest of occasions. But with more registered adult players than Australia, New Zealand and South Africa combined and with 30,000 players left over, England should always be competitive. Unfortunately, its rugby community has embraced professionalism with the same unthinking stupidity as the British cricket authorities. Like cricket, the rugby structure the British unions have allowed to develop since 1995 rewards lacklustre journeymen players.

The future for British rugby lies in the Rugbyocracy acknowledging that for 130 years it has got its thinking and practice wrong on the way rugby should be played. If the Rugbyocracy does this England, at least, will become a major player in world rugby on the field and off the field.

Use It Or Lose It
January 2000

The news that the International Rugby Board has accepted the law changes adopted by the Sydney Conference on the Game came to Australia through the laconic publication of an agency news story from Dublin. John Eales was quoted as supporting the changes (which was the correct response) which will see new sin-bin, lineout, scrum and tackle laws introduced for the

2000 Super 12 season and, significantly, for the 2000 Six Nations tournament.

The changes will undoubtedly quicken up rugby. They will give the momentum of play to teams that try to do something with the ball. In this sense, the law changes represent another and large step in the evolution of rugby from a game that primarily rewards kicking to a game that primarily rewards running with the ball in hand.

To take one example from the new laws: scrums will see a 'use it or lose it' principle applied, so if a scrum is wheeled more than 90 degrees or becomes stagnant forcing repeated resets, the team in possession will ultimately lose the ball.

In the continuing debate over the theory of rugby, this application of 'use it or lose it' to scrums as well as mauls represents an evolution in thinking about rugby that is on a par with the evolution of man from the apes. The 'use it or lose it' principle, by definition, is about getting on with the game and not allowing it to be bogged down with endless set pieces. In this respect, it is allied with the adjustments made to the lineout reforms, with players allowed to pre-grip jerseys before the ball is thrown in.

The Rugbyocracy, in favour of set pieces, has been prepared to defend its position with, on occasions, venomous rhetoric. I know this from personal experience. In 1999 I wrote an article in the *Herald* taking Paul Ackford to task for attacking the modern lineout laws. Ackford complained that the reformed laws took the brawling for possession out of lineout play and made them too predictable. Ackford, the rugby correspondent for the (UK) *Sunday Telegraph*, and a vigorous defender of old rugby, also pined for the days of 3–3 slogs in the mud.

I pointed out in my article that with the lineout reforms it was still possible to win the ball against the throw. But jumpers had to be clever to do so. I made the further point that under the old lineout laws about 80 per cent of the lineouts in some of the games in the 1995 World Cup tournament were inconclusive.

No game with pretensions to being a worldwide entertainment, I argued, could prosper with this messing about with what should be restarts.

A short time after this article appeared I got a phone call from Gary Carr, a sports journalist with the ABC. 'Have you read "Planet Rugby" recently?' he asked.

I told him I hadn't.

'Mate,' he said, 'you'd better read what Stephen Jones has written about you. It's a disgrace.'

So I called up the 'Planet Rugby' web site and was shocked at Jones's splenetic and personal attack. To begin with, he identified me with a character invented by a so-called British comedian Harry Enfield, 'Stavros, a dodgy Greek owner of a dodgy Greek kebab shop'. The implication was that my background was so woggish that I couldn't possibly write intelligently about rugby, or anything else. 'Some of my colleagues in the media covering the England rugby tour,' Jones wrote, 'and reading one of the grotesques last week in the *Sydney Morning Herald* actually suggested that Zavos was a real person. Very funny. Like Loadsamoney, no one can be that execrable. And how can he exist?'

Jones, who also occupies the lofty perch of rugby writer for the *Sunday Times*, claimed that I was an 'antipodean newspaperman strident of voice and excruciatingly bereft of a grasp of any aspect of modern rugby'. That lack of understanding, he went on, was demonstrated by the way 'Spiro Zavos prognosticates on the modern day lineout. He follows the line that the dire, sanitised, boring forklift of the current period is in some way good for the game. He attacks the views expressed by Paul Ackford who wants old-style facets to return to such a contest, not something your grandmother could win.'

Jones ended with a few drops of an attack on Super 12 rugby 'which violated every concept of the game and produced rugby of a feather-like intensity'.

At the Conference on the Game, Tim Gresson told me that

the northern hemisphere and southern hemisphere split was over. I was agnostic. But the haste with which the IRB adopted the new laws and the fact that they apply to the Six Nations tournament during a current European season suggests that the good of the game has possibly moved ahead of power play considerations, as far as the IRB is concerned.

If this is true it will mean, thankfully, the end to the hegemony of the Rugbyocracy. This will mean, in turn, that rugby will prosper in Europe, as it has in Australia, South Africa and New Zealand.

PART V: Australian Rugby into the Twenty-first Century

'Making a Little Winter Love'

What a deale of cold busines doth a man mis-spend the better part
of life in! in scattering complements, tendring visits, gathering and
venting news, following Feasts and Playes, making a little winter
love in a darke corner — Ben Jonson, 1572–1637

Billing the World Cup

On 7 January 2000 the Australian Rugby Union sent out a press
release to all the sporting media in Australia announcing:' "Bill"
to Visit Troops in East Timor'. 'Bill' is the William Webb Ellis trophy, the gold cup presented to the winning team in the 1999
Rugby World Cup tournament. Major-General Peter Cosgrove,
the commander of the Australian-led INTERFET forces in East
Timor, had sent the Wallabies an inspirational message before
their RWC final at Cardiff. 'There's no question,' said Dan
Crowley, one of the cup-bearers to East Timor, 'that the mes-
sages from East Timor had a big effect on the players. Here were
people involved in a difficult and potentially life-threatening
mission taking the trouble to encourage us. Peter Cosgrove's
message was unbelievably powerful.' Crowley suggested jocu-
larly, too, that they should 'hang Bill from the bottom of a Black
Hawk helicopter' so that as many as possible of the 9000
INTERFET force could see the trophy.

In the end, the players were transported around the various
posts throughout East Timor by helicopter and the sacred
golden trophy was lovingly exposed to the troops to gaze on
wherever they landed. Some New Zealand troops, in an act of
defiance and thwarted proprietorship, welcomed the trophy
with a stirring haka.

After the visit to East Timor, throughout 2000 the William
Webb Ellis trophy was transported around Australia, starting at
Parramatta in the western suburbs of Sydney, then going bush to
places like Wagga Wagga and Dubbo, on to Brisbane for the
World Series Sevens Tournament, to Adelaide, Melbourne,

Tasmania, Western Australia and finally back to Sydney in time for exhibition at the Sydney Royal Easter Show. This voyage of exploitation followed the earlier tickertape parades for the Wallabies and the William Webb Ellis trophy in the major cities.

There is clearly method in this determination by the ARU to show off the William Webb Ellis trophy as Australian rugby's most sacred relic, to as many Australians as possible. And this relates to the declaration made by John Eales as the Wallabies emerged, with the trophy, into the concourse at Sydney Airport after returning from their RWC triumph. 'This cup,' Eales told the crowd of supporters, holding the trophy aloft, 'is Australia's cup.' Australian rugby wants to identify rugby and its icons with Australian patriotism and nationalism as deeply as possible.

Britain transported its convicts to Australia. Australian rugby was reciprocating this malign gesture by transporting the World Cup trophy around Australia in the manner of a Roman general showing off his spoils of war.

From the beginning of rugby in Australia there has always been a sense that when Australians were playing it they wanted to make what was a British game created by upper-class public school boys into an Australian game. As early as 1908, in fact, there was talk of 'cutting the painter' with the IRB if Australian rugby interests continued to be thwarted.

A persistent theme in the practice and rhetoric of Australian rugby has been the identification of rugby and rugby players with Australia's involvement in the various wars throughout the twentieth century. Rod Macqueen, for instance, acknowledged this connection between rugby and the blood sacrifice of young Australians on the battlefields by taking the Wallabies to see war graves in France during the 1998 tour of Europe. Major-General Cosgrove's message to the Wallabies before the 1999 RWC final was made in a similar spirit.

Australian rugby teams, too, contested Test matches against England at a time when Australia as a constitutional entity did not exist. There was no Australian anthem and no Australian flag in 1899. The concept of a distinct Australian citizenship did not come into force until 1949. Australian rugby, therefore, had established its identity as an Australian construct before there was an Australia. This identification of rugby in Australia with Australian values – inclusiveness, bravery, cleverness, mateship, optimism and toughness – was one of the reasons, too, why Dr Moran rejected nicknames such as 'Rats' and 'Rabbits' for the Australian team in 1908. He did not want the team characterised as a rodent or a pest. He wanted something that was uniquely Australian, the Wallaby.

The British view of Australia, expressed through the actions of the Rugbyocracy, is summed up by the poet Samuel Coleridge who envisaged Australia as 'Old England with some elbow room'. This is a vision that does not conform to the way Australians view themselves. Or the way the Australian rugby community views every aspect of rugby.

David Malouf, in his 1998 Boyer Lectures, makes the point that once the colonies in Australia were established, the settlers and later the native-born inhabitants began to see themselves, in cultural terms, 'not as colonial but as confidently provincial, standing in the same relationship to London as the great provincial cities of England'. This identity, Malouf suggests, was expressed in two (conflicting) ways, either as confidence about Australia being in the world or anxiety about Australia's place in the world. Such a conflict of identity, he argues, means that Australia in a metaphorical sense is forever coming of age after being abandoned, perhaps, by a bad stepmother, Britain.

We can see these themes expressed by Malouf working themselves out in the difficult relationship Australian rugby has had with the Rugbyocracy. There has been a contrariness, ill-will and a tendency to bicker that lasted throughout the twentieth century. This endless rowing will probably be resolved early in the twenty-first century, in favour of the southern hemisphere way of playing and administrating rugby.

The symbol of the way Australian rugby is trying to Australianise the Home unions may be seen with the successful campaign to change the name of the RWC trophy from its Rugbyocracy intonations of 'William Webb Ellis' to the Ocker, good-bloke 'Bill'. It was the 1991 RWC-winning Wallabies who first labelled the trophy 'Bill'. But it was really the world championship victory in 1999 that gave the Australian rugby community the confidence to make the new name stick. So the players like Dan Crowley now routinely talk about 'Bill' as if the trophy were a person, and an Australian person at that. The ARU is pushing to establish (on an informal basis, obviously) a name change for the trophy as far as Australians are concerned.

My guess is that when the 2003 World Cup tournament is played in Australia most Australians will, naturally, call the trophy 'Bill'.

Australian Rugby's Five Stages

Aristotle postulated the theory that all institutions go through a similar life-cycle of birth, growth, maturity, decay and death. On this pattern, Australian rugby is still very much on the growth section of its life-cycle, as it enters its fifth stage of development, a stage that begins with the new century.

The first stage of Australian rugby, from the 1860s to 1914, was an era of the Cultural Cringe. Australian rugby saw England as the centre of the rugby universe and the fount of all knowledge and leadership in the game. There were exceptions to this generalisation, of course. Dr Herbert Moran was conscious of the need for Australian rugby to develop its own identity. But when important matters regarding the governance of the game arose, Australian administrators accepted the dictates imposed from Britain, even when – as in the case of professionalism – the dictate was against the interests of Australian players and the cause of rugby's advancement in Australia.

There was an element of the inevitable in some of this. The laws of rugby were developed in Britain and rugby players in Australia, until 1890 when the International Rugby Board was formed, had few options but to follow what had been laid down in Britain. To expect these rugby players to 'Australianise' rugby at this stage of its history would be like expecting Australian opera singers to change the conventions and practices of grand opera when they performed it in Australia.

So in the early days, as an example of this tendency to follow the leader, Australian sides adopted the English formation of two fullbacks, two halves and two quarters. Later in the nineteenth century when the New Zealanders developed their two five-eighths system, Australians opted for the British model of two halves and two centres.

In the early days, too, the Australian game, like the game in Britain, was 'confined mainly to the long scrum, sometimes lasting 15 or 20 minutes'. Luckily for the future of rugby in Australia this obsession with scrumming, which is still a feature of the British game, was dropped when the influence of New Zealand rugby began to assert itself, for the better, following a pioneering tour of New Zealand by NSW in 1882.

This era of the Cultural Cringe was the stage when Australian rugby lost its chance to establish itself as the national winter game in the way that cricket had established itself during this period as the national summer game. The main problem for rugby was that the provincial Melburnians had invented their own winter game, Victorian Rules. Rugby made little effort to try and ensure that this game was marginalised, even in Victoria, by the more global game of rugby. Even though rugby-playing Australians admired the game, with its 'Victorian science' methods, they allowed themselves to be swayed from taking it seriously as a threat to rugby by accepting the British opinion that there was not much substance to Victorian Rules.

The Victorian game, therefore, wouldn't last and wasn't a

threat. That was the British view and this view, unfortunately, was accepted by the Australian rugby community. A.E. Stoddart, the captain of a British rugby side that toured Australia in 1888, commented after watching Geelong play Melbourne, 'There is nothing in the game that our men cannot pick up in half an hour.' When Stoddart's team played the flag winner Carlton before a crowd of 25,000, they were thrashed.

This dismissal of the merits of Victorian Rules as a game meant that its threat to rugby was not realised until it was too late. By the end of the century, what Australian Rules historians have called the 'Barassi Line' had been established, separating NSW and Queensland from the rest of the nation. South and west of the Barassi Line is secure and devoted Australian Rules territory. In recent times the Barassi Line has extended into country areas of NSW and attacks from Australian Rules have been made across the Barassi Line against Sydney and Brisbane, with AFL teams playing out of these capitals.

The Cultural Cringe stage also saw rugby lose its hegemony in NSW and Queensland to rugby league. The Great Split of 1908 would not have happened if rugby administrators had rejected Rev. Mullineux's arguments for lilywhite amateurism and had continued with the system of payment for injuries and time off work that had been established in NSW and Queensland.

The first stage of Australian rugby ended with a symbolic appropriateness given its Cultural Cringe imperatives. The fourteenth Test between Australia and New Zealand (with the Wallabies winning only two in the entire series) was played in 1914 at the Sydney Cricket Ground. The Test started at 1.30 p.m., to enable the New Zealanders to catch a boat that was leaving Sydney before nightfall. The previous Saturday, during the NSW–New Zealand match, a chilling notice was posted on the SCG scoreboard: WAR DECLARED AGAINST GERMANY.

The second stage of Australian rugby was the period between the Wars, 1919 to 1939. For Australian rugby this was the era of State Rights, a time that fits David Malouf's paradigm of an Australia that was 'confidently provincial'. During this era NSW established itself as one of the major provincial powers in world rugby, defeating the All Blacks and the Springboks.

NSW's victory over the Springboks in 1937 represents one of the finest achievements of Australian rugby, for the 1937 Springboks defeated the Wallabies and the All Blacks, the first time the New Zealanders had lost a home rugby series, so the 1937 Springboks gained for themselves the compliment of being 'the best team ever to leave New Zealand'. NSW defeated this Springbok side in a mud bog at the SCG, running in five tries in a thrilling exhibition of Waratahs rugby.

The State Rights mentality of this era was shaped by the famous 1927–28 tour of Europe by the NSW Waratahs. This team established an Australian way of playing rugby – tough, expansive and clever – that has been the ideal for Australian teams ever since. Australian national teams, too, could now be expected to defeat any team in the world. In 1934 Australia defeated the All Blacks 25–11, for instance, scoring more points against the New Zealanders than any other team ever had. The Lions were defeated in 1930. And, of course, the Springboks by NSW in 1937.

During this era of State Rights, rugby was re-established strongly in NSW and not so strongly in Queensland after both state unions went into recess for the duration of the First World War. In Queensland it was not until 1929 that the state union was re-constituted. A Wallaby side included NSW and Queensland players in 1929, the first such side since 1914, and defeated the All Blacks 3–0 in a Test series, a feat not repeated until 1998.

The State Rights era saw Australian rugby move away from a ritualistic concession to British views. A vital link was established with New Zealand. This link, especially between NSW and NZ rugby, gave a pragmatic edge to the way Australians thought about rugby and the way they played the game. Professor G.V. Portus, writing in the *Sydney Mail* in 1924, made the point that the tours to Australia in 1920, 1922 and 1924 by the All Blacks, and other tours by the NZ Universities team, saved rugby in NSW by drawing great crowds to matches which, in turn, allowed the NSWRU to pay off its debts and set up the game as an alternative to rugby league at all levels of competition. Writing about the visit of the 1924 All Blacks side, which later toured the United Kingdom winning the title of 'The Invincibles' because of its unbeaten record, Professor Portus writes: 'A crowd of over 25,000 watched the first Test. By the time the second Test had been played, the expenses of the tour were covered . . . The third match provided the NSWRU the wherewithal to overtake its financial deficit and pay off a New Zealand loan. And the last match furnished an item of clean credit to be devoted to future organisation.'

Despite the successes of the 'confidently provincial' State Rights era, Australian rugby was still held back by residual elements of the Cultural Cringe. The manager of the 1930s Lions was the extremely rude and patronising James Baxter. He dismissed Australia's attempt to have a seat on the IRB with characteristic Rugbyocracy contempt. 'The Home Union has granted you and New Zealand several dispensations in regard to the laws of the game,' he told a rugby gathering at Tattersall's Club in the CBD of Sydney. 'We do not mind you playing a different game, but when you abandon them it will be the time to consider your representation. You have been knocking on the door of international control for some time. By coming into line with us in the matter of the rules under which you play, you will hasten the day of the formation of an international body.'

In other words, unless Australian rugby accepted the

hegemony of rugby by the Rugbyocracy, it could not take its place on the world governing body, the IRB.

The third stage of Australian rugby is the period from 1946 to 1978, the Anxious Era. In this era, provincial confidence gave away to an anxiety about the future viability of rugby in Australia. This anxiety was reflected in the performance of the Wallabies, which plumbed the depths with the 'Woeful Wallabies' of 1972, a team that played six Tests, drew one, lost four and finally defeated Fiji 21–19. The next year the Wallabies were defeated by Tonga, the lowest point in Wallaby Test history.

There was a successful tour of the UK in 1947–48, which culminated in a strong victory against England at Twickenham, 11–0. The 1957–58 tour of the United Kingdom and Europe, though, was a disaster with all five Tests lost. England was defeated at the SCG 18–9 in 1963, during the first tour of Australia by England since the Rev. Mullineux's team of 1899. The bitterness of the British–Australia rugby link was confirmed in 1975 at the 'Battle of Ballymore', when the Australian forwards decided that they would never again cop it sweet when being belted illegally by England's thuggish pack. The battle cry for action against the perfidious Albions was 'Bondi Beach', words that epitomised the Australian experience.

Anxious people and teams often take extreme risks in their desperation to achieve success. The 'Bondi Beach' manoeuvre was an example of this mentality in play. The fears about the future of rugby in Australia during this Anxious Era were well-based. Rugby league was thriving in NSW and Brisbane and league clubs presumed, with some justification, that they could buy any rugby union player they wanted. Interest in local rugby had collapsed so completely that a NSW–Queensland match at North Sydney Oval in 1971 drew only several thousand spectators and administrators wondered where their next dollar was going to come from.

A crisis conference was organised, with experts from New Zealand attending, and a document was produced outlining how rugby could survive. The main theme of the document was that Australian rugby had to look to South Africa and New Zealand for help and inspiration, not the United Kingdom.

Australian rugby needed success on the field, however, to rid itself of its anxiety. Up to the 'Battle of Ballymore', for instance, the Wallabies had lost 26 of their past 33 Tests, with only five wins and two draws. Constant defeat is the mother of anxiety.

The fourth stage of Australian rugby, from 1979 to 1999, is the Growing Strong era. It began with a victory against the All Blacks at the SCG in 1979, the first time the Wallabies had defeated the All Blacks in Australia since 1934. Several generations of supporters in Australia had played out their rugby careers, embarked upon their life's work, retired and, although they had followed every rugby Test through their lives, had yet to see the All Blacks losing to the Wallabies. The one-off Test win in 1979 changed that.

It set the stage for the most successful era of Australian rugby with the achievement of the Grand Slam in 1984, the 3–0 blackwash of the All Blacks in 1998 and the crowning glory of two Rugby World Cup triumphs (out of four RWC tournaments), in 1991 and 1999.

The hallmark of this era was the growing Australian determination to stand up for an Australian input into the world game of rugby. South Africa, New Zealand and Australia set up the Super 12 tournament which has, within five years, established itself as the most exciting provincial tournament in the world, with television audiences around the world tuning into its play. The NSWRU made this tournament possible – securing the future of Australian and world rugby – by stating in 1995 that 'rugby is no longer an amateur game'. This encouraged News Ltd to buy the television rights to South African, New Zealand

and Australian rugby, which, in turn, allowed these countries to offer professional contracts to their top players.

The Growing Strong era ended with the Wallabies the world champions of rugby. Rugby league is no longer in a position to steal the best rugby union players. In fact, this stealing process has been reversed with several rugby league players (including Andrew Walker who joined the Brumbies for the 2000 season) returning to Super 12 rugby after they became rugby league players because they wanted to be paid to play. The Bledisloe Cup Tests are one of the great sporting occasions for Australian sports lovers.

But by the turn of the millennium and going into the twenty-first century, there is still a great deal of unfinished business for Australian rugby. No Australian team has won the Super 12 tournament and the Wallabies are yet to win the Tri Nations series. The Wallabies, too, have yet to entrench themselves at the same level as the Springboks and the All Blacks, as one of rugby's consistently best teams year in and year out.

So the next stage of Australian rugby should be the Dominant Era. The ARU will establish its dominance, through control of the purse-strings, over the state unions. During this era, too, the Wallabies will want to win the William Webb Ellis trophy again and its share of Tri Nation tournaments. Off the field, Australian rugby administrators will want to impose the practices and ethic of the vibrant southern hemisphere rugby game over the dead-weight control of the northern hemisphere officials.

Destroying the Rugbyocracy

Simon Schama, the cultural historian, talks about the 'strange music of the diction of the past'. There is a 'pastness to the past', he argues. But in its 'splendid messiness' the diction of the past sings to us. It offers us themes and counterthemes that make sense of the past, despite its messiness, and offer insights for the way the future will become the present and then the past.

One of the strongest themes to emerge from the history of Australian rugby is its battle with the constricting and hostile power of the Rugbyocracy. This battle is literally a battle for the future of rugby. It is a battle that Australian rugby must win.

At the crux of the battle is the Golan Heights of the International Rugby Board. The Rugbyocracy has used the IRB, and still does, to impose its will on the game. When the IRB was established in 1890 the Rugby Football Union (the English Rugby Union) gave itself six seats and graciously allocated two seats each to Wales, Ireland and Scotland. Over a century this RFU control has evolved into the 'Home' nations control, with the current president of the IRB being a Welsh lawyer, Vernon Pugh QC, and most of the important committees of the IRB dominated by Home Unions delegates.

These delegates tend to make decisions with their personal agenda to the fore. Late in 1999, for example, an IRB Conference on the Game, which was held at Sydney, decided on the introduction of the sin bin for representative matches. This decision was supported by the coach of Ireland, Warren Gatland, and by a leading Irish official, Syd Miller. But Tom Kiernan, an Irish delegate on the IRB and the chairman of the committee with the authority to approve the Conference on the Game's decisions, made it clear to IRB members that he was opposed to the sin bin and would vote against it when his committee discussed the issue.

Tom Kiernan had no right to take such a personal and high-handed approach to the sin bin. But his behaviour was typical of IRB delegates throughout the twentieth century.

A View from the Top

The offices of the Australian Rugby Union are in Mount Street, just off the main business area of North Sydney. On the other side of the street is the convent where Mother Mary MacKillop spent the last years of her life. Inside the ARU's building, on the seventh floor, there are huge photographs of the Wallabies in action on the walls, plaques and cups in cases around the conference rooms and offices, and an air of pleasant bustle as people walk briskly from one meeting to the next carrying briefing papers. The office of the chief executive of the ARU, John O'Neill, is down a short corridor and on a corner with views of North Sydney and the harbour from two large windows.

O'Neill is seated at his desk, with banker's glasses slipping down his nose, scrutinising a document. The man described as the best rugby administrator in the world by New Zealand officials (who have a record for competence in their own right) is stocky, neatly dressed in a dark suit, has a high forehead and an open pleasant face. His demeanour is that of a genial but highly intelligent, no-nonsense leader.

O'Neill was educated at St Joseph's College, Hunters Hill, the famed nursery of Wallabies and professional men dedicated to being leaders in their field of work. He played for the Second XV for two years. 'They brought a ring-in, in my last year,' he says wryly. You sense that not playing for Joeys First XV is one of the great disappointments of his life. He went to university, taking a law/arts course, mucked about for two years and was told by his father that he'd organised a job for his son in the Rural Bank.

'There were nine kids in the family,' O'Neill explained, 'and you had to get through uni or work.' Within 15 years, by the age of 35, he was running the bank, which converted to the State Bank of NSW and was then prepared for privatisation by O'Neill. When he came into his top job he was mocked as 'The Boy Banker'. But by 1995, when he left to take up the job of chief executive of the ARU, the banking world was loud in its praise for his achievements.

The step from the tough, nerve-racking world of banking

took him into the tough, nerve-racking world of having to take the ARU through a difficult and critical phase from an amateur organisation running an amateur game to becoming a professional organisation running a professional game.

Our conversation, which seemed to me to be a view from the top of Australian rugby in every respect, with the 1999 RWC victory as a centrepiece, took place in January 2000, a day before O'Neill flew out to Dublin and an IRB meeting where he wanted agreement from the other delegates to thoroughly review the IRB, with a view to professionalising its operation.

'I came into the office of Chief Executive on 9 October 1995 off the back of the Murdoch deal with the ARU, the SARU and the NZRU of 24 June,' he told me. 'The first thing I had to do was clean up the mess at the ARU. We had to manage the transition from amateur to professional. This was not merely a matter of paying players. The game had to be managed professionally. This meant asserting the interests of the ARU, not an easy thing given the history of Australian rugby. What you have to remember is that until 1949, there was no ARU. The NSW and Queensland unions were affiliated with the IRB through the England union, the Rugby Football Union. In 1949 it was the IRB, not the Australian state unions, which insisted on an Australian Rugby Union.'

This history was intriguing to me for it explained, in part, why the NSW and Queensland unions have fought so bitterly with each other and then, later, against the ARU. The two state unions had a history of independence. They saw themselves as on a par with the Home nations like Scotland and Ireland, rather than as provinces like Auckland or Natal. This explains, too, why ARU delegates to IRB meetings sometimes pushed their own hobbyhorse ideas rather than those of the ARU.

'So when I became chief executive I inherited a governing body, the ARU, that was relatively benign. And because of the

long-standing influence in the case of the QRU and the dominance by the NSWRU, what I tried to do was challenged.
But with financial success, particularly, this has been changed
around. The ARU has become what I call "the central treasury"
of Australian rugby. As the dust has settled down after four years
and having success on and off the field, the ARU is now in a
sound financial position. These profits will cascade down
through the rugby system.'

I suggested to O'Neill that the ARU was basically bankrupt
in 1995. The costs involved with mounting a defence of the
World Cup (the 'Two-Peat') in South Africa could not be met
out of the small income stream the ARU had with its minimal
television rights. There was a vicious challenge, too, from rugby
league with the NSWRL announcing in early 1995, in the
wake of its expansion into a 20-team competition, that any
rugby league club buying a rugby union player would not have
to consolidate the purchase in its salary cap requirements. This
was a blatant attempt to strangle rugby union by denying the
code its star players.

John O'Neill agreed with these comments. 'The ARU lost
$800,000 in 1995,' he said, 'and in 1996, when we had to honour
the Ferrier Agreement with the players' payments and had to set
up and market the Super 12 and Tri Nations tournaments, we lost
$3 million. These losses wiped out our reserves. But since 1996
our finances have been growing strongly, increasing at about
10 per cent a year. We've gone from an income of $9 million in
1995 to $50 million in 1999. We've done this by developing new
Test venues in Melbourne, Perth, Canberra and Parramatta. We
created a world record rugby crowd for the Wallabies–All Blacks
match in 1999, about 108,000 spectators. When you think that
there were fewer than 18,000 at Concord Oval in 1987 for the
RWC semi-final between the Wallabies and the French, you can
see what tremendous gains we have made.'

I asked him to look into the future and give me an indication of where he saw Australian rugby in, say, 2003 when the Rugby World Cup final will be played at the Olympic Stadium, and perhaps even further ahead.

His answer was not a series of predictions but a statement of the objectives of the ARU up to 2010. Given the successful record of the ARU under O'Neill's clever and energetic leadership, there is the strongest possibility, in my view, that these predictions will be accomplished. So in a sense he was predicting the future.

'The ARU has four objectives into the next decade,' he said. 'First, we want Australia to be a world power in rugby on a continuous basis. We want the Wallabies to be with the Springboks and the All Blacks as a perennial top team. Second, we want rugby to be the number one participation winter sport in Australia. At present we have 115,000 men, women and youngsters playing rugby. This is a substantial jump from the 86,000 in 1995. Our aim is to have about 160,000 rugby players by 2003. The AFL has between 180,000 and 250,000, the figures are a bit rubbery. The RWC win and the 2003 RWC tournament should see our player numbers increase.

'If we get things right, too, rugby could be an Olympic sport, not perhaps in time for the Athens Olympics but certainly the Games in Beijing or wherever after that. We put a proposition to the Sydney organisers for rugby to be included for the Sydney Games but it proved too difficult at the time. The IOC has been insistent that it wants the 15-a-side game but we have to be careful not to compromise the Rugby World Cup. I think we'll have to be insistent that it's Sevens Rugby or nothing for the IOC. After the success of Sevens Rugby at the Commonwealth Games at Kuala Lumpur, the IOC should become receptive to the idea.

'Third, we have to be obsessed about growth. Growth of player numbers, growth of our revenue streams, growth in the interest in rugby through spectator numbers, television viewers, radio listeners and readers. Through growth we can generate career pathways for our players through a fourth Super 12 side. And, in turn, we can generate more mass entertainment. In terms of hours on television, the AFL and rugby league have about a 2-to-1 ratio over us, although the gap is narrowing.

'Fourth, we must strive to maintain our tradition, ethos and the values for the youth of Australia. Our players are, and will be, great role models for young people to emulate.'

I reminded him of his controversial statements about the demise of rugby league. During my researches, I came across a prediction made by J.J. Giltinan, the manager of the unsuccessful Rugby League Kangaroos on their tour of Britain in 1908, that within 'three years' rugby union would be dead in Sydney. Was the O'Neill prediction about the phasing out of rugby league as a major sport in its own right by 2020 in the same category as the Giltinan prediction?

'Not really,' O'Neill replied. 'I've always been a student of history. I know that history doesn't repeat itself but it does have a habit of rhyming. The Great Split of 1908 between rugby union and rugby league in Australia came down to money and social class issues. Into the twenty-first century rugby union players are now paid. Our top players are probably as well paid as their rugby league counterparts. In an egalitarian society like Australia, rugby league has gathered great strength from its boast that it's the working-class game. But our rugby teams now reflect all the classes. Rugby is no longer a rah-rahs game. The ethnic mix that makes Australia such a vibrant society and culture is reflected in the Wallabies. John Brass was telling me a few days ago that there is no need for rugby union players to go to league the way he had to.

'And then there's the fact that rugby union is a global game and rugby league isn't. This lack of reach is going to be the fatal weakness of rugby league. Johnnie Raper was making that point recently when he called for more international matches in rugby league. But rugby league is not a transportable product. Either you are a global game in a smallish local market or a big game in a big local market, like American football. But the television demographics of rugby league, essentially the C and D sections of the audience in NSW and Queensland, mean that its broadcasting is too narrowly based in the global era. This is not a criticism of rugby league. It is a statement of business realities in the twenty-first century.'

I told O'Neill that one of the themes of Australian rugby, in my opinion, was the long struggle of the ARU to untangle the control exercised by the Rugbyocracy over the game and through this overall control over rugby in Australia. Where, I asked him, did he see the future direction of the IRB and Australia's role in the governance of rugby as a world game?

'The preamble to the agreement that allowed Australia, South Africa and New Zealand into the IRB as member unions in 1949,' he replied, 'has the phrase "equality of membership". Since 1890, when the English grabbed control of the IRB and rugby, that has never been the case. And it is still not the case, despite the success of the ARU, the SARU and NZRU in every aspect of rugby and the failure of the British unions in every aspect of rugby. In Ireland, for instance, rugby has slipped down to be the number four sport. In Scotland rugby is in danger of being obliterated by soccer. The president of the IRB, Vernon Pugh, even though he is a Welshman, said after the 1999 RWC tournament: "We handed the Welsh Rugby Union a jewel and they failed to polish it." Most of the main committees on the IRB are chaired by Home Unions delegates. Many of these delegates still think that Australia's success in the World Cup is a temporary triumph.

'These delegates, too, hate the idea of professional rugby. If they had their way, they'd go back to the coarse rugby days when you played, got pissed and didn't worry about winning or entertaining the spectators. The IRB is poorly run. The accounts from the 1991 RWC tournament were finally presented just before the 1995 RWC. The IRB hasn't handled the transition to professionalism at all well. The IRB must honour its preamble and govern for everyone, not for the Home Unions. I am pushing for a McKinsey-type review of the objectives and practices of the IRB. The British diehards think I'll go away if they keep putting off the inevitable reconstruction of the IRB. But I won't.'

The Australian view from the top, it seems, is that the old Empire is determined to strike back.

The 'Darke Corner' of the Future

The future by definition is unknowable. But we can make some shrewd guesses about what will happen in the rugby world in, say, the first and second decades of the twenty-first century. The most important thing that will happen is that little will change with the way rugby is played. We can make this prediction or guess by pointing to how rugby has evolved since the 1860s. If Dr Moran or Rev. Mullineux were brought back to life by some magic timewarp and were taken to see a rugby Test, they would be able to follow play after a few minutes' explanation of the latest laws without much difficulty.

In *Tom Brown's Schooldays*, Old Brooke tells Tom that it will take him about a month to learn all the rules of the Rugby School football game. The modern game, and the game played by the Rev. Mullineux and Dr Moran at the turn of the twentieth century, retains this historical complexity. But the essentials of the game – the running, the passing, the tackling, the scrumming and the jumping – are much the same now as they were a hundred years ago.

There will be continual changes, more modifications, to the laws, for rugby is a game that is always evolving as clever players and coaches work out ways to exploit the laws. And there will be changes to the presentation of the game. Norman Harris ran an intriguing article in the *Observer*, 9 January 2000, in which he quoted a book called *Touchdown* in which leading British sports figures made predictions about rugby matters in the Year 2000. The predictions were made in 1970.

Teddy Tinling, famous for the dresses and lace knickers he designed for female tennis players, made these predictions: 'One day the dressing room might be re-named the paint room or the spray room. People spray-skin on themselves now, so it is a quite logical development that a form of clothing or covering for rugby could be evolved in the same way.' Harris suggests that the 'skin-tight shirt, making a player as slippery as an eel' – the All Blacks new Adidas jersey foreshadowed but not produced for the 1999 World Cup tournament – might fit Tinling's prediction.

One of England greatest forwards and a notable official, Lord Wakefield of Kendal, the W.W. Wakefield dropped for the England–Waratahs test on the 1927–28 tour, predicted: 'Not all innovations to win possession are necessarily cheating. I see nothing wrong with hoisting at the lineout . . . I can visualise rugby being played in a covered stadium. I also believe it will be played on artificial surfaces.' The 1999 RWC final, of course, was played in the Millennium Stadium at Cardiff, which had the capacity to pull its roof across to protect the players from the elements. For the RWC final, because there was no rain, the roof was open and exposed the occasional slanting column of golden sunlight.

Vivian Jenkins, the first fullback to score a try in a Five Nations Test and later, after he stopped playing rugby for Wales, a noted rugby correspondent for the *Sunday Times*, predicted for 2000: 'There could be a World Cup for rugby, though I for one hope it does not happen. A World Cup is quite an ordeal for our soccer players, whose living it is. For amateur rugby players it would introduce a much too demanding complication into their daily lives.' The pessimism in this prediction and its acceptance that rugby would always remain an amateur game is typical of the jeremiah approach to rugby favoured by the Rugbyocracy.

If I could dare to follow up these predictions with a tentative prediction about the next two decades of rugby I would make the point that the way rugby evolves depends very much on the ideological question of whether it is seen as a low-scoring game or a high-scoring game. The Rugbyocracy favour the low-scoring model. They see rugby as a form of soccer, with some handling thrown in. The Rugbyocracy, therefore, favours laws that lead to penalty kicks at goal. The southern hemisphere rugby community, particularly, see rugby as a form of basketball, with some kicking and no forward passes. This vision favours a game in which tries are encouraged.

'Scoring tries,' says Rod Macqueen, 'should be the point of the game.' He points to the discussion at the IRB's Conference on the Game a month after the 1999 RWC during which IRB delegates were amazed when the coaches at the conference told them they coached their sides to give away a penalty rather than concede a try. It was only after they took this admission into their thinking that these IRB delegates acknowledged the value of the sin bin proposal. Macqueen insisted that if the sin bin had been in operation during the 1999 RWC tournament there would have been many more tries scored than there were.

The soccer/basketball contest for rugby relates, too, to the future direction of law changes. Take the tackled ball law, for instance, which for the history of the game has been an area of contention. There is a need to provide a contest for possession of the ball at the tackle. There is also a need for some continuity in play to be allowed. The soccer approach, which is adopted by most British referees, tends to penalise the side going into the tackle with the ball. The basketball approach, favoured by most southern hemisphere referees, tends to penalise the side making the tackle.

Given that an inevitable imperative for rugby is that it retains its appeal as a mass entertainment, the likelihood is that the laws of rugby will be written in future to enhance the game's popularity. This means an endorsement of the basketball approach.

We can predict, too, that rugby will entrench its position as the second most popular football code in the world. It will always remain a Pepsi Cola to soccer's Coca-Cola but this will not prevent the code from having a Rugby World Cup tournament every four years that will be the biggest international sports event of that particular year.

Late in 1998 the IRB announced that Venezuela had become its eighty-fourth member nation. India (which played in the Asian championship in 1999, along with China), Peru, Cuba and a further eight other small nations have made applications to join the IRB. With the creation in 2000 of the IRB's Sevens Rugby worldwide series of tournaments, many of these smaller nations will get a chance to play international rugby. And they will be eligible, too, to compete in future Rugby World Cup tournaments through the extensive system of qualifying matches.

The takings for the IRB, as rugby has expanded into a genuinely world game, have moved from $8 million in the 1987 RWC tournament to a profit of about $150 million for the 1999 RWC tournament. Estimates of the television audiences for Rugby World Cups have increased from 300 million in 1987 to 3 billion, with 140 countries taking the television coverage, in 1999. Attendances at RWC matches have risen from 600,000 in 1987 to 1.5 million in 1999.

By 2011, when the RWC tournament may be held, perhaps, in Japan, China may have developed its national rugby team to the level where it is a contender for the main tournament. By then, too, the RWC tournament may be conducted at three levels, allowing up to 60 teams to experience play at the world championship of rugby.

The globalisation of rugby will eventually destroy the control of the Rugbyocracy. The new national rugby powers will identify more with Australia, South Africa and New Zealand than they will with the negativity of the British rugby unions. At the

1999 RWC tournament, for example, as a sign that this is already happening, no fewer than six sides had a New Zealander in a senior coaching position.

Not even the Home Unions were immune from this southern hemisphere influence. John Mitchell, the former All Black number 8, was a coach for England. Warren Gatland, another All Black, coached Ireland. Wales was coached by the former Auckland Super 12 coach, Graham Henry. And Scotland, with its all-Scots coaching staff, filled its national side with the 'kilted kiwis', New Zealanders like John and Martin Leslie being Scotland's best players, with John Leslie captaining the side.

Probably, however, the Rugbyocracy will remain tenacious in defending what it regards as its territory. A report in the *Sydney Mail* on 12 September 1909 discussed, under the heading 'Gossip' by 'Wanderer', the way NSW supporters of rugby did not 'feel kindly towards British authorities because of the actions of the Scottish and Irish unions in refusing to meet the Australian Wallaby team during their trip to England, and also in boycotting the Anglo–Welsh team which came to New Zealand and Australia.' The article contemplated a division of the rugby world into a southern and northern hemisphere split: 'From the foregoing facts it would appear that matters are ripening for a dissolution of partnership between the senior and junior members of the world of Rugby football. In the first place, the Rugby Union game must be made faster, whatever happens, or else Rugby Union will go to the wall. Secondly, there must be an alteration in that part of the constitution which provides for the payment of pin money. These amendments, it is almost safe to say will not receive the imprimatur of the English Rugby Union. Therefore, there will remain one course open, that is, the formation of an Australasian Rugby Union . . . There is no getting away from the fact that it is imperative that we must control the game, according to local conditions if we wish to survive the present invasion of the Rugby League into Rugby Union ranks.'

'Wanderer' got it right, 90 or so years ago. If we reverse the sentiments of his last sentence and re-phrase it to indicate the possibility of rugby union absorbing rugby league some time in the twenty-first century, his observations about the needed influence of Australian and New Zealand brainpower in the running of world rugby are as relevant now as they were in 1909.

Winter Love

In 1995, Gordon Bray, the voice of rugby through the 1980s and 1990s with his television commentaries, brought out a book of articles and essays on rugby by well-known players and writers called *The Spirit of Rugby: A Tribute to Australian Rugby Union*. The tone of the book was, rightly, celebratory. The foreword, written by Bray, captured the mood with an account of the 1927–28 Waratahs having an audience with the then Duke (later King George VI) and the Duchess of York. The Duke asked for his baby daughter, Elizabeth, to be wheeled into the audience room in her pram for everyone to admire. One of the Wallabies, a tough farmer, who had had a few beers to steady his nerves before the audience and was now over-fortified, asked for permission to hold the baby. For a while he cradled the child in his massive hands. Then he began to toss her into the air like a football, with the tiny princess laughing as the throws got higher and higher. The princess, of course, was later to grow up to become the Queen and present the William Webb Ellis trophy twice to Wallaby captains. 'In one brief moment,' Bray writes, 'the future Queen had been anointed by the "spirit of rugby" – Australian-style.'

Another anointment for the Queen surely came at Twickenham during the 1991 Rugby World Cup final when she and most of the main stand heard an anguished Bob Dwyer yell out to his players in that most Australian of expressions, 'Kick it to the shithouse!'

The Queen's experience with the spirit of Australian rugby has centred on its egalitarian spirit. For the princess–tossing Wallaby and the anguished coach, the future and present Queen was part of the rugby family to be treated with the interest and concern that is allocated to all the members of the family. But there is more to the spirit of Australian rugby than this admirable democratic instinct. There is the toughness of Frank 'Banger' Row, Australia's first rugby captain, who invited his father early on in his career to watch himself and his brother play. He noticed that his father left before half-time.

'Why?' he asked.

'Never seen such a bunch of ruffians,' his father replied.

And the spirit is found in the determination of Dr Herbert Moran to argue up and down Britain with referees and officials for acceptance of the tough, manly but fair tackling and rucking methods of his Wallabies. His point was that Australians were as competent to work out how rugby should be played as anyone in Britain.

The spirit is there, too, with the missionary zeal of Daniel Carroll taking the rugby culture to the gridiron heathens of California. It is in the desperate match-saving tackling of Cyril Towers, Trevor Allan, Phil Hawthorne, George Gregan and John Eales, who epitomised as a young Wallaby the traditional will to win by sprinting across the turf of Twickenham late in the 1991 RWC final to grass Rob Andrew as he was racing towards the Australian tryline to score, potentially, the winning try.

It is in the cheek of David Campese's goose-step and the daring of Dally Messenger diving over opponents to score a try. The spirit is revealed in the Rolls-Royce smoothness of Mark Ella running a backline. It is Phil Kearns giving Sean Fitzpatrick, his All Black opponent, a player who had mercilessly sledged him early on in his career, the upper cut sign after he scored the critical try at Wellington for the Wallabies in 1990.

The spirit of Australian rugby is in the courage and audacity of Tim Horan, feeling as sick as a black dog, tearing through the Springboks defence in the RWC semi-final at Twickenham in 1999. It is in the serendipity of Stephen Larkham in the same match, nonchalantly dropping his first goal in Test rugby to take the Wallabies through to the RWC final.

And the Australian rugby spirit is with all the rugby players who went away in the twentieth century to fight Australia's wars and took the morality of the rugby game, its emphasis on physical and mental courage, its respect for fortitude, its inclination towards cleverness and shrewd strategy, into their battles to sustain their determination to show they had the right stuff.

The winter love Australians have shown and will continue to show well into the twenty-first century for the rugby game is memorably expressed by Dr Moran towards the end of his chapter on his rugby experiences in *Viewless Winds*: 'For rugby is a great game, not ending with the blown whistle. Years after we see again the rift in the opposing defences. We get ready to break through with a sudden flash of speed. Long after events we still stretch ourselves full-length barely to reach the heels of a flying three-quarter, drag them to ourselves and him to the ground. We leap, once more, higher than the others on a long lineout, gather the ball on our fingertips, marvellously, and head the rush onward. We sink at the feet of the dribbling forwards and gather the ball as the attacking force tumbles pell-mell upon us: the situation is saved! We feel the joyous rapture of massed forwards taking it on in a fierce irruption, or of centre-threes swerving through and just reaching the white line as they hit the green turf. The earth trembles, but a try has been scored.'

'The earth trembles, but a try has been scored' is a rallying call, a cooee from one generation of players to the next and to the next and the next, that epitomises the enduring spirit of Australian rugby.

Appendix

Australian Rugby Milestones

List prepared by the Australian Rugby Union Archives

1823	Running with the ball reportedly introduced into the game of football at Rugby School in England.
1829	The *Sydney Monitor* of July 25 reports a game of football at the Barracks (modern-day Barrack St in Sydney) between soldiers.
1841	Running with the ball officially allowed in Rugby School's rules, providing the ball was taken on the bound. Passing was specifically forbidden.
1848	The first series of meetings held at Cambridge University in England for the purpose of formulating a code which would unite the players of the public schools, who were at that time playing with their own individual sets of rules.
1861	Rugby matches reported in WA between troops and visiting sailors.
1863	The Rugby Football Union (England) formed and meetings held in London to draw up a standard set of rules. Still very loosely framed.
1864	The first Australian rugby football club was established at Sydney University, colours blue and gold.
1867	The Brisbane Football Club was formed, followed in 1878 by the Excelsior Club and then the Queensland Wallaroos.
1870	The brothers R.A. and W.M. (Monty) Arnold formed the Wallaroo Club in Sydney to provide the first really regular opponents for Sydney University.
1870	Wellington (NZ) Club formed and the first inter-provincial match played with the Nelson Club under rugby rules of C.J. Munro.
1871	The first rugby match between England and Scotland. Twenty players a side, 13 forwards, three halfbacks, one three-quarter and three fullbacks.

1874   The first body to control the game of rugby in NSW, the Southern Rugby Union (SRU), was formed with R.A. Arnold as the founding Chairman; J.J. Calvert elected as the first President, a position he held for 40 years until 1914. The first SRU member clubs were: Balmain, Goulburn, King's School, Camden College (Newtown), Newington College, Sydney University, Wallaroo North Shore (St Leonards), Waratah – which incorporated the Sydney Club and won the first premiership in 1874.

1876   Up to this time, kicking for goal was more important than scoring tries. The SRU decided that when no goals were kicked, matches should be decided by the majority of tries. This followed similar trends in the UK.

1877   Player numbers in international matches reduced from 20 to 15.

1880   The total number of clubs under the control of the SRU exceeds 100.

1881   The game is organised on a regular basis in WA.

1882   The Northern Rugby Union (NRU) is formed in Queensland. The first SRU (NSW) team tours NZ with 15 players only. Played seven games, won four, lost three. The first inter-colonial match between the NRU (Q) and the SRU (NSW) played in Sydney, SRU winning 28–4.

1884   The first NZ representative team visits Australia and wins all eight matches.

1886   A numerical value was adopted by the Rugby Football Union in England for tries and goals. Three tries were made equal to one goal.

1888   Club rugby formally organised in Victoria and the Melbourne Rugby Union formed (MRU) against strong opposition from Victorian (Australian) Rules.

1888–89	A British team captained by R.L. Seddon, the first rugby team from Britain to tour abroad, visits Australia and NZ. In Australia it won 13 and lost two matches. Seddon was drowned in the Hunter River in NSW and the international MCC cricketer A.E. Stoddart took over (the trip was originally a professional cricket tour). To cover expenses when in Victoria, the team played a number of Victorian Rules matches with some success. There is no official recognition of this tour.
1888–89	The first team from NZ (known as the NZ Natives) toured the UK where they played 74 matches, winning 49 and losing 20. All told on tour in NZ, Australia and the UK, the NZ Natives played 106 matches, won 78 and lost 23. This is still the record of total matches played by any international team, any time.
1889	First team from Victoria to visit NSW. The SRU team won both matches, 13–6 and 17–14 against vigorous opponents.
1890	The International Rugby Board (IRB) formed.
1892	The foundation organisations for rugby in Australia, the SRU and the NRU, change their names to the NSW Rugby Union and Queensland Rugby Union respectively.
1892	Mauls in goal abolished.
1893	The WARU formally established in Western Australia.
1894	The NSW team travels to Victoria for the first time.
1896	The Metropolitan Rugby Union is created by the NSWRU to conduct and develop the game in Sydney.
1899	The first team endorsed by the Rugby Football Union of England tours Australia and the first

historic Test match featuring a combined Australian team is played at the Sydney Cricket Ground on 24 June, Australia winning 13–3, although the tourists won the other three Tests.

In this year the Victorian Rugby Union is established and plays against the visitors.

1900   The first district grade competition is established in Sydney based in defined residential qualifications and the first premiership won by the Glebe Club (now incorporated with Balmain into the Drummoyne Club).

1903   The first Test match between Australia and NZ is played at the Sydney Cricket Ground on 15 August, won by NZ, 22–3. This tour greatly increased the popularity of rugby and large crowds started attending grade matches in Sydney and Brisbane.

1904   The first visit to Australia by a champion NZ schools team, Te Aute College, which played seven matches, winning four. They played Fort Street Model High School, St Joseph's College, Newington College, Combined Bathurst Schools, Combined GPS and Sydney University.

1905   The first visit to NZ by the Australian team, won three matches and lost four, including the Test, 14–3.

1905–06   Bouncing the ball into play from touch eliminated. Scoring values of 3 points for a try, 5 points for a converted try and 3 points for a penalty universally adopted.

1907   A then record crowd of 52,411 attended the 13 July match between NSW and NZ at the SCG.

1907–08   Financed by newspaper proprietor Joynton Smith and a group of Sydney businessmen, rugby league is established as a professional variant of the game of rugby union in NSW and Queensland. Enticing the most famous rugby player in Australia, Dally Messenger, to defect, they are able to attract a number of other prominent Wallabies.

1908–09   The First Wallabies tour the United Kingdom. They won 25 of their 31 matches, beat England 9–3 but lost to Wales 6–9. They did not play Scotland or Ireland. They scored 438 points on tour to 149 against, scoring 104 tries in the process and averaging better than three tries per game, with 80 scored by the backs and 24 by the forwards. The First Wallabies competed in the Olympic Games rugby tournament at the London Olympics of 1908, winning the Gold Medal.

1911   Simultaneous visits to Australia by NZ, the Maoris and USA Universities.

1912   To bolster the popularity of rugby union against the growing inroads being made by the new professional game, the Australian team visits the United States and Canada, winning 11 matches and losing five.

1914–18   During the Great War, Australian senior rugby went into recess, with strong appeals to players to support the patriotic cause. Seven former Wallabies were killed at Gallipoli, along with Major J.F. McManamey, President of the NSWRU. Long lists of deaths of rugby players on the Somme in France were regularly published by the NSWRU. These losses drastically affected the strength of the code, particularly as rugby league continued its regular competitions throughout the war years, taking over and later retaining many of the grounds formerly devoted to rugby union.

Restarting the game in 1919 in NSW proved difficult but even more so in Queensland and

Victoria, which were unable to regroup until 1929 and 1926 respectively. The Victorian Rugby Union was assisted by the defection of all the rugby league clubs in their state.

1919   Australia's famous AIF team takes part in the King's Cup Victory tournament at the end of the war in Europe against 'teams from all parts of the Empire and France' and is the only team to beat NZ, the eventual winners.

1921   South Africa visits Australia and NZ for the first time, winning four out of four in Australia and 15 out of 19 in NZ.

Memorial for all rugby union players killed in the Great War unveiled in London by the King.

1922   First full tour by the Maori team of Australia.

1923   Centenary matches to celebrate 100 years since that day in 1823 when young William Webb Ellis allegedly first ran with the ball. The principal centenary match was played at Rugby School, where combined England and Wales (21) beat combined Scotland and Ireland (16).

The Shute Memorial Shield for competition between first-grade clubs in Sydney, still one of the strongest club competitions in the world, was inaugurated, with Sydney University Club the first winners.

1926   Australia wins the right, along with all the other Dominions, to separate representation at the Imperial Rugby Conference. Waseda University from Japan tours NSW for three matches.

1927–28   The NSW team, the Waratahs, make an historic tour of the UK, France and North America. Play 31 matches, won 24, drew two. They beat Ireland, Wales and France but lost to England and Scotland. They made a great impression with superb running, passing and relentless backing up which is still recalled today and created that rugby style with which NSW and Australia has long been associated.

1928–29 The Queensland Rugby Union resumes operations and its re-emergence immediately makes a forceful impact on the performances of the Australian team, which defeated NZ in all three Tests for the first time. This was the first occasion when the Australian team comprised representatives of the states of Queensland, NSW and Victoria and began a strong decade for the game in Australia.

1930 A British Lions team tours Australia and NZ. In Australia they won five and lost two, including the Test match, which Australia won 6–5.

1931 The Bledisloe Cup was presented by the then Governor-General of NZ, Lord Bledisloe, for competition between Australia and NZ.

1933 The Wallabies tour South Africa for the first time, playing 23, winning 12, losing ten, with one drawn. Of five Tests, South Africa won three and Australia two.

The South Australian Rugby Union formed.

1934 Australia wrested the Bledisloe Cup from NZ, winning the first Test 25–11, with the other being drawn 3–3.

The Australian Universities team tours Japan, winning four out of seven in front of crowds up to 60,000 as the game grows in popularity in that country.

The diamond jubilee of the NSWRU draws a great gathering of former players and officials.

1936 The Imperial Rugby Conference is held in London. A forward program for international tours is discussed for the first time.

Queensland plays Victoria for the first time in Sydney and wins a very tight match 16–15. NZ regains the Bledisloe Cup. The King's School tours England and Scotland.

1937   NSW defeats the Springboks for the first time but South Africa wins the Tests 9–5 and 26–17. The ACT Rugby Union is established.

1939   The Wallabies travel to the UK for a full tour but arrive by ship on the eve of the Second World War, returning home without playing one serious match (they played friendlies only in Ceylon and India).

1939–45   Having careful mind to the damage done to the life of the game by the decision at the outbreak of WWI to suspend all senior matches, rugby administrators elected to continue playing the game (other than representative matches) throughout the period of hostilities and thus not repeat handing impetus to rugby league, as they had during 1914–18.

1947–48   The Third Wallabies tour Great Britain, Ireland, France, Canada and the United States. They are the only team to complete all internationals without having had their line crossed. The Third Wallabies scored 500 points in 35 matches, running in 98 tries.

1948   Australia invited to join the International Rugby Board.

1949   On 26 November, the Australian Rugby Union is formally established with the union of the six states and the ACT.

The Wallabies play their one-hundredth test, defeating the NZ Maoris at Melbourne 18–3.

1952   Australia hosts the first visit by a team from Fiji and what a rugby revelation this turned out to be, as the visitors dazzled the rapidly growing crowds with their sparkling, breathtaking open style. The game in Australia receives a much needed lift. The Test series is drawn.

1958   The first Test match ever played in Melbourne takes place at Olympic Park against the Maoris, who win 13–6.

1963   Following a very disappointing tour in 1961, Australia again tours South Africa and draws the series 2–2, its best result to date.

1966   The Ballymore Ground is opened in Brisbane.

1967   The first of many successful overseas tours by an Australian Schoolboys' team takes place to South Africa, winning five out of seven.

The Fifth Wallabies tour to the UK and Australia beats Wales for the first time. The lure of touring becomes rugby union's most important defence against the depredations of the professional game.

1971   Australia wins its first Test against France in France, 13–11 at Toulouse, but then slides into a period of decline on the international scene, reaching the bottom by being beaten in 1973 in Brisbane by Tonga.

1972   Four-point try introduced.

1973   A major reappraisal begins in Australia of coaching techniques and playing styles to arrest and turn the decline around.

1975   Australia plays its first Tests against Japan in Australia and wins the series 2–0 over spirited opponents. The second test at Ballymore, Brisbane, won by the Wallabies 50–25, is the two-hundredth Test played by Australia.

1978   Australia defeats Wales 2–0 for the first time in a Test series in Australia. It then goes on to beat NZ 30–16 for what was at that time a record score against the All Blacks in the third Test in Auckland.

1979   Australia travels to Argentina for its first Test series there and squares the two Tests.

The Wallabies win the Bledisloe Cup for the first time since 1949.

1980   The Wallabies again win the Bledisloe Cup, setting a new winning margin of 26–10 in the third Test.

1981   Australia defeats the touring French team 2–0 in the Test series. First tour of Australia by an Italian team takes place. The Wallaby tour selectors for the first time chose three brothers in a touring side, Mark, Gary and Glen Ella.

The Seventh Wallabies tour the British Isles with only six matches lost out of 23 played but involving only one Test win. Poor goalkicking regularly resulted in losses in games which this good side was in a strong position to win.

1984   The disappointments of 1981 were reversed when the Eighth Wallabies completed the Grand Slam of wins during this year's tour of Great Britain. This was the most successful Australian team to date and its record featured a try in every Test by Mark Ella and 42 points in the four Tests by Michael Lynagh.

1987   The first Rugby World Cup was an idea first floated by Australia with NZ's support but which aroused only negative views in the northern hemisphere. This inaugural competition, played in Australia and NZ, was won by NZ.

1991   Now adopted by even the most sceptical of earlier detractors, as in fact the world championship of rugby, the second World Cup is held in the northern hemisphere. Australia defeats England 12–3 in the final at Twickenham and is hailed as one of the greatest sides in the history of the game.

The RWC pool-round Test against Wales, at Cardiff, won by the Wallabies 38–3, is the three-hundredth Test played by Australia.

1992   The Wallabies visit South Africa to put their world champion status on the line against a South Africa recently readmitted to the world rugby community. They silence their South African doubters with a masterful 24–3 victory at Cape Town. Australia then successfully defends its world champion title for the next three years.

1993   Five-point try introduced.

1995   Now an enormous moneyspinner, drawing a global TV audience of over one billion potential viewers, the third World Cup takes place in South Africa but Australia goes down to England on the bell in a quarter-final. During the tournament, rumours abound of an entrepreneurial proposal to create a worldwide professional rugby structure. In the ensuing months, frenzied negotiations between the entrepreneurs, players and national rugby administrators take place. The calm and deliberate handling of this crisis by the national bodies wins the day. Although the entrepreneurs came close to success, it became apparent that they never really had their funding in place, so that the narrow success of their 1908 predecessors was not repeated.

In the shadow of all this drama, the 1995 World Cup was won by South Africa in front of President Nelson Mandela wearing a Springbok jersey.

Under the mounting pressure of the TV dollar promised by the networks to rugby league, the IRB decides that 'rugby is no longer amateur'. Players given contracts and the brave new world of professional rugby begins.

1996	The inaugural seasons of Super 12 and the Tri Nations tournaments begin.
1997	Rugby league is split by the Super League battle.
	The ARU plays a Bledisloe Cup Test at the Melbourne Cricket Ground before a crowd of 83,000 spectators but few members.
1998	The Wallabies defeat the All Blacks 3–0 in a Test series for the first time since 1929.
1999	A world record crowd of 107,042 spectators in the Olympic Stadium at Sydney watch the Wallabies defeat the All Blacks.
	Australia wins the World Cup at the Millennium Stadium at Cardiff, defeating France in the final 30–12. The Wallabies become the only team to win two World Cups and enter the twenty-first century as the world champions of rugby.

Index

A

ABC, 181, 221, 249
Aborigines, 52, 197–200
    dance, 108–9
Ackermann, Jessie, 37
Ackford, Paul, 194, 248–9
ACT, 198, 231
    Brumbies, 7–8, 11, 210, 222, 231, 263
    players, 185
Adamson, C.Y., 92
advantage law, 228–9
advantage line, 22, 65, 175
    Sevens, 167
AFL see Australian Football League
age teams, 236
AIS see Australian Institute of Sport
    (AIS)
All America, 120
All Blacks see New Zealand
Allan, 'Slab', 180
Allan, Trevor, 95, 178–80, 277
amateurism, 97, 99–100, 103, 106,
    121–2, 176–8, 258
Andrew, Rob, 69, 188, 277
angles, running at, 10, 228
anthems, 9, 255
Apia, 62
Argentina, 16, 40, 145, 164–5
    in World Cup
        1991, 59–60, 63
        1997, 8
ARU see Australian Rugby Union
    (ARU)
ASDA see Australian Sports Drug
    Agency
Athletic Park, 127, 136
Auckland Rugby Union, 182
Auckland Warriors, 241
Australian, the, 195
Australian Dispensation, 128
Australian Field, 97

Australian Football League (AFL),
    215, 258, 268–9
Australian Imperial Forces (AIF), 121,
    142
Australian Institute of Sport (AIS), 50
Australian Jewish Times, 129
Australian Rugby Union (ARU), 48,
    122, 151, 183, 256, 263, 266–7, 270
    and—
        coaches, 190
        International Rugby Board
            (IRB) 266
        players, 185
        professionalism, 181, 183
        Rugbyocracy, 33, 270
        William Webb Ellis trophy, 254
        World Rugby Corporation, 185
    archives, 113, 122–3, 141
    CEO, 6, 45, 235–6, 265
    drug-use policy, 48–9
    finances, 235–6, 266–7
    history, 266
    law changes, 244
    objectives, 268
    slogan, 16
Australian Rules football, 88–9, 200,
    215–16, 258 see also Victorian
        Rules football
    New Zealand, 89
Australian Schoolboys, 189, 198
Australian Sports Drug Agency
    (ASDA), 48
Ayres-Smith, A., 93

B

Bachop, Graeme, 71, 172
bag snatching, 20, 38
Baker, Reginald 'Snowy', 85, 111,
    120–1
Ballymore, 155, 190, 197, 206
    Battle of, 261–2
Balmain, 151, 154
Barassi Line, 258
Barbarians, 146

Barnes, Simon, 49
Batchelor, Denzil, 179–80
Baxter, James, 260
Belfast, 16
Belson, F. C., 93
Bennett, Wayne, 14
Bentham, Jeremy, 52
Best, John, 10, 42, 48
Bevan, Derek, 29
Bishop, David, 59
biting, 38–9
Blackheath, 105
Blanco, Serge, 149
Bledisloe, Lord, 132–7
Bledisloe Cup see New Zealand
Bolger, Jim, 181
Bond, Graeme, 198
'Bondi Beach', 261
Booth, Ernest 'General', 113
Booth, William, General, 101
Bowen, Scott, 161
Bowman, Tom, 233–4
Boyce twins, 129
Boyer Lectures, 255
Bradman, Donald, Sir, 60, 149, 214
Brass, John, 269
Bray, Gordon, 183–4, 276
Brennan, Trevor, 17
Brial, Michael, 57, 205
Brisbane, 136
Britain, 8, 33, 63–4, 90, 105, 145, 180,
    225, 261–2
British Columbia, 123
British Lions, 96
    games against Australia—
        1930, 131–2, 134, 136, 259–60
        1989, 132, 157
        1990, 148
British Rugby League, 201
Brockhoff, David, 45, 77, 147, 160,
    198
Broncos, 14
Brooke, Zinzan, 171
Brumbies, 7–8, 11, 210, 222, 231, 263

Bucher, A. M., 92–3
Buenos Aires, 8
Bulletin, 35, 85
Bunce, Frank, 159, 206
Burke, Matt
    games against—
        New Zealand
            1996, 205–6
            1998, 234
            1999, 241–3
        South Africa
            1993, 167
    in World Cup
        1995, 18
        1999, 31, 48
            games against—
                France, 13, 42, 45
                South Africa, 30
Bush, Ron, 135
Byrne, Norbert, 45

C
Caloundra, 12, 14–16
Calvert, J. J., 104
Campese, David, 22–3, 60, 95, 147–9,
    195–7, 213–14, 225, 247, 277
    accolades, 148, 214
    and Bob Dwyer, 147
    and John Kirwan, 149
    as fullback, 57
    background, 36
    games against—
        Lions 1989, 132
        Manu Samoa
            1994, 168–9
        New Zealand
            1982, 148, 214
            1991, 57, 144
            1993, 159
            1994, 170
        Queensland
            1997, 213
        South Africa
            1993, 161, 166–7

in Britain
    1988, 148
in World Cup
    1991, 60–1, 65, 69–71, 73, 77–8,
        144
        against—
            New Zealand, 29, 213–14
    masks, 213
    mistakes, 148–9
    retirement, 214
    try-scoring, 60, 149, 213
Canada, 142, 188, 193
    1908, 90
Canberra, 236, 267
Cardiff, 3–8, 20, 31, 38, 82, 253, 272
Cardiff Arms Park, 59, 66, 75
Cardiff Institute of Higher
    Education, 193
Carew, P., 94
Carisbrook Park, 136, 158
Carling, Will, 244
Carlton, 258
Carne, Willie, 240
Carozza, Paul, 149, 155–6
Carr, Gary, 249
Carrington, Governor, 34–5
Carroll, Daniel, 116–23, 130, 277
    birthday, 122
    death, 123
    in US, 123
Carson, James 'Jum', 94–5
Carter, Alun, 193
Catchpole, Ken, 143–4, 169
Cavanagh, Vic, 128
Charters Towers, 98
China, 187, 222, 274
Christchurch, 76, 232
Churchill, Winston, 34, 36, 51
Clarke, David, 235
Clarke, Don, 162
Clendinnen, Inga, 36
coaches and coaching, 7, 50, 146, 164,
    177, 191, 212, 243, 273
    honours, 117

Cockbain, Matt, 47, 231
Cockerill, Richard, 237
Coker, Troy, 63, 78
Colton, A., 94–6
Commonwealth Games, 268
Connors, Mark, 242
Coogee Oval, 74, 226
Cookson, G., 92, 96
Cornwall, 106, 109, 112–14, 117
Cosgrove, Peter, Major-General, 41,
    253–4
Coughlan, Timothy, 37
Courtenay, Bryce, 216
Cowley, Ken, 184
Craig, Greg, 10, 164
Craven, Danie, 193, 243
Creatine, 47–8
Crittle, Peter, 45, 124, 143
Crouch, Glen Alfred (Paddy), 199
Crowley, Dan, 234, 253, 256
Cuba, 274
Cullen, Christian, 206, 242
Cultural Cringe, 256–8, 260
Curtin, John, 34
Cutler, Steve, 58, 63, 146

D
Daily Mail, 34
Daily Telegraph, 39, 112, 194
Dalton, James, 219
Daly, Tony, 57, 74, 78
Davies, Gerald, 148
Davies, Jonathan, 201
Davis Cup, 49
Davis, W., 94
de Beer, Jannie, 25–30, 219
de Bono, Edward, 14
de Courey Laffan, R. S., Rev., 106
de la Hunty, Shirley (née
    Strickland), 116
defensive skills, 10–13, 45, 68–9, 76
Dempsey, Tony, 158
Diehm, Ian, 87
Domoni, Sam, 198

Doohan, Patricia, 123
Doran, G. P., 92–3
Douglas, J.W. H.T., 120–1
Dowd, Craig, 234
drug-use policy, 48–9
Dublin, 16, 58, 67, 70–71, 76–7, 80–1,
144, 213, 266
Dunedin, 128, 136, 158–9, 224
Dunlop, Edward, Sir 'Weary', 209,
215
Dwyer, Bob, 6, 20, 151, 153, 165, 191,
195
and—
David Campese, 147
George Gregan, 167
Geoff Mould, 189
as coach, 62, 146, 190–1
against—
New Zealand
1993, 160
South Africa
1993, 163
in World Cup
1991, 58–9, 61, 63–4, 73–4,
76, 276
New Zealand
1991, 150

E
Eales, John
and—
laws, 247
national anthem, 9
as number 8, 57
background, 36
captain, 107, 115
games against—
Argentina
1997, 8
New Zealand
1966, 206
1992, 156
1994, 170
1998, 233–4

in World Cup
1991, 45, 58, 60, 62–3, 78
games against—
England, 277
1999, 4, 53
games against—
France, 41–4
Romania, 17
South Africa, 28
victory, 254
East Timor, 41, 253
Eastes, Charlie, 95
Easts, 57
Eden Park, 58, 135–6
1991, 150
Edinburgh, Duke of, 3
Egerton, Rob, 57, 71, 78
Ella, Gary, 200
Ella, Glen, 190, 198, 200
Ella, Gordon, 225–6
Ella, Mark, 19, 76–8, 146, 167–8, 175,
190, 198–200, 225–6, 277
Ellis Park, 24, 181
Ellis, Charlie, 94–5
Empire Games
1938, 129
Enfield, Harry, 249
England, 26, 142, 180, 237, 245–7, 275
and—
rugby league, 201
games against Australia—
1899, 52, 91–6, 102–4
1908, 90, 108
1927–8, 126
1927–8, 125
1947–8, 180, 261
1963, 261
1966–7, 144
1991, 57, 227
1997, 8
1998, 226–8
1999, 236, 238–9
in World Cup
1991, 69–70, 72–6, 78, 158, 233

1995, 18, 186, 188, 193
1999, 5, 31, 82
    South Africa, 25
Ensor, E., 177
Erickson, Wayne, 229
Evans, Alex, 10, 43, 154
Evans, Gil, 20
Evans, W. T., 94, 96
Evers, E. V., 93
eye-gouging, 38, 43, 53

F

FA Cup, 117
Farr-Jones, Nick, 79, 146–7, 153, 164
  and—
    David Campese, 148
  games against—
    Argentina, 165
    New Zealand
      1990, 191
      1992, 156, 164
    Queensland
      1992, 155
    South Africa
      1993, 161, 166–7
  in Britain
    1984 Grand Slam, 80, 164
  in World Cup
    1991, 47, 68, 78, 81
Fenton, Peter, 124
Fenukitau, Ipolito, 198
Fepuleai, Feesago, 61
Ferrier, Ian, 185
Ferrier Agreement, 267
Fiji, 186, 198, 261
Finau, Fili, 198
Finegan, Owen, 43–4, 213
Fishman, Roland, 152
fitness, levels of, 10, 14, 21, 43
Fitzpatrick, Sean, 172, 205, 243, 277
FitzSimons, Peter, 77, 164–5, 235
Five Nations, 272
Fleck, Robbie, 26
Fleming, Jim, 38–9, 232

Flett, John, 57
Foley, Michael, 44
Football Association, 202
Ford, Eric, 126
Ford, John, 126
foul play, 38–9, 166, 246
Fox, Grant, 71, 150, 159
Foxtel, 241
France, 244, 247
  and amateurism, 178
  in Olympics, 118–19
  in World Cup
    1991, 72
    1995, 186
    1999, 3, 5, 112
      games against—
        Australia, 32–3, 38
        New Zealand, 30–1, 38–40,
          44
      in final, 13, 42–7
  record against Wallabies, 43
Francis, Neil, 66–7
Francombe, J. S., 93
Fraser, Dawn, 116, 118, 214
Fraser, Jane, 137
Frith, J. P., 228
front row, 17, 136

G

Gallaher, David, 64, 157
Gallipoli, 37, 142, 147
Gatland, Warren, 16–17, 264, 275
Gavin, Tim, 46, 58
Geelong, 258
Geoghegan, Simon, 66
George, Harold, 141
Gerrard, W. G., 96
Gibson, G. R., 93
Giltinan, J. J., 269
globalisation, 241, 274
goals and goal-kicking see also kicks
  and kicking, 29
  conversions, 69
  drop, 11, 25–6, 28, 31, 69, 231–2

Neil Jenkins, 22
penalties, 63
Gordon, 180, 195
Gordon, Harry, 110–11, 117, 120–1
Gordon, Strath, 47
Gould, Phil, 207–8
Gould, Roger, 190, 206
GPS *see* Greater Public Schools (GPS)
Gralton, A., 94, 96
Gray, H. G. S., 92
Great Split, 100, 217, 258, 269
Greater Public Schools (GPS), 88,
    103, 129, 207–8
Greening, Phil, 237
Gregan, George, 198
    and—
        Bob Dwyer, 167
    background, 36
    games against—
        Manu Samoa
            1994, 169
        New Zealand
            1994, 29, 169–170, 172–4, 277
            1998, 233
            1999, 242
    in Sevens, 167–8
    in World Cup
        1995, 188
        1999, 4
            games against—
                France, 13, 41–2, 44
                Wales, 21
    vice-captain, 115
Gresson, Tim, 244–5, 249
Grey, Nathan, 30, 237
Grobler, Juan, 18
Growden, Greg, 8, 13, 17, 19, 27, 152,
    183
Guiney, David, 122
Guscott, Jeremy, 243, 245

H
haka, 109, 170, 216, 242, 253
Handy, Chris, 73

Harris, Norman, 271–2
Harrison, Scott, 10, 40
Hart, John, 182
Hastings, Gavin, 70
Hawke, Colin, 21–2, 243
Hawkins, Chris, 196
Hawthorne, Phil, 144, 277
Hay, Peter, 36
Henry, Graham, 5, 20, 22, 243, 246,
    275
Herbert, Daniel, 17, 45, 48, 52
Hewitt, Bruce, 133
Hickie, Thomas, 89, 101
Hill, Alfred, 129
Hill, Rowland, 106
Hoeft, Carl, 234
Home unions, 32, 132, 256, 264,
    270–1, 275
Hong Kong Sevens, 167, 187, 209
Honiball, Henry, 25–6
Horan, Tim, 95
    and—
        Stephen Larkham, 17
    games against—
        England
            1997, 8
            1999, 237
        New Zealand
            1991, 150
        NSW
            1992, 154–5
        South Africa
            1993, 166–7
            1998, 232
            1999, 239
    in Sevens, 168
    in World Cup
        1991, 45, 60, 70–1, 73–4, 78
            games against—
                New Zealand, 29, 214
        1999, 47
            games against—
                France, 41
                Ireland, 17

South Africa, 26, 30, 278
  Wales, 21, 23
  player of the tournament, 18
Hosie, Alan, 148, 245
Howard, Fred, 59
Howard, John, 130
Howard, Pat, 159, 168, 206
Howarth, Shane, 22, 171, 173
Hughes, Robert, 35–6

I

Independent Monthly, 196
India, 274
Inglis, Gordon, 50–1
injuries, 98, 202, 217, 258
International Rugby Board (IRB), 100,
  136, 240, 243, 245, 261, 264, 270
  and—
    ARU, 266, 270–1
    laws, 192–3, 243–7, 250, 257
      advantage law, 229
    and Rugbyocracy, 32, 246, 260,
      264
    professionalism, 100, 181, 271
    referees, 245
    sin-bin, 264, 273
    World Cup, 187
  affiliations, 266
  balance, 230
  finances, 270, 274
  Great Split, 100
  Home unions, 264
  members, 274
  set up, 264
  Sevens, 274
  Sydney Conference, 243–7, 264,
    273
International Rugby Hall of Fame,
  182, 200
IRB *see* International Rugby Board
  (IRB)
Ireland, 246, 264, 266, 270, 275
  and—
    law changes, 244

games against Australia—
  1899, 92–3
  1908, 90
  1927, 124
  1927–8, 125
  1999, 239
  in World Cup
    1991, 64, 66–8, 72–4, 77
    1999, 16–17
Italy, 18
  and amateurism, 178
Ivory Coast, 186–7, 193
Ivory, Frank, 199

J

James brothers, 97
Jamrozik, Wanda, 195–7
Japan, 168, 186–7, 274
Jarman, J.W., 92–3
Jeffreys, John, 72
Jenkins, Neil, 22
Jenkins, Vivian, 272
jerseys
  Australian, 208–9, 215, 235–6
  New Zealand, 272
Jones, Alan, 18–19, 61, 145–6, 152,
  164
  and *Sydney Morning Herald*, 151–4
Jones, Bob, 78–9
Jones, Lloyd, 14
Jones, Michael, 62, 158, 171
Jones, Stephen, 31–2, 230, 249
Jones-Hughes, Jason, 22
Jorgensen, Peter, 208
Joubert, Andre, 167, 219
Judkins, W., 93
Junee, Darren, 208

K

Kafer, Rod, 243
Kahl, Paul, 155
Kangaroos, 33, 76, 269
Karam, Joe, 170
Kearns, Phil, 78, 184

games against—
    England
        1998, 226
    New Zealand
        1990, 190, 277
        1993, 158
        1994, 174
    South Africa
        1993, 162, 166
    in World Cup, 185
        1991, 60, 63, 78
        1999, 17
Kefu, Toutai, 17, 27, 36, 41, 198, 243
Kelaher, Tim, 159
Kelly, A., 94, 96
Keyes, Ralph, 66
kicks and kicking *see also* goals and
    goal-kicking, 63, 128–9, 142, 147
    drop, 11, 29
    goals, 45, 65, 162
    penalties, 63
    quick taps, 165
    out on the full, 128
    tactical, 17, 29–30, 45, 67, 69, 75,
        149, 193
        England, 237
    vicious, 39
Kiernan, Tom, 264
King's Cup, 120
King's School, The, 152, 207–8
Kirwan, John, 57, 71, 149, 171
Knox, David, 79–80, 168–71, 219
Kronfeld, Josh, 38

L
Laidlaw, Chris, 101
Lancashire, 202
Lane, Tim, 10, 28, 41
Lansdowne Road, 16, 67
Larkham, Stephen
    and—
        Tim Horan, 17
    games against—
        New Zealand

1997, 224
1998, 234
Scotland
    1997, 8, 224
South Africa
    1998, 231
in World Cup
    1999, 47
    games against—
        Ireland, 17
        South Africa, 11, 26, 28–31,
            278
        Wales, 22
Lawrence, D. H., 33
Lawrence, Keith, 59
laws, 257
Lawson, Henry, 37
Leeds, 180
Leigh, 180
Leslie, John, 275
Leslie, Martin, 275
Levy, Geoff, 185
Lillicrap, Cameron, 10
Lindsay, Maurice, 201
lineouts and lineout skills, 40, 42, 44,
    63, 66–7, 156, 272
    laws, 193, 244, 247–8
    lifting in, 207
Little, Jason, 45, 47, 68, 78, 155,
    162–3, 165–6, 168, 170
Little, Walter, 233
Llanelli, 59, 105
Loane, Mark, 145
Loftus Versfeld Stadium, 6–7
Lomu, Jonah, 206
Lord, David, 184
Luyt, Louis, 23–4
Lynagh, Michael, 79, 129
    games against—
        All Blacks
            1992, 156
        New Zealand
            1990, 191
            1991, 150

in World Cup
  1991, 63, 65, 67–8, 73, 77–8, 80
  1995, 188
  kicking, 159

M

MacDougall, Adam, 236
Mackenzie, Compton, 37–8
Macqueen, Rod, 10, 14, 221–2, 243,
  245, 254, 273
  and—
    John Eales, 115
  as coach, 8–15, 211, 236
    ACT Brumbies, 7, 11
    against South Africa
      1998, 232
    appointments, 7, 220–2
    defensive skills, 11–13
    fitness, levels of, 14
    in World Cup
      1999, 81–2
        final, 39–42
        against France, 38–41,
          44–5
        South Africa, 27
        victory, 5
      NSW, 7, 210
  as player, 210
  background, 211–13
Magne, Olivier, 41
Maitland Daily Mercury, 102
Major, John, 81
Malcolm, Syd, 124, 137, 189
Mallett, Nick, 25–7, 30, 243
Mallon, Bill, 122
Malouf, Bruce, 225
Malouf, David, 255, 259
Mandela, Nelson, 181
Manly rugby league club, 76
Manu Samoa, 20, 59, 61–3, 65, 72,
  167–9, 174, 191, 198
Manu, Daniel, 197–8, 204
Marks, H., 94
Marshall, Justin, 206, 242

Marshall, Peter, 229–30, 243
Martelli, E., 92, 96
Martin, Greg, 149
Matraville High School, 200, 225
mauls and mauling, 11
  laws, 244
  rolling, 160
Maxwell, John, 225
McCall, Rod, 58, 62, 78
McCartney, Ken, 150
McDermott, Lloyd, 199–200
MCG *see* Melbourne Cricket
  Ground
McGeechan, Ian, 243
McGown, Bob, 94–5
McGown, T. M., 93
McGruther, Dick, 235–6
McGwire, Mark, 48
McKay, John, 7, 10
McKenzie, Ewen, 74, 78
McLean, T. P., 143
McLean, Paul, 129, 190
McManamey, James, Major, 142
Mehrtens, Andrew, 206, 242
Melbourne, 89, 91, 122, 215, 267
Melbourne Australian rules football
  club, 258
Melbourne Cricket Ground, 89–90,
  216, 236
Messenger, Dally, 95, 103, 208, 214,
  277
Millar, Syd, 245
Millennium Stadium, 3, 5, 16, 20,
  23–4, 42, 46–7, 82, 272
Miller, Jeff, 10, 14, 27, 41, 58, 63
Miller, Ross, 222
Miller, Syd, 264
Mitchell, John, 275
Moffet, David, 183
Montgomery, Percy, 231
Moran, Herbert, 108, 119, 255–6,
  277–8
  1908 tour of Europe, 33–4,
    105–12, 114, 116, 122, 131

and—
   amateurism, 121–2
   foul play, 33
at Sydney University, 52
autobiography, 107
background, 107–8
captain, 115
Morrison, Ed, 63
Mould, Geoff, 189–90, 200
Muggleton, John, 10–11, 13
Mulford, John, 113, 141
Muller, Pieter, 26
Mullineux, Matthew, Rev., 33, 93, 97,
   103, 237–8, 258, 261, 271
   1899 tour by England, 90–4,
      98–100, 102, 104, 112, 127, 132
Murdoch, Rupert, 178, 183–4, 201,
   266
Murrayfield, 8, 223–4

N
Nance, Steve, 10, 14, 21
Nasser, Brendan, 58
Natzka, Oscar, 130
New Zealand (All Blacks), 124, 186–8,
   195, 230, 241, 244, 259, 263, 267–70
   and—
      David Campese, 213–14
   Bledisloe Cup, 134–7, 175, 263
      origins, 133
   games (including Bledisloe Cup
   games) against Australia—
   1882, 87
   1903, 104
   1905, 64, 93, 109, 209
   1910, 120
   1913, 141
   1914, 258
   1920, 260
   1922, 260
   1924, 260
   1928, 127, 242
   1929, 134, 259
   1931, 135–6
   1932, 136, 189
   1934, 136, 215, 259
   1936, 136
   1949, 178–9
   1962, 199
   1979, 262
   1980, 157, 242
   1982, 147–8
   1984, 206
   1986, 80
   1988, 157–8
   1990, 76, 149, 190, 277
   1991, 57–8, 150
   1992, 156, 158, 164
   1993, 159–60
   1994, 169–73, 191
   1995, 182–3, 191, 194, 196–7
   1996, 205–6
   1997, 210, 216, 224
   1998, 4, 9, 14, 232–4, 259, 262
   1999, 4, 12, 242
   in World Cup
   1991, 59–60, 70–2, 74, 76, 80–1,
      144
      against Australia, 29
   1995 final, 181–2
   1999, 5, 19, 31, 81–2
      against France, 30–1, 38–41, 44
      pool rounds, 18
   Sevens, 168
   women players, 175
New Zealand Herald, 135
New Zealand Natives, 89, 125
New Zealand Rugby Union
   (NZRU) 134–6, 183, 198, 266, 270
   and professionalism, 181
New Zealand Schoolboys, 198
Newcastle, 108, 124
Newcombe, Barry, 230
Newington College, 85
News Ltd, 100, 241, 262
Nicholls, E. Gwyn, 92–3
Nicholson. E.T., 92–3
nicknames, 255

North Sydney Oval, 175, 261
North Sydney rugby league, 180
Northern League, 97, 177–8, 202
Northern Transvaal, 24
NSW, 270
  and—
    Australian Rules (football), 258
  games against—
    Queensland
      1882, 87–8
      1883, 88–9
      1908, 119
      1971, 261
      1992, 154–5
    South Africa
      1937, 259
    New Zealand
      1882, 257
  Super 12, 7
NSWRU, 90–2, 103–4, 124, 141, 153,
  190, 213–14
  and—
    amateurism, 99–100
    ARU, 235–6
    IRB, 266
    players, 185
    professionalism, 100, 176, 178,
      181, 262
    World Rugby Corporation, 185
  clubs, 101
  finances, 260
NZRU see New Zealand Rugby
  Union
NZ Universities, 260

O
O'Brien, Paddy, 6
O'Neill, John, 6–7, 45, 47, 110, 115,
  235, 240, 265
O'Reilly, Tony, 214
Obolensky, Prince, 148
Observer, 271
Ofahengaue, Willie, 58, 63, 68, 74, 78,
  154–5, 168, 197–8, 232

Olympic Games, 268
  1912, 112
  Antwerp 1920, 117–18
  Helsinki 1952, 116
  London 1908, 90, 105–6, 109–14,
    117–18, 120, 131
  Melbourne 1956, 116
  Paris
    1900, 118
    1924, 117–18
  Rome 1960, 116
  Sydney 2000, 50
  Tokyo 1964, 116
Olympic Stadium, 4, 236, 241, 247, 268
Osborne, 148
Osler, Bennie, 25
Otago, 128, 135
Owen, Dicky, 20

P
Packer, Kerry, 185–6
Parramatta, 236, 267
Parramatta rugby league club, 11
passes and passing, 75–6, 87–8, 96, 102,
  136, 143–4, 147–8, 162, 189, 193, 195
  and Rugbyocracy, 33
  cut-out, 33, 156
  David Campese, 29
  George Gregan, 169
  pretending, 192
Paterson, Ian, 200
Paul, Jeremy, 17, 36, 43–4
PBL, 186
Pembroke, David, 10
penalties, 63, 129, 149–50, 242–3
  France, 72
People's Liberation Army, 222
Perkins, Charlie, 199
Perkins, Kieren, 205
Perth, 230, 232, 236, 267
Peru, 274
Petersham Rugby Club, 46
Pienaar, Francois, 181
Pilecki, Stan, 145–6

'Planet Rugby', 249
Players' Union, 47
Poidevin, Simon, 58, 62–3, 76, 78, 157–8, 225
Pollard, Jack, 93, 102, 119, 122, 208
Porter, Cliff, 127
Portmarnock, 16
Portus, Garnett Vere, 131, 260
Potter, Gareth, 193
Pretoria, 219
Princess Anne, 3, 47
professionalism, 13, 32, 97–100, 176–7, 200, 211, 245, 247, 256, 271
1899, 97
Prosser, Ray, 145
Pugh, Vernon, QC, 228, 264, 270

Q
QRU, 141
and
ARU, 235–6
establishment, 87
IRB, 266
Norbert Byrne, 45
players, 185
Queen, the, 3–4, 15, 46–7, 74, 276–7
Queensland, 88, 141, 198, 213, 259, 270
and—
Australian Rules (football), 258
games against—
NSW
1882, 87–8
1883, 88–9
1908, 119
1971, 261
1992, 154–5
Quinn, Keith, 135
Quinnell, Scott, 201

R
Rand, A.W., 90–1
Randall, Terry, 76
Randell, Taine, 39
Randwick, 57, 144, 147, 168, 189, 195, 225–6
Ranfurly Shield, 134–5
Raper, Johnnie, 269
Reebok, 208–9, 235
Rees, Vivienne, 175
Referee, 91–2, 113, 135–6, 141
referees, 58, 149, 229, 245
British, 63–4
in World Cup
1991, 63
RFU *see* Rugby Football Union
Rockhampton Bulletin, 98
Roebuck, Marty, 57, 66, 68, 78, 160, 166
Roff, Joe, 204, 206
Romania, 16–17, 118
Rosenblum, Myer, 127–30
Rosenblum, Rupert, 129
Ross, Alex, 206
Rossouw, Pieter, 219
Row, Frank ('Banger'), 45, 94–5, 277
Royds, Percy, Admiral, 127
rucks and rucking, 38, 128
laws, 244
Rugby Football Union (RFU), 100, 106, 124, 144, 264
rugby league, 194, 199–200, 208, 240, 260–1, 269, 276
and—
Trevor Allan, 180
Dally Messenger, 214
coaches, 69
establishment, 86, 103
fitness, levels of, 14
Great Split, 269
injuries, 217
laws, 202–3
rugby union, 201, 240–1, 261, 263, 267, 269–70
'defections' ('conversions'), 112, 119, 178, 180
numbers, 178

passing techniques, 76
skills, 10, 13
tackling, 76
television, 240, 269–70
New Zealand, 103
Northern League, 177
Queensland, 141
referees, 151
Super League, 100, 178
Rugby News, 230
Rugbyocracy, 36, 136, 180, 247,
    255–6, 260–4, 272–5
and—
    Australians, 35, 49
    passing, 33
    rough play, 34
    southern hemisphere rugby, 32
    IRB, 246
    laws, 248, 250
    negativity, 274
in
    1899, 97
    1908, 115
Runyon, Damon, 66–7
Ryan, Warren, 69

S
Salvation Army, 101
Samania, Toa, 169
Samoa *see* Manu Samoa
SANZAR, 183, 244
SARU *see* South African Rugby
    Union
Sayle, Jeff, 225
Scates, Bruce, 142
SCG *see* Sydney Cricket Ground
Schama, Simon, 263
Schmidt, Uli, 166
scoring, level of, 273
Scotland, 190, 246, 264, 266, 270, 275
and—
    law changes, 244
    games against Australia—
        1899, 92–3

1927, 124, 223
1927–8, 125
1970, 129
1997, 8, 223–5
in World Cup
    1991, 64, 66, 69–70, 72
    1995, 186
Scots College, 129
scrums and scrummaging, 40, 104,
    136, 143–4, 192
    defined, 192
    front row, 17
    laws, 244, 247–8
    referees, 64
set pieces, 73, 150, 229, 248
Sevens Rugby, 167–8, 178, 268,
    274
SFS *see* Sydney Football Stadium
Sheehan, Paul, 211
Shelford, Wayne, 63, 157–8
sin-bin, 247, 264, 273
Singapore, 222
Six Nations, 245, 248, 250
Skinstad, Bobby, 27
Slack, Andrew, 148–9
Slater, Gordon, 135
Slattery, Peter, 65
Small, James, 166–7
Smith, Greg, 6–7, 15, 190, 210,
    219–21
Smith, Lee, 244
Smith, Sean, 39
soldiers' teams, 142
South Africa (Springboks), 143, 230,
    242, 244, 263, 267–8, 270
    games against Australia
        1896, 92
        1921, 134
        1937, 209
        1993, 158, 160, 162–3, 165–7
        1996, 203–5
        1997, 6, 14, 219, 221, 234
        1998, 230–2
        1999, 238–9, 243

in World Cup
    1995, 19, 24
        final, 181–2
    1999, 5, 6, 11, 18, 23–5, 29, 278
        games against
            Australia, 26–8, 30–1
            England, 25–6
            preparation, 24–6
South African Rugby Union, 24, 266, 270
Spencer, Carlos, 226
Spindler, Ben, 10
Spragg, Alfonso ('Lonnie'), 94–6
Springboks see South Africa
Spurr, Barry, 217
St Aloysius' College, 108, 119, 122
St George, 11
St Joseph's, 45, 108, 207–8, 265
State of Origin, 240–1
Stead, Billy, 64
Stoddart, A. E., 258
Stokes, Leonard, 33
Stout, F. M., 92–3
Stransky, Joel, 162
Stuart, T. P. Anderson, Professor, 51–2
Sun, 195
Sun Herald, 49–50, 133, 151
Sunday Telegraph, 248
Sunday Times, 31, 148, 230, 249, 272
Super 12, 48, 195–8, 210, 212,
    228–30, 245, 248–9, 262–3, 267–9,
    275
    strength of, 5–6
Super League, 100, 178, 184, 240
Swannell, B. I., 93
Swansea 154
Swarbrick, D. W., 180
Sydney City, 208
Sydney Conference of IRB, 243–7
Sydney Cricket Ground, 11, 52, 94,
    102–4, 129, 131, 136, 169, 214–15,
    258–9, 261–2
Sydney Football Stadium, 165, 168,
    173, 195, 197, 203, 213

Sydney Mail, 87, 90, 92, 95, 131, 260,
    275
Sydney Morning Herald, 8, 17–19, 90,
    96, 100–2, 121, 132, 135, 172, 195,
    235, 248–9
    and Alan Jones, 151–4
Sydney Sunday Times, 85
Sydney University, 45, 51–2, 85, 88,
    108, 119, 131, 147

T

Tabua, Ilie, 167, 197–8
tackles and tackling, 11, 76, 142,
    147–8, 167
    George Gregan, 29
    high, 61
    laws, 193, 244, 247
Tancred, Arthur, 179
Tanner, Hayden, 143
Tanner, William 'Doey', 94
Tasker, William 'Twit', 141–2
Tatz, Colin, 199–200
Tavalea, Timote, 198
Taylor, Helen, 176
Teague, Mike, 76, 158
Teichmann, Gary, 24–6
television, 144, 161, 187, 241, 262,
    267–70, 274, 276
    rights, 100, 262, 267
Templeton, Bob, 79–80, 82, 145
Thompson, C. E. K., 92
Thring, J. C., 202
Times, The, 31–2, 49
Timms, A. B., 92–3
Timu, John, 71
Tinling, Teddy, 272
Tonga, 186, 193, 198, 245, 261
Tournaire, Franck, 39
Towers, Cyril, 95, 126, 128, 131, 189,
    277
Transvaal, 195
Tregenza, John, Dr, 52
Trevor, Major, 112
Tri Nations, 234, 238, 263, 267

strength of, 5–6
Trinity College, 80
Trotter, Russell, 244
Truth, 93, 98–9
Tucker, J. S., 126
Tuigamala, Va'aiga, 149
Tune, Ben, 13, 22, 43, 48, 95, 130,
    206, 231
turnovers, 41
Twickenham, 8, 28, 48, 72, 74, 76,
    126, 148, 276–8
    in World Cup, 6, 11, 23, 27, 30–31

U

Umaga, Tama, 242
Underwood, Rory, 69, 188
United States, 18, 90, 142, 187
Uppingham School, 202
Uruguay, 28
Uttley, Roger, 227

V

van der Westhuizen, Joost, 24–7, 29, 220
van Straaten, Braam, 239
Venezuela, 274
Venter, Brendon, 28
Victorian Rules football, 85, 87–9,
    257–8 *see also* Australian Rules
    football
Vodafone, 9

W

Wakefield, W. W. (Lord Wakefield),
    125, 272
Wales, 204, 246, 264, 272, 275 *see also*
    Welsh Rugby Union
    and amateurism, 178
    games against Australia
        1899, 92–3
        1908, 20, 90, 115, 122
        1927–8, 125
        1991, 57
        1996, 197
    games against Manu Samoa, 20

in World Cup
    1991, 59, 61–7, 75
    1999, 4–5, 16, 19, 21–3, 31
Walker, Andrew, 200, 208, 263
Walker, Lloyd, 200
Wallace, A. C. 'Johnnie', 124–6
Wallach, Clarrie, 141–2
Wallaroo club, 87, 95
Wallaroos, 175–6
Waratahs, 127, 272
    in
        1927–8, 123, 125–7, 142, 179,
            259, 276
        1996, 196–7
    match against South Africa 1937,
        259
Warbrick, W., 94
Ward, Chris, 151
Ward, P., 94–5
Warringah, 211–12
Watson, Andre, 3, 5, 43, 243
Waugh, Stephen, 30
Webb, Jonathan, 73
Webster, Jim, 152
Webster, Tom, 126
Wellington, 136, 190, 277
Welsh Rugby Union, 42, 106, 228,
    270
Wendt, Albert, 62
West Harbour, 200
Whitaker, Chris, 44
White, C., 94
Whitton, Evan, 132, 148, 152–4
Wickham, S., 95
Wigan, 201
Wilkins, Phil, 210
Wilkinson, Jonny, 237
William Webb Ellis trophy ('Bill'),
    3–4, 53, 134, 246, 253–4, 263, 276
    1991, 9, 11
    1999, 6
        victory, 44
    winners, 19
Williams, Ian, 149

Williams, Tasha, 175
Williamson, John, 4, 242
Wilson, David, 173
Wilson, Harold, 154
Wilson, Jeff, 169–71, 173–4, 242
Wilson, Stu, 147, 149
'Woeful Wallabies', 261
women players, 175–6, 268
World Cup, 39, 71, 82, 188, 272
  1987
    games against—
      France, 267
  1991, 47, 57–60, 64–6, 69–70,
    73–4, 79, 81, 191, 256, 276
    games against—
      Ireland, 72
      NewZealand, 9, 213–14
    finals, 3
    Manu Samoa, 62–3
    victory, 7, 262
  1995, 100, 167, 186, 188, 191, 193,
    235, 241, 267
    England, 18, 193
    final, 24, 181–2
    lineouts, 248
    New Zealand at, 195
  1999, 19, 111, 220, 225, 230, 240–1,
    243–5, 253–4

  final, 8, 13, 29–33, 38
  games against
    France, 3, 32–3, 38, 40–1,
      43–7, 112
    South Africa, 26–30
    Wales, 20–3, 247
  pool rounds, 15–19, 21
  programs, 10
  semi-finals, 6, 26–31, 244
  victory, 5, 43–7, 262, 270
  2003, 221, 245, 256, 268
  2007, 247
  attendances, 274
  coaches, 117
  host nation, 5
  marketing, 186–8
  television, 274
  tries, 12
World Rugby Corporation, 184–6
World Series Sevens Tournament, 253
Wyllie, Alex, 8
Wynnum–Manly, 199

Y
York, Duchess of, 195
Yorkshire, 202

The Taylor Years
Ken Piesse

When Mark Taylor inherited Australian sport's most coveted position in May 1994, the Australian cricket team was finally able to deliver the ultimate knockout blow against the long-running champions, the West Indies. Taylor and his ambitious XI then embarked on a run of success never before seen in Australian cricket – winning nine series in a row to become the undisputed power of the world game.

Award-winning cricket writer Ken Piesse's *The Taylor Years* celebrates Australia's Test achievements under Mark Taylor's captaincy and captures all the highlights of the period, including:

- Taylor's first months as leader of the team after a decade under Allan Border's rule
- his disastrous batting slump in 1996 and courageous career revival in England in 1997
- his famous 334 not out at Peshawar, which equalled the highest Test score of all, by the legendary Don Bradman.

Here are recollections of the stars of Taylor's team, including Michael Slater, Glenn McGrath, the Waugh twins and Stuart MacGill, as well as memorable photographs and fascinating statistics to please cricket fans of every age.

The Taylor Years is an entertaining, illuminating record of one of the finest periods in the annals of Australian cricket.